Florian Carl

Berlin/Accra

KlangKulturStudien
SoundCultureStudies

herausgegeben von

Lars-Christian Koch
und
Raimund Vogels

Band 3

LIT

Florian Carl

BERLIN/ACCRA

Music, Travel, and the Production of Space

LIT

Umschlagbild: Ofei Ankrah und Gruppe. Auftritt im April 2004
in Berlin
Foto: Florian Carl

∞

Gedruckt auf alterungsbeständigem Werkdruckpapier entsprechend
ANSI Z3948   DIN ISO 9706

Bibliographic information published by the Deutsche Nationalbibliothek
The Deutsche Nationalbibliothek lists this publication in the Deutsche
Nationalbibliografie; detailed bibliographic data are available in the Internet at
http://dnb.d-nb.de.

ISBN 978-3-8258-1905-7
Zugl.: Hannover, Hochschule für Musik und Theater, Diss., 2007

A catalogue record for this book is available from the British Library

©LIT VERLAG Dr. W. Hopf Berlin 2009
Fresnostr. 2   D-48159 Münster
Tel. +49 (0) 2 51-620 32 22   Fax +49 (0) 2 51-922 60 99
e-Mail: lit@lit-verlag.de   http://www.lit-verlag.de

Distribution:
In Germany: LIT Verlag Fresnostr. 2, D-48159 Münster
Tel. +49 (0) 2 51-620 32 22, Fax +49 (0) 2 51-922 60 99, e-Mail: vertrieb@lit-verlag.de

In Austria: Medienlogistik Pichler-ÖBZ GmbH & Co KG
IZ-NÖ, Süd, Straße 1, Objekt 34, A-2355 Wiener Neudorf
Tel. +43 (0) 22 36-63 53 52 90, Fax +43 (0) 22 36-63 53 52 43, e-Mail: mlo@medien-logistik.at

In Switzerland: B + M Buch- und Medienvertriebs AG
Hochstr. 357, CH-8200 Schaffhausen
Tel. +41 (0) 52-643 54 85, Fax +41 (0) 52-643 54 35, e-Mail: order@buch-medien.ch

Distributed in the UK by: Global Book Marketing, 99B Wallis Rd, London, E9 5LN
Phone: +44 (0) 20 8533 5800 – Fax: +44 (0) 1600 775 663
http://www.centralbooks.co.uk/html

Distributed in North America by:

Transaction Publishers
Transaction Publishers
New Brunswick (U.S.A.) and London (U.K.)

Rutgers University
35 Berrue Circle
Piscataway, NJ 08854

Phone: +1 (732) 445 - 2280
Fax: + 1 (732) 445 - 3138
for orders (U. S. only):
toll free (888) 999 - 6778
e-mail: orders@transactionpub.com

Für meine Eltern

Contents

Acknowledgments   ix

1 Introduction: Music and Mobility   1

2 Africa and the Zoo   20

3 Musical Geography   34

4 Approaching Urban Space   56

5 Black Atlantic Worlds   76

6 Mapping the Scene   100

7 Symbolic Economies   121

8 Traveling With Culture   143

9 Conclusion: Music, Power, Space   167

   References   181

Acknowledgements

This study grew out of the research project "Processes of Musical Transformation and Identity Construction in Migrational Settings: The Music of Ghanaian Migrants in Germany and its Transcultural/Transnational Connections." The research cooperation was based at the University of Music and Drama Hanover, Germany, and the University of Ghana, Legon, and it was funded by the Volkswagen Foundation. Within this framework I have been a research fellow in Hanover from March 2004 to August 2007. I am very grateful to the Volkswagen Foundation for the material support without which this study would not have been possible.

This study was first handed in as my Ph.D. dissertation at the University of Music and Drama Hanover. I am particularly indebted to my supervisor Raimund Vogels in Hanover for his constant advice, encouragement, and friendship which exceeds the work in this project. I also thank Willie Anku for his support during my time in Legon. To my other colleagues in the research project, particularly Matthias Eger and Martin Ziegler, I am thankful for fruitful discussions, ideas, suggestions, but more importantly for their friendship and the beautiful time I had over the course of three and a half years. After all, much of my own thoughts in this thesis reflect views we collectively arrived at, though I alone am, of course, responsible for what is written here.

For his corrections, comments, and the detection of linguistic oddities I would like to thank Dennis Newson in Osnabrück, who took the effort to read through all chapters. Having lived in Ghana some forty years before I got to know the country, under completely different political and infrastructural conditions, the feedback I got from Dennis was particularly valuable for me and our exchange, largely by email, was, I think, highly interesting for both of us. It goes without saying that for any mistakes that are left in the text I alone am, of course, accountable.

I also wish to acknowledge a number of people in Berlin and Accra, where I carried out the bulk of my research, without whom this study would have hardly been possible: Ofei Ankrah, Judith and the family Bögelsack, Gordon Odametey, Mark Kofi Asamoah and all members of Adikanfo, Lina Bundrock, Kay Boni, Margareth Dzikpor, Charles Kwame Konu and all members of Nortseme. There were many others who shared their views, knowledge, and time with me and whom I might have forgotten to mention here. My sincere thanks to all.

Finally, without the love and support of my family I would not have been able to finish this work. The trust my parents, to whom this book is dedicated, put in me and my work is a constant motivation, not to mention the material support they have been giving me over all these years. And lastly, without the love, care, patience, and encouragement of my wife, Hornam, I would not have accomplished the often arduous task of sitting down and write. My gratitude to all of you is beyond words.

1 Introduction: Music and Mobility

The World in Motion

> This century has seen a drastic expansion of mobility, including tourism, migrant labor, immigration, urban sprawl. More and more people "dwell" with the help of mass transit, automobiles, airplanes. In cities on six continents foreign populations have come to stay — mixing in but often in partial, specific fashions. The "exotic" is uncannily close. Conversely, there seem no distant places left on the planet where the presence of "modern" products, media, and power cannot be felt. An older topography and experience of travel is exploded. One no longer leaves home confident of finding something radically new, another time or space. Difference is encountered in the adjoining neighborhood, the familiar turns up at the ends of the earth. [...] "Cultural" difference is no longer stable, exotic otherness; self-other relations are matters of power and rhetoric rather than of essence. A whole structure of expectations about authenticity in culture and in art is thrown in doubt. (Clifford 1988:13f)

This is how James Clifford describes the predicament of culture and the conditions of ethnographic modernity in the twentieth century. All the more at the beginning of the twenty-first century, we find ourselves "off center among scattered traditions," in a world in which "the conditions of rootlessness and mobility" are "an increasingly common fate" (ibid.:3); a world in which "[p]eople and things are increasingly out of place" (ibid.:6) and in which, as Clifford, quoting a poem by William Carlos Williams, puts it, "pure products go crazy."

"Globalization" has become one of the keywords in today's political debates. Employees, it is held, have to position themselves vis-à-vis multinational corporations, national economies to compete for "the best heads" in Marshall McLuhan's often evoked "global village"; the "war against terrorism" can only be won by an international "coalition of the willing," and "global warming" only stopped by the concentrated forces of the international community. The outgrowths of transnational migration can be watched every other day on the evening news. And while thousands of young Africans risk their lives on over-loaded boats heading north in hope of a better life, thousands of Europeans cross the Mediterranean by airplane in the other direction every year on their way to the tropical beach resorts and game reserves of the south. The world is shrinking, it is said; the near has become the far, and the far the near. There is virtually no place on earth where we would not encounter familiar sights, no place where one could not drink Coca-Cola, watch CNN, or listen to the music of Michael Jackson. On the other hand groups stubbornly, and in some places increasingly aggressively, insist on their cultural, ethnic, or religious differentness, as do nation-states on their particular national interests, and individuals on their individuality. The fear of modernity has always been indifference and "alienation," hence the concerns about the particular, the individual, the unique.

This is roughly how the now often recounted story of globalization goes. Many see the distinctiveness of places disappearing in a single globalized mass culture, and reactions to the finding of this "global homogeneity" range from regret over different forms of salvage attempts to anxieties to the point of hostility. We cannot deny and should not ignore that global processes increasingly affect each of us in our daily lives. Yet, there are also less dramatic versions of the narrative about global interdependence. Social anthropologist and prominent analysts of transnationalism Ulf Hannerz, for example, is skeptical about the withering away of cultural diversity. As he remarks:

> The people in my favorite Nigerian town drink Coca Cola, but they drink *burukutu* too; and they can watch *Charlie's Angels* as well as Hausa drummers on the television sets which spread rapidly as soon as electricity has arrived. My sense is that the world system, rather than creating massive cultural homogeneity on a global scale, is replacing one diversity with another; and the new diversity is based relatively more on interrelations and less on autonomy. (Quoted in Clifford 1988:17)

Cultural pessimists would hold that the products of this "new diversity" are less "authentic" than the ones they replace; they are condemned as commercialized, standardized, artificial, fake. As Clifford comments in the initial quotation to this chapter, with the former "pure" products going "crazy," a "whole structure of expectations about authenticity in culture and in art is thrown in doubt" (Clifford 1988:14). The world is not what it used to be — such comments seem a little bit like what every generation says about the one by which it is superseded. After all, every discipline constructs its own authenticities.

Modernity harbors some real paradoxes, and the global might not be the right place for purists. Yet, for many people who live with what is said to be the consequences of globalizing processes — migrants, professionals, artists, musicians, cosmopolitans; people who try to manage their professional and personal lives translocally between at times contradictory worlds — globalization is not so much an ideological, but a very concrete organizational and logistic problem. Thus, while acknowledging that there is a new quality to movement, mobility and global travel traffic as compared to two hundred, one hundred, or even fifty years ago, the question for us should not so much be whether we like this fact or not, but rather how we and other people deal with these new conditions both conceptually as well as practically.

Reconsidering Ethnography

If we principally accept Clifford's characterization of the predicament of culture in the world we live in, it seems legitimate to ask whether ethnography — an awfully old-fashioned-sounding term once referring to the description of the customs and beliefs of other peoples and cultures — makes sense at all within this world of extremes and rapid change. It seems easier to reflect upon ethnographic modernity than to actually practice an ethnography that takes modernity and globalizing processes into account. Yet still, for social anthropologists and ethnomusicologists alike, ethnography as "the observation and description (or representation) of culture" (Cooley 1997:4) is still the disciplinary key concept and the prime method by which we approach social reality. Following Merriam's seminal definition of ethnomusicology as "the study of music in culture" (Merriam 1964:6), ethnomusicologists still attempt to "engage living individuals in order to learn about music-culture" (Cooley 1997:4).

One consequence ethnographers drew from the insight that the world and cultural processes taking place within it are highly interdependent and cultural formations therefore rapidly changing, was to search for the remnants of cultural traditions that would soon completely vanish — and there are still people looking for the last "survivals" of some long forgotten cultural past. There is certainly nothing wrong with preserving the cultural heritage of mankind for future generations, which is the main task of museums and other archival institutions. But in contrast to a "salvage ethnography," which is indeed often based on the assumption that "authentic" and "pure" cultural expressions more and more disappear in today's globalized and commercialized world, we can also follow a different path. An approach that tries to make sense of cultural complexity rather than searching for — or even worse, inventing — presumably lost self-depending cultural systems is not so much concerned with questions of authenticity in a purist sense, but rather how different authenticities are positioned against each other and in opposition to supposedly inauthentic, artificial, impure products. An ethnography of the kind we have in mind is, in other words, interested in relations and not in essences. As Clifford writes:

> Intervening in an interconnecting world, one is always, to varying degrees, "inauthentic": caught between cultures, implicated in others. Because discourse in global power systems is elaborated vis-à-vis, a sense of difference or distinctness can never be located solely in the continuity of a culture or tradition. Identity is conjunctural, not essential. (Clifford 1988:11)

If people and things are, as Clifford argues, increasingly "out of place," one task of modern ethnography is to scrutinize how people, nevertheless, constantly put things as well as themselves back into place, how things and people relate. This is, after all, what debates about authenticity are all about: about positioning. And to position oneself, to define one's identity in a — more or less — self-determined fashion is becoming increasingly important. We can, today, choose who and what we want to be, or, this is at least what we are told. While the propagated freedom of the individual often seems rather a *de jure* than a *de facto* reality (cf. Bauman 2000), it is true that the sphere of the cultural, of public meaning, is increasingly invaded by individualism. Cultural identities have become more idiosyncratic and more dynamic, a matter of bricolage, of style and personal choice.

Cultural positions might therefore not be as self-evident as they used to be before the advent of the digital age, and they are hardly stable. But at the same time people are not as lost as philosophical disquisitions on "identity construction" and the "postmodern subject" might make it appear at times, though for some people defining their cultural as well as individual identity vis-à-vis the "global power system" is certainly more difficult and troublesome than for others. But we should not expect people to occupy only one single place, to dwell in their particular cultural niche, detached from time and space. "Just about every person," as Charles Keil has remarked, "is less mono-ethnic and much more complicated musically, historically and culturally than we think" (Keil 1994:176). We have to resist, thus, a view in which cultures are conceived of as enclosed meaning systems, as things rather than a process, something we can find somewhere "out there" if we just search hard enough.

Understood in this sense, cultures cannot "clash"; as a process culture always happens "in between," in the encounter of two or more people, where meaning is generated, reproduced, negotiated, and sometimes fought over.

As an empirical method of observation, reflection and description that focuses on social interaction while the observer interacts him- or herself with living individuals, ethnography can be, in our view, a way of accessing the idiosyncrasies and dynamics of cultural processes as well as remaining well grounded while discussing the effects and challenges of so-called globalization in the lives of individuals and groups. Though "participant observation," being a highly microscopic, qualitative approach, might lack the clarity and straightforwardness of more rigid quantitative research tools, it has the potential of bringing the ambiguities and paradoxes of cultural processes into focus which might otherwise remain hidden under the assumed homogeneity of a larger analytical entity or a chosen "sample." As Mark Slobin has remarked, rather than being interested in rigid definitions, doing ethnography is more about "match[ing] terms with reality" (Slobin 1993:12f). Ethnographies are therefore necessarily idiosyncratic themselves; we cannot pretend to be neutral observers while we engage ourselves in social interaction. As second-, third- and sometimes fourth-order interpretations, ethnographic texts are, as it has been remarked, as fictitious as they are realistic accounts of social life (cf. Geertz 1973:15f). After all, ethnography "appears as writing, as collecting, as modernist collage, as imperial power, as subversive critique," as a

> mode of travel, a way of understanding and getting around in a diverse world that, since the sixteenth century, has become cartographically unified. One of the principal functions of ethnography is "orientation" (a term left over from a time when Europe traveled and invented itself with respect to a fantastically unified "East"). But in the twentieth century ethnography reflects new "spatial practices" […], new forms of dwelling and circulating. (Clifford 1988:13)

Focusing on "spatial practices" (cf. de Certeau 1984), the scope of this ethnography, then, is to consider music's role in the production of space. In its attempt to go beyond the often assumed isomorphism of place, space, and culture (cf. Gupta & Ferguson 1997:34f), that is, in arguing that cultural formations are not isolated meaning systems in space but rather hierarchically interconnected within the global cultural economy, my own study can more generally be understood in the context of an "anthropology as cultural critique" (Marcus & Fischer 1986). While it represents itself a "mode of travel" (and in fact my own travels over the course of the last three years), the following dis-

cussion concentrates on the interrelation between musical practices and different forms of mobility that characterize our present, namely transnational migration, tourism, and urbanism. My argument is based upon the assumption
that music, understood as social practice, plays a crucial role in the production
of space, and it particularly brings into focus the significance of music in the
German-African encounter. As such it can be understood as a contribution to
a musical geography that examines the nature and maps the relative arrange-
ment of places and sites established through musical practice and discourse,
which is to say, through the "musical construction of place" (Stokes 1994).

Migrational Flows: The Ghanaian Diaspora

More concretely: This study is the outcome of three and a half years work in a
research project on the music of Ghanaian migrants in Germany.[1] The project
was a cooperative initiative by scholars from the University of Music and
Drama Hanover, Germany, and the School of Performing Arts at the University of Ghana, Legon. For me it provided the framework and, more importantly, the means to collect material for my doctoral thesis. The overall aim of
the project was to inquire into the musical practices within the Ghanaian immigrant community in Germany, to trace the transnational links between
Ghana and Germany that inform these practices, and to investigate the
transcultural configurations that transform them.

The preliminary idea of the project was based on the statistical fact that
in the last three decades or so, Germany has become one of the preferred destinations for Ghanaian migrants in Western Europe. With roughly 20,000
people officially registered at the end of 2006, Ghanaians represent the largest
group of immigrants from sub-Saharan Africa in Germany.[2] Germany is
therefore the most important host country for Ghanaians in Europe after the
United Kingdom. Considering the fact that there is a significant number of
immigrants without legal resident status and also that naturalization rates have
gone up since a change of German citizenship laws in 2000, we have to keep
in mind, though, that when we speak of Ghanaian migrants in Germany, the
official figures are clearly underestimates. The actual number of people with a

---

[1] The full title of the project, which was funded by the Volkswagen Foundation, was "Processes of musical transformation and identity construction in migrational settings: The music
of Ghanaian migrants in Germany and its transcultural/transnational connections."
[2] All statistical data referred to here and in the following was, if not indicated otherwise,
provided by the Federal Statistical Office in Germany (*Statistisches Bundesamt*).

Ghanaian background might well be thirty percent higher. Outnumbered only by immigrants from North Africa, Ghanaians are the largest African population in Europe (Akyeampong 2000:203f), which is quite remarkable in view of the rather small West African country with a total population of perhaps twenty to twenty-two million people.

Ghana, a former British colony which as the first sub-Saharan nation gained independence in 1957, is the country with the highest emigration rate in West Africa. Most Ghanaians in Europe emigrated in the 1980s and early 1990s. Beginning in the late 1970s and then rapidly increasing in the following decade, we see constantly rising numbers of Ghanaians in then West Germany, which is connected to the political and economic crisis in Ghana by that time. As Akyeampong discusses in more detail, in the early 1980s "Ghana's already weak economy collapsed totally, and in late 1983 the UN Food and Agriculture Organization reported massive hunger. […] Because of these conditions the exodus of Ghanaians abroad for political and economic reasons gathered full stream" (Akyeampong 2000:205). According to estimates, by the mid-1990s between twelve to twenty percent of Ghana's total population was living abroad. Today we find Ghanaian communities all over the world, the largest in western Europe and North America, but on a smaller scale also in North Africa, the Middle East, and as far as Southeast Asia and the Far East. In recent years, travel traffic in south-south direction, particularly towards the rapidly developing Asian economies, is considerably on the increase (Akyeampong 2000, Peil 1995). As for Germany, in the last decade the Ghanaian community appears to have stabilized, and the number of Ghanaian nationals in the country did not increase significantly.[3] More rigid immigration laws make it currently extremely difficult for West Africans, or, for that matter, people from the so-called "developing world," to legally enter the states of the European Union.

Today, Ghana is politically and economically relatively stable. In the African context the country is often discussed as exemplary with regard to "good governance," fight against corruption, and economic development. Since 1992, Ghana has a democratic multiparty system. Though there is a north-south divide in terms of socioeconomic development and the country remains heavily dependent on international financial and technical assistance, in the last few years Ghana had a steady economic growth. The "brain drain" that

---

[3] The average age of Ghanaian nationals residing in Germany is 34.3 years and the average length of their stay in the country is 11.6 years (figures for 2006). This indicates that most immigrants who came in the 1980s and 1990s have come to stay and founded families by now. Most newborn children automatically acquire the German citizenship and do not, therefore, appear in the statistics.

was part of the massive emigration of the past decades still constitutes a major problem in many professional occupations. The riches and lifestyle of the Western world, transported in media representations, fuel the popular imagination in Ghana, and "going abroad" continues to be an omnipresent theme in public discourse. And yet, "abroad" is more than just vivid popular images or some vague desired elsewhere. Transnational connections to the global Ghanaian diaspora[4] are a social reality very much present in everyday life. If you talk to people in Ghana, virtually everyone has at least some distant relative living outside the country, and modern telecommunication technologies make it now very easy to stay in touch. There has even been a weekly show on television, *Greetings From Abroad*, where expatriates send their regards to family and friends at home. The cash flow from the Ghanaian diaspora to the home country, most visible in the massive building boom in the coastal urban areas, has by now become one of the major economic factors for Ghana.[5]

Over the course of the last forty years the largest Ghanaian community in Germany has established itself in the city of Hamburg. Encompassing officially roughly 6,000, unofficially maybe about 10,000 people, the Ghanaian community in Hamburg is the second-largest in Europe after London. We find another larger community in Amsterdam where maybe seven to eight thousand Ghanaians live and a respective infrastructure of shops, businesses, churches, associations and so on has been established. Larger numbers of Ghanaians are also based in other European countries such as Italy, Spain or Sweden. On a global scale we find the largest communities in cities like London, New York or Toronto, and all of these communities are interlinked both among themselves as well as with the home country by a multiplicity of social ties (cf. Peil 1995).

The German Debate

With regard to ethnographies on the music of immigrant communities in Germany there is still much left to be desired. Though particularly in North

---

[4] I use the term "diaspora" here in the sense as it has been developed by Clifford, involving a sense of community as well as of homeland, constructing thereby "alternate public spheres, forms of community consciousness and solidarity that maintain identifications outside the national time/space in order to live inside, with a difference" (Clifford 1994:305f; see also Akyeampong 2000:184ff).

[5] Foreign remittances reached an estimated eight billion US dollars by the end of 2006 (Kwarteng 2006).

American academia research on music and migration has attracted considerable attention in the last two decades or so,[6] with regard to Germany's "internal Others" and, moreover, their representation in German musicology or ethnomusicology, the research project clearly broke new grounds (cf. Vogels 2005). Apart from Greve's detailed study on the musical life among Turkish immigrants (Greve 2003), there are only few attempts and hardly any profound study scrutinizing the musical practices of migrants in Germany.[7] We find a few surveys of what is (implicitly or explicitly) conceptualized as the music of "ethnic minorities," suggesting thereby that we could identify anything like the music of "the majority" in Germany (would that be the music of Beethoven or André Rieu? That of "Ballermann" star DJ Ötzi or rather the teenager band Tokyo Hotel?).[8] If we consider Turkish popular music — regrettably only marginally represented in Greve's otherwise extensive study — and the worldwide success of performers like Tarkan, who conquered not only the Turkish and the German charts, or that of Turkish-German "R'n'Besque" star Muhabbet from Cologne, terms like "minority music" seem, however, to obscure more than they explain.

The relative lack of substantial studies on music and migration in Germany has certainly to do with the marginal role of a discipline like ethnomusicology in the country. But it might also be linked to the somewhat paradoxical way immigration and immigrants have been dealt with over the course of several decades. If we look at the political debates, much of what has been said in this connection seems irrational, and often the low social status of immigrants has been misused for other political and ideological ends. In popular discourse we can also observe a certain uneasiness in the way issues concerning foreigners, or, as they are called, *Ausländer*, are discussed. One can sense uncertainty as to how to relate to immigrants in the way they are referred to. Sometimes

---

[6] To give but a few examples, see the studies on migrant workers in South Africa by Erlmann (1991) and Coplan (1994), Turino's (1993) extensive study on the music of Andean migrant workers in Peru, Reyes' (1999) study of the music on Vietnamese refugees, or Flores' (2000) work on Puerto Rican identity and music in New York.

[7] See the survey of individual musicians and the music of "ethnic minorities" in then West Berlin edited by Baumann (1979), a similar compilation of Turkish music in Germany (Baumann 1985), and a publication on immigrant musicians in Hamburg, which offers valuable insights into the personal life histories of 32 musicians from 15 different countries (Schedtler 1999). Ghanaians and their music are represented in none of these publications.

[8] See also Hermetek (2001) for an ambitious attempt to map the musics of "ethnic minorities" in Austria. Hermetek reminds us of the political importance of the establishment of minority statuses in multi-ethnic nations like Austria (or, for our concern, Germany). There is, however, a significant difference between indigenous minorities such as the Sorbs in Brandenburg and Saxony or the Danish in Schleswig-Holstein, and the new immigrant populations from the "Global South" that entered Europe in the past three to four decades.

one can hear strange composite terms from the mouth of politicians, talking about *unsere ausländischen Mitbürger* ("our foreign fellow-citizens"), which represents a paradox in itself. It is only in the last few years that issues concerning immigration and immigrants are discussed with more equanimity.

Hosting over seven million people without a German passport, which represents about nine percent of its total population, Germany has been at the top of international immigration statistics for several years. Since the end of World War II roughly fifteen million expellees and refugees immigrated to the territory of then West Germany, and about a third of Germany's current population can be said to result from these migrational flows. Approximately a third of all immigrants in Germany have been residing in the country for more than twenty years and have, by now, become an integral part of society (Bade 1992; Meier-Braun 2002). The official governmental report on migration for 2005 states that today every forth newborn child in Germany has at least one parent from abroad. In the major West German urban centers about forty percent of the youth at age fourteen has what is now commonly referred to as "migrational background" (*Migrationshintergrund*). In some of the larger urban centers such as Frankfurt (Main), immigrants represent about a third of the total population (Ausländerbeauftragte 2005:21f).

The most paradoxical aspect of the German debate is the fact that until recently conservatives insisted that Germany is not a country of immigration. Right-wing political groups have been using such misrepresentations to foster xenophobic anxieties, dwelling on images of "Germanness" where cultural, ethnic, and national identity form a homogeneous, purified whole. Such a racialized conception of nationhood is also implied in ideas such as that of a German "leading culture" (*Leitkultur*). A parliamentarian of the conservative party (CDU/CSU), Friedrich Merz, introduced this term, which is related to nineteenth-century notions of a *Kulturnation*. Assuming an unwillingness to "integrate" themselves, he called for the assimilation of immigrants to the "German leading culture" if they wanted to stay in the country. Though Merz and others employing the term could not specify what they meant by *Leitkultur*, it seems clear that we are dealing here with some kind of Christian, national-conservative middle-class version of what culture is and what it is not. Paul Gilroy remarked that such "crude and reductive notions of culture that form the substance of racial politics today are clearly associated with an older discourse of racial and ethnic difference which is everywhere entangled in the history of the idea of culture in the modern West" (Gilroy 1993:7).

These debates are not new. In a suggestive essay Ha reminds us that immigration was discussed in almost identical terms during the Bismarck era, when the image of Germany as a non-immigrant nation was "articulated [...]

as a national dogma" (Ha 2003:81). The image of the nation unified by "common blood" was the basis for the German citizenship law until recently. Grounded in the principle of nationality by descent and not by birth, the law was put into operation as early as 1913 and has only been modified, but not completely abrogated, in the year 2000. Children of immigrants of the second and third generation have now the right to acquire German citizenship, though dual citizenship is still rejected. The historical reductionism of political discourse often conceals that immigration is by no means a new phenomenon. The formulation of national immigration politics in Germany goes hand in hand with the establishment of the German colonial empire at the end of the nineteenth century (Ha 2003). Debates preceding the formation of the German Empire in 1871 were most concerned with the massive emigration of millions of Germans predominantly to the New World. Though today a "place under the sun" (*ein Platz an der Sonne*) is rather associated with the national lottery than Germany's colonial endeavors abroad,[9] if we want to understand current migrational flows and debates on immigration, we cannot ignore the broader historical dimensions of the phenomenon and Germany's role in the global power system.

In Search of a Field

In March 2004, when I began my work as a research fellow, I moved to Berlin, identifying the city and what I called "Ghana in Berlin," for the time being, as my "field." It was particularly in the 1980s, during the times of the Cold War, that for Ghanaians Berlin served as a point of entry to West Germany and other countries in western Europe, as it is described, for example, in Amma Darko's novel *Beyond the Horizon* (1995), and as Ghanaians told me in personal conversations. Traveling to East Berlin, the capital of the GDR, political circumstances made it relatively easy for Africans to cross the border to West Berlin, where some decided to stay, and many moved on to other desired destinations in western Europe. Today, Berlin hosts between two (officially) to four thousand (unofficially) Ghanaians, which makes them the largest African immigrant group in the city. Particularly in districts with large numbers of immigrants such as Neukölln, Kreuzberg and Wedding, where the African

---

[9] The phrase goes back to the German foreign minister Bernhard von Bülow who in 1897, in a speech at the *Reichstag*, insisted on Germany's legitimate right to have colonial possessions. The same phrase (and associated palm tree images) is nowadays used in advertisements for the national lottery where people can win a holiday abroad (cf. Meier 1984).

community is predominantly based, there is a Ghanaian infrastructure in place, if on a somewhat smaller scale than in Hamburg and in its differentiation hardly comparable with a group like Berlin's Turkish population.

Over the course of the following three years I tried to make sense of the cultural complexity I was confronted with, concentrating mainly on the urban musical landscapes in Berlin and Accra and searching for connections between the two. Both cities were unknown territories for me until then. I visited Ghana for the first time on a three-months stay from November 2004 to February 2005, traveling together with Ofei Ankrah, a Ghanaian musician and dancer whom I had worked with in Berlin and who had a drumming and dancing group in Accra he wanted to bring to Germany to perform. Back in Germany, I spent most of 2005 in Berlin where I continued my research on the city's music scene. Together with two of my colleagues in Hanover, in March 2006 I accompanied a group of ten German music students on an excursion to Ghana. In June 2006, then, for more personal reasons, I permanently moved from Berlin to Accra, where I completed my research and finally "wrote up" the results. As a matter of course, the research project predetermined my movements between Germany and Ghana which I would otherwise not have been able to afford. And it made me become a migrant myself. So, whatever else the following chapters are about, they have been profoundly shaped and impacted by the basic focus of the project.

However, my own project followed a slightly different path than the research project as a whole, at least how I envisioned it in my initial understanding. Not that I didn't find Ghanaians in Berlin — they are there, to be sure. I roamed Ghanaian-owned stores, visited church services almost exclusively attended by Ghanaians, and I also witnessed other social events such as funeral celebrations and outdoorings (naming ceremonies). It might be due to a lack of ability or ethnographic vigor, but as I moved on, my field kept moving and shifting, and the immigrant community I initially had in mind seemed reluctant to present itself as a homogeneous entity to me. Though we will touch aspects of it in the discussions that follow, this ethnography is decidedly *not* about the musical practices within a Ghanaian community or the music of the Ghanaian diaspora in Germany. To me it seemed that the terms I was operating with — such as "music culture" or "migrant community" — just did not match reality. What I found where people who, just like me, made their way through the sometimes confusing diversity of urban space, and who introduced me by and by to the African music scene first in Berlin and then later also in Accra. There were Ghanaians among those people, but there were also many others, Africans, Europeans, immigrants, natives.

Initially searching for "Ghanaian music," I realized that people are rather into "African music," be it "traditional" or "modern." So I also went into Afri-can music, trying to practice what I had learned ethnographers do, that is, "participant observation." Following and interacting with individual musi-cians, performance groups, workshop participants, audience members, and others involved in the scene, I focused on African music and what people in Ghana call "cultural music" or just "culture" (which includes dance). I visited concerts, parties, clubs and festivals, and regularly participated in drumming and dancing workshops as well as in rehearsals; I recorded performances, en-gaged people in conversations, wrote over one thousand pages of notes and conducted more formal recorded interviews with fifteen musicians, dancers, and others involved in the "Afro" business. I also discovered other sources of information: during my excursions in Berlin's music scene I became a collector of flyers, distributed to advertise music workshops, parties, and concerts, which reveal specific politics of representation and constitute a kind of cartography of the city's musical landscape if taken as a whole. I followed media reports, read newspaper articles, listened to radio programs and traveled cyberspace, though the mediascape is only marginally represented in my account. Finally, at different points in the following discussion I will also dwell on earlier histor-ical research on the discourse on African music in German literature of the nineteenth and early twentieth century (cf. Carl 2004 & 2006).

This ethnography, then, deals with a transnational music scene that cen-ters around a relatively general and often vague notion of "African music." This transnational music scene, localized as "Afro" scene in Germany and as the "culture" scene in Ghana, stretches across the space paradigmatically marked by the cities of Berlin and Accra. Rather than being concerned with musical communities, cultures, or minorities, I focus on the points of contact between different cultural formations. In fact, I argue that cultural identity is itself something that is "made" only in the encounter between people. I am interested in how notions of "culture," "ethnicity," "race," and "nation" are produced by means of musical performance in the encounter between Ger-mans and Ghanaians in particular, and between Europeans and Africans, which is to say, Whites and Blacks, more generally. I am, in other words, in-terested in how space constitutes itself through musical practice in the trans-national field between Germany and Ghana.

Considering music principally as a transnational spatial practice raises a number of questions, as Guilbault has noted with regard to the phenomenon of "world music." She asks: "What is the relations between musics, a popula-tion's identities, and the issue of ethnicities? Confronting these complex reali-ties calls not only for a redefinition of culture but also for a redefinition of bonds, boundaries and borders" (Guilbault 1997:34). Employing the concept of (social) space might help finding answers to questions of how collective identities, often in the form of territorial concepts, are articulated through musical performance and discourse. Following Henri Lefebvre I understand social space as follows:

> (Social) space is not a thing among other things, nor a product among other products: rather, it subsumes things produced, and encompasses their interrelationships in their coexistence and simultaneity — their (relative) order and/or (relative) disorder. It is the outcome of a sequence and set of operations, and thus cannot be reduced to the rank of a simple object. At the same time there is nothing imagined, unreal or "ideal" about it as compared, for example, with science, representations, ideas or dreams. Itself the outcome of past actions, social space is what permits fresh actions to occur, while suggesting others and prohibiting yet others. Among these actions, some serve production, others consumption (i.e. the enjoyment of the fruits of production). Social space implies a great diversity of knowledge. (Lefebvre [1991] 2004:73)

Space is "cultural" in that it implies and comprises knowledge and meaning. As Lefebvre notes, "[s]pace may be marked physically, as with animals' use of smells or human groups' use of visual or auditory indicators; alternatively, it may be marked abstractly, by means of discourse, by means of signs. Space thus acquires symbolic value" (ibid.:141). As a marker in and of space, music can indicate difference as well as identity, and this through the exclusion or inclusion of other elements in space. It is through musical performance as a sensual and emotive experience that space is "at once conceived, perceived, and directly lived" (ibid.:356). Social space is at first a theoretical construction, just as the transnational space that expands between Berlin and Accra, with which this ethnography is primarily concerned, is an abstraction. "Considered in isolation," Lefebvre notes, "spaces are mere abstractions. As concrete abstractions, however, they attain 'real' existence by virtue of networks and pathways, by virtue of bunches or clusters of relationships" (ibid.:86). Such "clusters of relationships" can range from worldwide telecommunication networks to the social networks of individuals. Thus, not only for the people I encountered on my way through the space I am about to describe, but also for myself, "Berlin/Accra" is a very concrete abstraction, embodied in relationships, biographies, memories and anecdotes, in places and sites.

Concrete abstractions form therefore the intersection between theory and practice for any ethnographic endeavor (cf. Bourdieu 1977). As an empirical

approach that is based on participant observation, face-to-face contact, dialogue, and the movement between different sites, ethnography is necessarily
relational, itself concrete and abstract at the same time. Although it is a key-
word that came up only in recent methodological discussions with regard to
"globalization" or the "world system," ethnographies have always been
"multi-sited" (Marcus 1995), in the sense that they explore social networks,
different subject positions, and the interconnections between different sites.
During "fieldwork," which in the anthropological disciplines has always "essentially […] been a messy, qualitative experience," as Marcus and Fischer
(1986:22) phrased it, the relation and tension between the abstract and the
concrete level is always present. It manifests itself in the inconsistency of concepts when applied to reality, and in the contradictions — at times conflicts —
that arise in concrete relations to other people and things in space.

Yet, in the space of writing the concreteness of relations remains often abstract. For the more solitary phase of the ethnographic process, which is to say,
in ethnographic writing, relations become a matter of representation, of textual strategy and style. I have tried to retain the quality of the concrete and
contradictory, which was an essential part of my own "fieldwork experience,"
at least rhetorically by interspersing my rather abstract discussions of the production of space through travel and music with accounts of more concrete encounters that took place during my own travels between Germany and Ghana.

*   *   *

As a matter of consequence, my account might at some points appear eclectic,
as it abruptly moves between sites and times. We will explore a number of
contexts in which the performance of African music takes place, or, how different places are constructed through the performance of African music. As a
multi-sited endeavor, this ethnography is both heterotopic and heterochronic,
which is to say, it focuses on how places as well as time are inscribed in space,
and how through the evocation of place space is produced. From a spatial perspective, time is only one possible parameter for the distribution of elements in
space. Thus, while exploring the place(s) of African music within a globalized
popular culture, we will also ask about the connections and relations that are
established between places and sites through performances and representations, and how different spaces thus come into being, how they are produced
through music.

The next chapter will take us to the zoo, as one of the sites where African
music emerges. In the nineteenth and early twentieth century in Europe and
North America the performance of African music took place in the form of

ethnographic shows that were also part of colonial and world exhibitions. Ethnographic shows or what in the German context is called *Völkerschauen* were staged at fairs, in circuses, and also in the newly emerging zoological gardens. While in the twentieth century this form of popular entertainment was partly replaced by other media, above all the growing film industry, in recent years we increasingly find performances of African music in zoos again.

Since its world premier in December 2005, the production *Afrika! Afrika!* by André Heller, "the magical circus adventure from the amazing continent,"[10] has attracted hundreds of thousands of visitors in Germany, Austria, Switzerland, France, Britain, and Spain, and the show will soon also tour the United States. Due to its immense commercial success, the event has been copied in a number of smaller productions of "Africa circuses" touring throughout Germany and other countries. Considering the unbroken popularity of the staging of Africa as a miraculous, magical, mysterious, and adventurous continent, we will ask about similarities and differences between nineteenth-century performances and representations of Africa and those we witness today. How can we make sense of the performance of African music in zoos? What are the continuities and the discontinuities between staged performances by Africans in the nineteenth, the twentieth, and the twenty-first centuries?

The third chapter will discuss the representation and performance of African music in a broader historical as well as theoretical perspective. It will scrutinize the role of academic disciplines in the discovery and appropriation of African music, in fact its very invention, and critically discuss the interdependence of colonial and scientific endeavors in the nineteenth and twentieth century. Particularly in the anthropological disciplines, the academic involvement in processes of colonization has been critically discussed in the wake of the so-called "crisis of representation." Taking the power relations that are produced and reproduced in and through academic accounts into consideration, the consequences scholars draw from the insight that the production of knowledge is never "objective" or "neutral" differ. In any case, as ethnomusicologists these insights compel us to critically reflect on our role in the production of cultural, ethnic, and racial difference. In how far and in what ways are we, as scholars, involved in the production of cultural, ethnic, and racial spaces through the theorization of music and musical practices?

The history of the idea of African music leads us from the European discovery of so-called "primitive music" in the age of exploration to later appro-

---

[10] Quoted from the official webpage at http://www.africancircus.de (accessed on July 7, 2007).

priations of it as the very antithesis to European "art music," as the racial Other. In Germany this difference became institutionalized in the distinction between "comparative musicology" in contrast to "historical musicology," a distinction which persists in universities up to today. As a possible response to the insight that African music has over a long period been fabricated not only as the cultural, but commonly as the ethnic or racial Other, in the last section of the third chapter we will try to come to terms with music in the context of a musical geography that situates contemporary musical practices as localized social practices on the one hand, yet that on the other hand considers these localized and localizable practices vis-à-vis the global cultural economy.

Chapter four represents a first exploration of urban space. It discusses both the practical and theoretical implications of the fact that musical practices today take place predominantly within what Henri Lefebvre (2003) characterized as "urban society." It is intriguing and revealing that the images produced through African music often denote some sort of pastoral, rustic and rural space, whereas its performance takes place mostly in an urban environment. What are the implications of the thus produced ambivalence? As a matter of fact, "globalization" and "urbanization" are two sides of the same coin, and the epicenters of what is discussed as globalizing processes are the major urban conglomerates as we find them around the globe today. Urban centers are also the nodal points in transnational migrational movements. Resulting from such movements, we will more particularly engage ourselves in the multiethnic realities of Berlin, and outline some of the debates that arise around this reality in the German context.

What from a German perspective is sometimes portrayed as menacing, inconceivable parallel worlds (*Parallelwelten*) or isolated migrant communities, are in fact parts of much broader social networks that are interlinked transnationally over several continents. As for the Ghanaian case, we find thriving social networks in many urban areas in Germany today that are not only linked to one another on a national scale, but to the international Ghanaian diaspora more generally. Media networks and shared social practices help in creating such "imagined communities" transnationally. As a diversion we will read colonial space as it inscribed itself in the urban landscape of Berlin. Finally, considering the multiethnic and transnational urban reality, we will discuss the consequences of these developments for ethnography and ethnographers, who were once rather thought of as traveling to some dead-end village where they would then "go native."

Aside from transnational formations based on common nationality or ethnicity, which produce their particular spaces, there are other networks and interconnections that also go beyond the scope of definite-bordered nations or cultures. One such space is what Paul Gilroy coined the "Black Atlantic," which expands between Africa, Europe, and the Americas and which is interlinked historically and culturally in manifold ways. Based on the global dispersion of Africans, which took its violent beginning in the transatlantic slave trade and which finds a continuation in current migrational flows, it was particularly music and expressive cultural forms that played a significant role in the constitution of the Black Atlantic. The mutual musical influences of musical practices and styles between black communities around the Atlantic are widely visible and audible in the global cultural economy today, and while African music has inspired African American musicians since long, American and European modernity has likewise played a significant role in transforming musical practices on the African continent. Resulting from the experience of displacement, particularly for African Americans African music has also become an important means in the search for their cultural roots. These are some of the issues we will discuss in the fifth chapter, in which we will also outline Germany's involvement in the Black Atlantic.

From the exploration of a number of different Black Atlantic worlds we will return to urban space more specifically and discuss the networks of people, places, and musical practices that constitute the "Afro" scene. How can we characterize the networks of a musical scene and how do individuals establish themselves in relation to others within these networks? Through more general considerations of urbanism and metropolitanism, we will try to come to an answer to the question how musical practices, understood as spatial practices, might themselves be an integral part in the production of urban and transurban spaces and identities. We will also ask about the roles of music festivals in the constitution of urban society and how culture becomes "festivalized" through musical practice.

Our engagement in the networks particularly of Berlin's "Afro" scene will be followed by a more detailed account of the symbolic economy of this cultural formation. While in chapter six we consider the musical production of space by focusing on concrete social networks and urban geography, in the chapter that follows we will concern ourselves more with the symbolic production of space. Questions as to how strategic positions are created by the employment of different politics of style and what kind of spaces are produced within symbolic economies will therefore be our preoccupation in chapter seven. The last two sections of that chapter will focus on questions of identity formation. How are identities and representations of space, for example, produced, mediated and appropriated? Or how are identities performed and transformed, and how are representations of space actually lived through performance?

In chapter eight then, lastly, we continue our travels in and our exploration of performative spaces in Africa. Even on the African continent, finding and capturing "Africa" is, as we will see, not always a simple task. Chapter eight will scrutinize the musical scene and the discourses built around the phenomenon of "culture" in Ghana. We will ask in how far "culture" differs from "tradition," for example, and will explore how "African culture" is produced as a symbolic space and a counter-image to an imagined West or the "white man's land." While one pervasive theme running through the preceding chapters is the production of racialized spaces through the musical construction of blackness, in chapter eight we will focus more on the production of race by way of the construction of whiteness. Both processes are, of course, mutually related. Looking at how "culture" functions as a means of contact between Ghanaians and Europeans, or Blacks and Whites more generally, within Ghana's growing tourist sector, we will finally come back to questions about our own involvement in the production of knowledge. The interplay between the academic production of knowledge and the performance of music and culture is, after all, a persistent theme throughout all of the following chapters.

As it might have already become obvious, the contexts in which we encounter African music could hardly be more diverse. From the great colonial and world exhibitions at the end of the nineteenth century, where amazed European audiences were confronted with staged exotic shows, to "African markets" put up in German zoos today; from funeral celebrations in urban settings in Ghana, where cultural troupes are hired to entertain guests with a pan-ethnic repertoire of African music and dance, to workshops and classes, where Germans are taught African drumming and dancing; from world music festivals to African American tour groups traveling to Africa in search of their cultural roots via music and dance; from televised Independence Day celebrations in Africa to the nightlife of European metropolises, where Whites and Blacks meet each other in search of exotic sexual adventure as well as potential marriage partners in order to secure their resident status in the "Fortress Europe" — in all these cases we are confronted with African music and images of Africa indicating specific patterns of identification. Considering all these different contexts, we will throughout be concerned with questions of how spaces are produced through performance and representation and what kind of spaces emerge through music as a spatial practice.

2 Africa and the Zoo

Nubians in Wilhelmine Germany

In 1876 a group of "Nubians" performed in Germany and their show became a great success. Because of its popularity this so-called *Völkerschau* toured in the country several times in subsequent years. The ethnographic show business was, after all, flourishing. From the display of corpses of people of non-European descent on fairs and in museums to folkloristic performances and the reconstruction of "native's villages" in zoos and other locations: The exhibition and performance of human difference attracted large audiences in Europe and North America throughout the nineteenth and in the early twentieth century.[1] The success of ethnographic shows depended largely on the audience's desire for the exotic. The logic of the *Völkerschauen* was based on an ambivalent fascination with the Other, the appeal of the unknown, which could appear threatening, at times erotic, yet which was ultimately harmless and under control in its appropriated form. Staged performances by Africans in Wilhelmine Germany such as that of the "Nubians" are clearly a part of this tradition.[2]

Curiosity about the Other was not restricted to popular culture. The popularization of ethnographic shows in the nineteenth century goes hand in hand with an increased scientific interest in human difference in disciplines like biology, ethnology, or anthropology. Philosophers of the European Enlightenment developed theories that explained the variation between the dif-

---

[1] The most prominent example for the exhibition of a corpse is probably the case of Saartje Baartman. Ranking as a medical sensation, the woman of the Khoi people was brought forcefully from South Africa to Europe in 1809 and became famous as the so-called "Hottentot Venus." She was exhibited almost naked at country fairs. After 1816, when she died at the age of only 26, her corpse was still displayed in England and France (Nederveen Pieterse 1998:172-187). The case was discussed recently in the media, because parts of Baartman's body were still exhibited in the Musée de l'Homme in Paris until 1981. Even after protests of human rights activists she was still kept in the archive of the museum. Finally, the South African government claimed back the corpse in order to bury Baartman in dignity, almost 200 years after she died. A plaster cast of her body is still kept in Paris (Oltmer 2007).

[2] On the tradition of the ethnographic shows see Brändle (1995), Haberland (1988), Lindfors (1999), Staehelin (1994), and Thode-Arora (1989).

ferent "human races" (Eze 2000). In the nineteenth century, scholars formulated evolutionary schemes that elucidated how the world's cultures evolved, and physicians argued about the pathologies of "primitive" peoples. There was generally an increased interest in "man" in academic discourse, a category of thinking Foucault (1973) identified as a distinctively modern invention. In the academic models, people from outside Europe were conceptualized as racially inferior, as "contemporary ancestors" on a lower evolutionary stage, or, sometimes as little children who still had to mature.

Museum displays and *Völkerschauen* helped to implement the logic of social Darwinism and racialism in public consciousness. While some shows turned out to be mere exotic spectacles, sensationalism was often combined with the claim that the performances were educational. This is particularly true for the ethnographic shows that were part of the great world and colonial exhibitions at the end of the nineteenth century (Debusmann & Riesz 1995; Meinecke 1897). Intended to promote the colonial and missionary project, the images transported in these shows reinforced the imperial worldview in which the superiority of European civilization over the rest of the world was an unquestioned assumption. *Völkerschauen* therefore played their part in popularizing the ideologies of imperialism and colonialism (Arnold 1995).

The show of the "Nubians" was organized by Carl Hagenbeck, founder of the zoological garden in Hamburg, and one of the most successful entrepreneurs in Germany around the turn of the century. Initially concentrating on the trade in exotic animals, Hagenbeck began to also ship in "exotic people" to Germany in 1874. Motivated by the success of his first "anthropological-zoological" exhibition of a reindeer herd and a family from Lapland, together with their complete household effects, Hagenbeck concentrated more and more on the profitable business of organizing ethnographic shows. Performances by people from Africa, reenacting hunting and war scenes, "ecstatic" dances, or indigenous village life — all scenes that were already known from travel accounts and other popular literature — always promised a success. Overall, German audiences were amazed to see "Somali warriors," Douala people from Cameroon, "fifty wild Congo women," or a whole "Amazon corps" on stage.[3]

Performances of this sort took place in circuses, zoos and other locations and clearly had an impact on the production and reinforcement of images of Africa and Africans. Lindfors (1999), in his essay about a group of Zulus from Natal which came to London in 1853 and subsequently also toured France

---

[3] For an overview of African ethnographic shows in Germany see Thode-Arora (1989:34ff & 168f).

and Germany, illustrates how colonial propaganda and popular images of the wild and fierce African met in ethnographic shows. Though there were, particularly if compared to Germany, a considerable number of Blacks living in Britain in the nineteenth century, "real" Africans were still a sensation. Due to the military conflicts between the Zulus and the British in South Africa, the Zulus had the reputation of a warlike people, as it was promoted in the European press. As Lindfors shows, this reputation only added to the success of the ethnographic show of the Zulus, and it comes with little surprise that in the newspaper reviews we see common clichés about "wild" and "fierce" dances, the "naturalness" of Africans, and similar epithets reproduced. Interestingly enough, the South African musical *King Kong* which toured Europe in the 1960s as well as similar productions of "Zulu musicals" in the 1970s were discussed in almost identical terms as the ethnographical shows that were staged a century before.

As a clever businessman, Hagenbeck was well aware of the stereotypes ascribed to Africans and made therefore extensive use of them in the promotion of his shows. In his memoirs, published in 1909 under the consistent title *Von Tieren und Menschen* ("Of Animals and Humans"), Hagenbeck reminisces about the arrival of the "Nubians" in Europe, a troupe that was actually made up of people from various ethnic groups in Sudan, a territory then under Egyptian occupation. He writes:

> In June 1876 the shipment of people and animals arrived at Trieste. The beautiful people belonged to different tribes; they came from our former animal paradise, the Sudan, which was closed down a few years later because of the Mahdist rebellion. Among the troupe was also a woman, Hadjidje, the first Nubian woman who came to Europe. In the ornament of their own wild personalities, with their animals, tents, household and hunting utensils, the guests presented a highly interesting anthropological-zoological picture from the Sudan. The exhibition always started in Hamburg and toured different cities from there, causing the same sensation everywhere. Here and there, I have to admit, some preparations were made. In Breslau for example I had the idea to drive my Nubians, all in the pompous ornament of their weapons, feathers, and coats, around the city in the noblest equipages one could get in Breslau. In the first carriage sat Dr. Schlegel, the director of the zoo, myself, and the beautiful Hadjidje. Next to every coachman throned a Sudanese warrior in gloomy majesty with a looming lance. Ten carriages drove one after the other. On the way we stopped at the best café in town, which

was immediately filled to the last corner with curious guests.[4]

Hagenbeck understood the attraction "his Nubians" had on the German audience, and he obviously understood how to choreograph otherness effectively. In the promotion of the Nubian show, the "beautiful Hadjidje" was particularly highlighted and pictures of her in postcard format sold well as merchandise. Representations of half naked people and women with bare breasts were clearly a taboo at the end of the nineteenth century in Europe and in Wilhelmine Germany. They could only be marketed with reference to their "ethnographic" interest. Hence, sexual desire and the allure of the black body was, after all, one of the main elements that African ethnographic shows brought into play. Not surprisingly, there was some overlapping of the markets in exotica and that in erotica during that time.[5]

If we analyze Hagenbeck's description of the promotional campaign for the "anthropological-zoological" performance in Breslau, we see that on a structural level the contrast between "civilization" and "savagery" is strategically widened, as for example through the employment of luxury carriages in which the Africans in their "wild" costumes were placed. Alterity and distance is consciously produced here. What we can observe in this particular instance is at the same time the more general effect of ethnographic shows taking place in zoos, namely the tendency to de-humanize the performers. Some of these

---

[4] "Im Juni 1876 traf der Menschen- und Tiertransport in Triest ein. Die schönen Leute gehörten verschiedenen Stämmen an, sie kamen aus unserem damaligen Tierparadies, dem Sudan, der einige Jahre später durch den Mahadistenaufstand geschlossen werden sollte. In der Truppe befand sich auch eine Frau, Hadjidje, die erste Nubierin, welche nach Europa gelangte. Im Schmucke ihrer eigenen wilden Persönlichkeiten, mit ihren Tieren, Zelten, Haus- und Jagdgeräten boten die Gäste ein hochinteressantes anthropologisch-zoologisches Bild aus dem Sudan. Jedesmal begann die Ausstellung in Hamburg und bereiste von hier aus verschiedene Städte, überall das gleiche Aufsehen erregend. Hier und da wurde freilich, wie ich gestehen will, etwas vorgearbeitet. In Breslau zum Beispiel kam ich auf die Idee, meine Nubier, alle im pompösen Schmuck ihrer Waffen, Federn und Felle, in den vornehmsten Equipagen, die man in Breslau haben konnte, durch die Stadt spazierenfahren zu lassen. Im ersten Wagen saßen Dr. Schlegel, der Direktor des Zoo, ich selbst und die schöne Hadjidje. Neben jedem Kutscher thronte in finsterer Majestät ein sudanesischer Krieger mit ragender Lanze. Zehn Wagen fuhren hintereinander. Unterwegs kehrte man im ersten Café der Stadt ein, das sich sofort bis in die entferntesten Winkel mit neugierigen Besuchern füllte" (Hagenbeck [1909] 1928:50). All translations from German to English in the following are, if not indicated otherwise, my own.

[5] Another striking example how sexism came into play in the promotion of ethnographic shows is a poster from 1913. It shows a lasciviously lying black woman with bare breasts and was used to advertise an event at the Passage-Panoptikum in Berlin entitled "50 wilde Kongoweiber" ("50 wild Congo women"). See illustration in van der Heyden & Zeller (2002:134).

shows attracted up to ten thousand visitors around the turn of the century. In the most extreme cases, people were exhibited in cages like animals, though this was clearly the exception.[6] Most of the performers in ethnographic shows were hired on a contract basis, and we can assume that they played the "savage" quite consciously. Nevertheless, in the *Völkerschauen* in the zoos of Europe as well as North America, Africans in their "villages" were placed next to lions and apes, to be gazed at through a fence. Clearly separated from the distanced observer, audiences were merely confronted with an accumulation of "exotic creatures," some bearing more resemblances with themselves, others less.

A Colorful Afternoon in the Zoo

The organizers had asked for something "colorful," Asamoah told me, and something colorful is what they eventually got. I had been rehearsing with Adikanfo for quite some months, not as a regular member, but rather as an apprentice who tried to comprehend some of the rhythms and dances the group was specializing in.[7] I learned bell and drum patterns which Ofei, who introduced me to the group in the first place, and the other members taught me, trying my best to reproduce them while playing along with the group. Everyone knew that I was the "university guy" who wanted to learn more about Ghanaian music. By and by we became acquainted through the weekly rehearsals. Some of the members urged me after a while to involve myself more in the group, to perform gigs with them as well. I was reluctant about that. It would have been Asamoah's decision anyway, since it was his group. Apart from that, I didn't feel I was ready to perform on stage yet. It might well be that the position of the observer was a much more convenient one, but I actually also wondered in how far a "white man" like me — an *oburoni*, as people in Ghana call me — would fit into an all-black group playing "traditional music and dance" from Ghana. My attendance at rehearsals was one thing, but in terms of public performances I was clearly out of the marketing concept of Adikanfo. I knew it and Asamoah was, of course, well aware of it, too.

---

[6] An African man, Ota Benga, from Central Africa was put on display in a monkey cage in the Bronx Zoo in New York City in 1906, for example (Nnaemeka 2005:100f).

[7] The group Adikanfo, specializing in Ghanaian drumming and dancing, is based in Berlin and led by Mark Kofi Asamoah. Introduced to the group by one of its former members, Ofei Ankrah, I started regularly attending rehearsals in April 2004 and continued working with the group throughout 2005. For more information on Adikanfo see Mark Kofi Asamoah's website at http://www.asamoah.de (accessed on May 8, 2008).

As far as the performance in Leipzig is concerned, what the organizers meant by "colorful" were rather black people in "African" costumes, performing "African" music and dance. Thus, nobody would have a problem with Abdul playing Ghanaian music, although he was from Burkina Faso and therefore the only non-Ghanaian member of Adikanfo. Ofei and Kay told me that performing with him was sometimes difficult. It wouldn't be wrong what he played, they assured me; he would definitely be a good drummer. But they just didn't share the same rhythmic "feel." Yet, nobody in the audience would be able to make out such nuances. In any case, when we loaded the instruments and the equipment from the rehearsal room in Berlin-Kreuzberg into the rented bus and prepared to take off that Saturday morning, it seemed clear that I would witness the performance from among the audience, taking pictures and maybe recording the show on video, while the others would be on stage. Our journey to Leipzig, about two hours drive southwards from Berlin, was relaxed. When we approached our destination, there was still a lot of time to make out the location for the gig before the sound check would start.

"Where are we going?" I asked, since nobody had told me yet where the performance would actually take place. I didn't know Leipzig. It was years ago, still in the times of the GDR, that I visited the city with my parents, and the only thing I could remember was the penetrating smell of lignite, which they used for the heating systems and which made me feel sick anytime I recalled it. The place had definitely changed.

"We have to go to the zoo," Asamoah said. "The place should be signposted." To the zoo? I was a little perplexed, but it seemed that nobody except me found the location somehow odd. So we went to the zoo.

It was a hot, sunny day in early August 2004. The summer had finally arrived and people slowed down as they went about their daily affairs and made their way through the city. It wasn't as hot as the summer before, when some editors of the *Bild*, the country's best-selling daily newspaper, started wondering (for want of a better story and possibly affected by the heat) whether we, the Germans, would now all become Africans, which is to say, black, due to the tropical temperatures (Hülskötter & Klostermann 2003). Anyway, the weather seemed proper for a "Dschungelnacht," that is, a "jungle night," as the organizers called the event set up in the Leipzig zoo for the last few years now in order to attract more visitors to its premises. While in previous years Adesa — another Ghanaian group that makes its way through the German cultural market — had performed here, this year Adikanfo had been booked to add some "African flair" to the event.

To get an impression what the "jungle night" is all about it is worth quoting the promotional text announcing the event in 2002 at some length, which went under the header "The Drums Are Calling":

> Hot rhythms, fiery dances and wild acrobatic shows are waiting for
> the visitors in the whole premises of the zoo. At 5 p.m. the Ghanaian
> group "Adesa" will enter the concert garden with a Gamashino pa-
> rade in the style of the Asafo warriors. Director of the zoo Dr. Jörg
> Junhold will open the Jungle Night there at 6 p.m. On a mystic cult
> place (concert garden) an international firework of high-powered ar-
> tistic performances by the Myth Company (South Africa) and Ndux
> Malax (Ghana), Latin American and African music by DJ Bongo,
> and a splendidly colorful parrot revue can be expected. The absolute
> highlights of the evening are the groups "Badenya" from Burkina
> Faso with songs, dance, and acrobatics starting at 9 p.m. and hot
> reggae with Root B Tama at 11 p.m.
>
> Outside the concert garden the zoo will be covered in torchlight.
> Artists animate with music and dance for a nightly walk and to the
> popular special tours into the tropical houses and to Pongoland […].
> Close to the Hacienda Las Casas the mystic sounds of voodoo per-
> cussion resonate in the shine of a campfire. A happy and colorful Af-
> rican celebration with hot rhythms, songs, games for children, and
> information about the black continent will take place in the jungle
> village of Pongoland.
>
> The zoo gastronomy as well as the scene gastronomy "Basa Mo"
> will provide all kinds of exotic food and cocktails.[8]

---

[8] "Im gesamten Zoogelände warten auf die Besucher heiße Rhythmen, feurige Tänze und
wilde Akrobatikshows. Um 17.00 Uhr zieht die ghanaische Gruppe 'Adesa' mit einer Ga-
mashino-Parade im Stil der Asafo-Krieger in den Konzertgarten. Dort eröffnet Zoodirektor
Dr. Jörg Junhold um 18.00 Uhr die Dschungelnacht. Auf einem mystischen Kultplatz
(Konzertgarten) wartet ein internationales Feuerwerk aus Hochleistungsartistik der Myth
Company (Südafrika) und Ndux Malax (Ghana), lateinamerikanische und afrikanische Musik von DJ Bongo und eine farbenprächtigen Papageien-Revue. Die absoluten Höhepunkte
des Abends sind ab ca. 21.00 Uhr die Gruppe 'Badenya' aus Burkina Faso mit Gesang,
Tanz und Akrobatik sowie ca. 23.00 Uhr heißer Reggae mit Root B Tama.
    Außerhalb des Konzertgartens hüllt sich der Zoo in Fackelschein. Kleinkünstler ani-
mieren mit Musik und Tanz zum nächtlichen Rundgang und zu den beliebten Spezialfüh-
rungen in die Tropenhäuser und ins Pongoland (jeweils 19.00; 20.00; 21.00 und 22.00
Uhr). In der Nähe der Hacienda Las Casas erklingen im Schein eines Lagerfeuers die mystischen Klänge von Voodoo Percussion. Ein farbenfrohes, afrikanisches Fest mit heißen
Rhythmen, Gesang, Basteleien, Kinderspielen und Informationen zum schwarzen Kontinent gibt es im Urwalddorf von Pongoland.

Hagenbeck hardly could have done a better job. It almost seems that the organizers in Leipzig copied his idea of "anthropological-zoological" exhibitions. From "hot rhythms," "fiery dances," and "wild acrobatic shows" to the encounter with wild animals and the visit in a "jungle village," where visitors are educated about the "black continent" that is emblematically represented by "Pongoland" (which, to make matters worse, seems reminiscent of Togoland, Germany's former *Musterkolonie*): in the description of the event in Leipzig we find every element of a nineteenth-century *Völkerschau*. The overall picture is complemented by the fact that most buildings in the zoo, founded over a century ago, are fashioned in colonial architectural style. The problematical historical link was not thematized by the organizers with a single comment, neither in the program notes nor at the event itself. The message of the "Dschungelnacht" seems clear: Africa is the jungle and its music and dances are hot, wild, mysterious, occult — come and enjoy an exotic spectacle.

We soon arrived at the zoo, though I should add that the promotional text quoted above makes the setting sound much more exciting than it actually was. Anyway, that is what promotion is all about. A young German woman in charge of coordinating the artists lead us to the backstage area where some snacks and drinks were provided. We dropped our bags in the dressing room that was reserved for Adikanfo and went back to the car, starting to unpack the drums. The group's performance was scheduled for the afternoon and was supposed to take place on the main stage, which was put up close to the entrance area. Other "African" performances, including drumming and dancing workshops, were placed along the paths through the zoo, between food stands and people dealing in all kinds of "ethno stuff" — figurines, masks, beads, carved giraffes and elephants, batiks, and the like. After a short sound check there was not much time to prepare for the actual performance. Everyone was dressing for the show.

Maggie, one of the dancers, had asked me to record the performance and was still explaining to me how to handle her video camera, when Asamoah came in, announcing that there was a slight change of plans. The organizers had asked him whether three of the nine members could drum at the zoo's entrance while the rest would perform on the main stage. This led to some protest and confusion in the group: if the organizers wanted two groups, they should pay for two groups, was one opinion. Apart from that, those playing at the entrance would be needed on stage. Asamoah looked at me and asked me to help out. With seven people they could still perform on stage. Ofei could

Die Zoogastronomie und die Szenegastronomie "Basa Mo" sorgen für allerlei exotische Speisen und Cocktails" (Leipzig Online 2002).

join the drummers and only the three women would dance. Thus, if Abdul, Kay, and I would drum at the entrance, everything would be fine. I was grateful for all Asamoah and the others in the group had done for me, so I hardly could have denied this request.

And this, then, is how I eventually found myself together with Abdul and Kay at the entrance of the zoo. Dressed in "African" costume, we played more or less "hot" rhythms, while East German families, some stopping for a moment to watch us before they entered the zoo (and probably wondering what the White was doing there), passed by in expectation of a "colorful" event. When the other members of Adikanfo finished their show on the main stage, they came to join us at the entrance for two or three more pieces. The drums were calling after all, and everyone, it seems, played his or her part.

After the performance everyone was in a jovial mood. We enjoyed the drinks that waited for us backstage and made fun of my uneven tanned arms, which betrayed I had been wearing a T-shirt anytime I went into the sun, and which made me look quite stupid in the sleeveless "African shirts" we were performing in. At least my involvement in the performance had a fraternizing effect. I asked the others whether they were aware of the tradition of the *Völkerschauen*. This wasn't the case and though Kay felt that the setting of the zoo was a little strange they didn't see a significant difference to other performances they do. The setting for performances of a group like Adikanfo is indeed often similar, be it at the *Karneval der Kulturen* (Berlin's yearly multicultural street festival), at world music festivals throughout Europe, the beach resorts along the Ghanaian coast, or at Accra's "Arts Centre" (Centre for National Arts and Culture). The repertoire, the audiences, "ethnic markets," drumming and dancing workshops, after-show parties: all this is an integral part of the business.

Maggie, who had formerly worked at the Centre for National Arts and Culture in Accra, brought her view of the event to the point: "You know, Florian, we're doing this for ourselves. Most people for whom we're playing don't really understand what we are doing anyway. But it's very important for us." Making a living of social aid and perhaps occasional low-paid jobs to provide money for herself and her little son, for Maggie performing with Adikanfo was clearly a way to take a break from the everyday realities she shares with many immigrants in Germany. Performing on stage is something that earns you respect, something that gives you recognition. And though people might not really understand the rhythms and dances they performed, audiences enjoyed and appreciated their shows nonetheless. "Culture" was something Maggie had already done at the "Arts Centre" in Accra. Most of the members of Adikanfo are professionals, working in the business with African culture since long before they came to Berlin or to Europe. Playing gigs like the one in Leipzig, for them, was merely a question of adjusting to the needs of the local market.

The Zoo Revisited

In May 2005 a heated debate came up in the German press and the scholarly community centering on an event in the Augsburg zoo. The event, not unlike the one in Leipzig, was announced as "African Village" and also offered a supposedly African cultural program including musical performances to attract visitors. At the event, the organizers wrote in their announcement, "artisans, silversmiths, basket makers and traditional hairdressers are grouped in a unique African savannah landscape."[9] It was particularly because of the label "African Village" in connection with the setting of the zoo that the organizers in Augsburg saw themselves confronted with harsh critique that came especially from the side of the Afro-German community: neo-colonialism, racism, and even fascism were among the reproaches. Alarmed by circulating bulk e-mails that also called my attention in the first place, within a short period of time the protest against the event was organized on an international scale. African-German organizations, human rights organizations, academic associations, Nobel Prize winner Nadine Gordimer, and individuals from several countries expressed their opposition to the "African Village."[10] After my own experiences in the Leipzig zoo the summer before, the massive protests actually came as a surprise to me, all the more since the event in Leipzig — which was just the same kind of event, namely an "African" market within the setting of the zoo, framed by an "African" cultural program — went on largely unnoticed.

In an open letter to the director of the Augsburg zoo, Barbara Jantschke, the Afro-German organizations ISD (Initiative of Black People in Germany) and ADEFRA (Initiative of Black Women in Germany/Black German Women) referred to the tradition of the *Völkerschauen* which, they argued, the event in Augsburg continued conceptually as well as practically. As they wrote:

---

[9] The announcement was published on the official website of the zoo at http://www.zoo-augsburg.de, but any hint of the "African Village" was removed from that page.

[10] The debate can be reviewed on the Internet at http://www.cybernomads.net (accessed on March 05, 2007), an online portal for the black community in Germany. See also a study by the Max Planck Institute about the "African Village" in Augsburg (Dea et al. 2005), and discussions of the incident in media reports (Hawley 2005; Schallenberg 2005; Schwarzer 2005; Zekri 2005).

It is obvious that the conveners do not understand the historical implications of their project. Even in Germany the ongoing impact of
German colonialism and racism on African peoples are nowadays
debated in public. Reproducing colonial perspectives, which turns
people of African descent into exotic objects, into sub-humans or
non-humans, harmoniously embedded in a perpetual village life,
serving as objects of observation and as inspiration to members of
the dominating, so-called majority population for future tourist expeditions, can hardly be interpreted as an encounter on equal foot-
ing. After forty years of German colonialism and twelve years of National Socialism the racist gaze is still very much alive in Germany.
(Quoted and translated in Nnaemeka 2005:90)

Another commenter on the "African Village" retrospectively wrote: "The ex-
hibit/event purporting to 'nurture tolerance and understanding among peoples' was nothing short of a reminder of the outrageous, racist, eugenic practices of Nazi Germany and the exoticizing of Africans in freak shows in
Europe" (Nnaemeka 2005:90). But regardless of the strong words employed by
its critics, the director of the zoo did not change her mind about realizing the
"African Village." She rejected reproaches of racism and insisted that there
was a great interest particularly among Africans themselves to participate in
the event as exhibitors. The organizer would actually be "a born African with
black skin" himself.[11] And she finally added that she considered the zoo exactly
the right place to convey, as she wrote in her reply to the letter of the ISD and
ADEFRA, "the atmosphere of the exotic."
   This in turn lead to even more enraged reactions and the protesters
called for a boycott of the event. On the other side were the organizers, supported by politicians and members of the city council of Augsburg, who considered the reproaches "absurd." Due to the large media attention, there were
also contributions to the debate based on actual visits to the zoo. One journalist, for example, wrote about his observations:

The village everybody is talking about does not exist. It is simply not
there. [...] All that is there are the usual suspects, as one knows
them from the alternative "Tollwood-Festival" in Munich's Olympia
Park, the "Afrika-Tage" which took place recently at the Interna-

---

[11] She referred to Medhat Abdelati, a born Egyptian and manager of the company *maxVita
GmbH*, which organized the event in Augsburg as well as similar African markets in Munich
before (cf. Dea et al. 2005:10f).

tional Handicraft Fair in Munich, from the tourist quarters in Johannesburg, or any given Africa market or Africa festival anywhere
in the country. (Schallenberg 2005)

For this observer the event didn't display Africans but showed only "the usual
suspects, in remarkably unimaginative accumulation" (ibid.). While about two
dozen protesters put up stands in front of the zoo, condemning the racist colonial gaze which in their eyes the event fostered, nobody inside the zoo, for this
journalist, was presented as "sub-human" or "aboriginal" to the visitors. As he
continues:

> What they see instead are — not too many — black people in one of
> the few roles that they are allowed to play in Germany: as hawkers
> and service providers who sell a little African folklore. Like any form
> of folklore, be it with reference to Bavaria or Africa, all this has little
> or nothing to do with the social and cultural realities of the respec-
> tive region. (Ibid.)

Other comments based on actual visits to the zoo came to similar conclusions.
"One could see what one had seen many times before, if, however, not in front
of antelopes: arts and crafts and ethno knickknacks, leather bags, beads, carved
warthogs, and fortune cards, tents for water pipes, and South African wines"
(Zekri 2005). When this reporter asked one of the African sellers in the zoo
about her feelings regarding the debates about the "African Village," the
Senegalese woman replied that she would display her products and not herself.
She wouldn't feel as an object. And, she added, she would have to earn money
to make a living. Formerly she used to have a shop in Berlin-Weißensee, the
woman told the journalist, but most of the Africans living there left because of
the growing presence of neo-Nazis in that part of the city. "Believe me," she
finally added, "sometimes it is better to live among animals than to live among
humans" (quoted in ibid.).

There were also other, more critical voices in the zoo, as a study of the
Augsburg event by scholars of the Max Planck Institute for Ethnological Research shows (Dea et al. 2005). But most of the exhibitors in the zoo selling
their products — most of whom were actually white Germans, and only the
minority of whom were Blacks, that is, African immigrants living in Germany
and Germans of African descent — were most concerned with the economic
side of the event. Some feared that the protest against the "African Village"
would prevent visitors, and thus potential buyers, from coming. Others found
the setting at least a little strange, but quite some traders in the zoo, regardless

of the color of their skin, considered the setting actually good for their business. Reactions like that of one trader, stating: "The place is not good. [...] We are no objects or animals you can look at. The city should give us a proper place. This is not correct. The time when Blacks were used is over [...]. Slavery has been abolished" (quoted in Dea et al. 2005:28), were clearly the exception. However, since the traders had paid quite high rents for their stands in advance (between 700 and 1000 Euro), they were economically dependent and thus not really in the position to protest against the politics of representation employed at the event.

With regard to the perception of the "African Village," the same study shows that some of the common stereotypes ascribed to Africa and Africans were clearly reproduced. Asked about their associations with Africa on exiting the zoo, most visitors put the continent in close connection to the animal and natural world (which is hardly surprising considering that they just came from the zoo). Most visitors knew little about Africa and, though the organizers had claimed the event would nurture tolerance and mutual understanding, stated that the event in the zoo had added nothing to their knowledge about the continent. Though the "African Village" in Augsburg was not a *Völkerschau* like those organized in Wilhelmine Germany (which is to say that Africans were not exhibited themselves), there are, then, nonetheless parallels. The image of Africa as exotic Other was, for example, used to attract visitors to the zoo in all three cases recounted in this chapter. Africa as well as Africans themselves became a kind of trademark at the events in Breslau as well as in Leipzig and Augsburg. As Dea et al. note, "[i]n this respect continuing colonial and racist stereotypes and the history of ethnographic shows overlap with current forms of marketing and lead to a racialization" (2005:43).

Another observation of the authors of the study was the high popularity of drumming workshops in the zoo. In contrast to the stands selling products, where the visitors passed mostly by and at best bargained about prices of particular items, drumming workshops were actually instances where a more substantial interaction between Africans and the visitors of the zoo took place. As Dea et al. write:

> One of the main attractions in Augsburg was drumming. Adults as well as children enjoyed drumming with Africans. Some visitors were obviously happy about the opportunity to interact with "friendly" Africans. It seemed that the participation in African culture in the zoo offered them a break from the stress of everyday life in Germany. They enjoyed the opportunity to have "a party" or to spend "a holiday" with Africans. Pictures of the interaction in con-

nection to drumming were the most numerous images in newspaper articles about the event. (2005:43)

The same observation holds true for the "Dschungelnacht" in Leipzig. Considered in this context, we can see that the place of African music, just as that of Africa more generally, is a highly ambivalent one in contemporary popular culture. While it serves, on the one hand, as a means of mediation between people and therefore goes beyond simple stereotypes, the encounters encouraged and facilitated by music are, on the other hand, often framed by highly problematic patterns of representation. As becomes most obvious in the case of the zoo, many of these representations have their roots in European imperialism and colonialism. They reinforce racialized images of the Other and produce Africa and Africans as fundamentally different in nature than Europe and Europeans. Hence, African music, it is often said, is essentially different from Western music — less intellectual and more energetic, natural, spontaneous, physical, intuitive, so some common clichés.

As for the *Völkerschauen*, most authors agree that this tradition disappeared from the scene in the 1940s. In the wake of the colonial revisionist movement, the National Socialists had launched the so-called *Deutsche Afrika-Schau*, which was used as a propaganda instrument and, at the same time, an apparatus to control those few "colored" people who were left in the country under the Nazi dictatorship.[12] The "German Africa Show," more or less the last income possibility for Blacks in Nazi Germany, was finally given up in 1940. And this was basically the end of the *Völkerschauen* in Germany as they had become popular in the nineteenth century. Eventually, the film industry took over in the sector of "exotic" entertainment. On the other hand, it can be argued — and we have, indeed, done so above — that representational patterns employed in the ethnographic shows of former times find their continuation in folkloristic events and musical performances today. And these continuities are, as we will see, by no means restricted to Europe's zoos.

---

[12] On the *Deutsche Afrika-Schau* see Möhle (2002:249ff). We will expand on this issue in a later chapter.

3 Musical Geography

Representing and Performing Africa

Music plays, as we have already seen, a vital role in the performance and representation of identities. Musical performance is therefore also one of the major means in the production, circulation, and consumption of Africa, understood here not so much as a geographical entity but rather as a discursive trope. Thus, in this chapter we will scrutinize the history of the idea of African music and examine how this category of thinking has been produced and reproduced particularly since the nineteenth century. Towards the end of this chapter, then, we will come to an outline of a more general theory of (social) space as a way of approaching the place(s) of African music within the global cultural economy. Stressing the spatiality of musical practice and thereby placing the emphasis on the social before the cultural realm might open a way, as we will argue, to escape forms of culturalism that lend to the racialization of performance practices and musical forms.

   The history of the representation and performance of Africa has attracted a lot of attention in recent literature. In this regard, Mudimbe's extensive studies *The Invention of Africa* (1988) and *The Idea of Africa* (1994) are certainly outstanding. His argument is based on Michel Foucault's notion of Power/ Knowledge (cf. Foucault 1979 and 1980) and he takes up a postcolonial approach as advocated by Edward Said ([1979] 1995) in his book on Western concepts of the Orient. In accordance with Said's definition of Orientalism, understood as "a way of coming to terms with the Orient that is based on the Orient's special place in European Western experience" (Said [1979] 1995:1), Mudimbe lays out the epistemological field he identifies as Africanism, that is, the production of knowledge about Africa in Western discourse. He comes to conclude that the

> "idea" of Africa [...] is a product of the West and was conceived and conveyed through conflicting systems of knowledge. From Herodotus onward, the West's self-representations have always included images of peoples situated outside of its cultural and imaginary fron-

tiers. The paradox is that if [...] these outsiders were understood as localized and far away geographically, they were nonetheless imagined and rejected as the intimate and other side of the European-thinking subject, on the analogical model of the tension between the being In-Itself and the being For-Itself. (Mudimbe 1994:xi)

Stimulated by these insights, other researchers have also begun to analyze the production of knowledge about Africa. There is a growing body of literature on the history of representations of Africa and Africans in Western popular culture as well as on the images of Africa produced and reproduced in staged performances in Europe and North America.[1] In a recent publication, Paulla Ebron (2002) has laid out the geographical and sociocultural scope for performances of so-called *jali* or griots.[2] She focuses on a variety of contexts in West Africa as well as in North America in which griots from The Gambia perform today, and particularly stresses the importance of travel traffic — in the form of concert tours, the migration of musicians, and tourism — in the production, circulation, and consumption of Africa within the global cultural economy.

In line with Mudimbe's argument, most authors agree that while we are dealing with constructions of Africa as the Other, the representational modes employed in performances and displays are, at the same time, self-constructions of a Western subject. As Kirshenblatt-Gimblett has noted with regard to museum exhibitions and folkloric performances:

Exhibitions, whether of objects or people, are displays of the artifacts of our disciplines. They are for this reason also exhibits of those who make them, no matter what their ostensible subject. [...] Museum exhibitions, folkloric performances, and folklife festivals are guided by a poetics of detachment, in the sense not only of material fragments but also of a distanced attitude. The question is not whether or not an object is of visual interest, but rather how interest of any kind is created. All interest is vested. (Kirshenblatt-Gimblett 1991:434)

What most of the studies of the representation of Africa reveal is the interdependence of the academic production of ethnographic knowledge on the one

---

[1] See for example Nederveen Pieterse (1998) and Lindfors (1999).
[2] For a general account on the significance of this West African caste of musicians and a description of their numerous social functions as chroniclers, story-tellers, advisors, praise singers, and so on, see Hale (1999).

hand and popular representations of the ethnic and cultural Other on the other hand. Holding the constructivist view that ethnography not merely represents, but rather actively constructs its very object of knowledge, this literature must be considered in the context of a more general revisionary process in the anthropological disciplines that has taken place in the wake of what has come to be known as the "crisis of representation" (cf. Marcus & Fischer 1986). The critical examination of anthropology's involvement in the colonial process (Asad 1973) and the role of representational modes in setting up and reinforcing power relations (Clifford 1988 and Fabian 1983) was subsequently also taken up in a number of publications in the field of music studies. Following Clifford Geertz' dictum that "if you want to understand what a science is, […] you should look at what the practitioners of it do" (Geertz 1973:5), the academic "writing culture" (Clifford & Marcus 1986) also of ethnomusicology came to the fore (cf. Bohlman & Nettl 1991). In a recent collection of essays the construction of the Other in a wide range of genres of Western music has been highlighted (Born & Hesmondhalgh 2000), and Bohlman and Radano (2000) edited a volume on the construction of racial difference in music and musical discourse.

A number of scholars working on African musical idioms have also taken up this disciplinary critique (cf. Waterman 1991). Blum (1991), for example, has shown how the employment of European musical terminology has shaped our understanding of musics from Africa. Agawu (2003) has examined the impact of colonialism on the representation of African music in academic discourse and gives us important insights into the history of the invention of this category. Carl (2004) has contributed to the archaeology of the German colonial discourse on African music in the nineteenth and early twentieth century. Radano (2000) has shown with regard to African American music how the idea of "black rhythm" evolved within American modernism and Waterman (2000) has examined the category of "race music." What these analyses show is that by the nineteenth century African music and "African musicality" had already acquired the status of a modern myth — a status that arguably continues to exist up to this day. As we have seen in the preceding chapter and will further elaborate on in the following, as a discursive as well as performative trope African music and its substitutes such as black music are powerful means of identification and effective metaphors signifying difference. African music plays a central role in the production of "Africanness."

The voices that contribute to the construction of Africa are many and they come from many different positions. A general observation is that after World War II, with the successive independence of African nation-states and the increase in migrational movements between Africa and Europe, the contexts in which the representation and performance of Africa took place highly diversified. Roughly from the 1960s onward, performing groups from Africa such as newly formed National Ensembles began to tour Europe and other parts of the world to represent the independent African nations rather than the "primitive" Other or the colonial subject. On the African continent itself music, dance, and "traditional culture" in the form of consumable commodities have become important marketing factors for the evolving tourist industries. "African culture" has become a major element in the self-representations and self-images of African nations. The impact of colonialism and its effects on representational patterns are, after all, complex and manifold.

Scholars and others professionally engaged in African music have mostly criticized its commercialization while consciously working on the construction and Africanization of tradition. This discourse, assuming some sort of natural biological (rather than social and historical) link between cultural expressive forms and groups of people as the carriers of cultural knowledge, has always involved processes of racialization. Not only European or Western scholars, but also Africans working in this field have often stressed biological factors when explicating the "distinctiveness" of musical practices in Africa.[3] As early as the 1920s Erich M. von Hornbostel, one of the early scholars of African music (cf. Carl 2004:131ff and Grupe 1998), complained that "the dances of the West Africans, who are rhythmically superior to all other races, have been completely assimilated after they went through the machine culture of the Yankees" (1921:177). In contrast to such forms of cultural criticism, which can still be heard from the advocates of authenticity in music and culture, we could in fact argue that the scholarly engagement by Hornbostel and his successors — Europeans as well as Africans (whatever these attributes might mean) — also contributed to the very process of commercialization of culture these intellectuals are criticizing. It is not only questions of representation we are dealing with when considering African music, but also claims to ownership both in the sense of copyright as well as a broader and much more vaguely defined right to one's cultural identity. Whose music are we actually dealing with when we speak of African music, and who is its legitimate representative?

In the realm of popular music, African musical forms (re)entered the Western market under the label of world music in the 1980s (cf. Taylor 1997). African music, or what is commonly referred to as such, is today an integral part of the global cultural economy. We find a host of local scenes centering

---

[3] See for example Avorgbedor (1983) who speaks about "bio-ecological" factors presumably distinguishing Ghanaian and more generally African musical practices from what he thinks of as Western musical forms.

on African musical styles in many countries of the so-called West. Since the days of the *Völkerschauen*, African music and cultural performances more generally have become a means to travel — for Africans to temporarily or permanently migrate to the metropoles in search of education, work, or sometimes mere adventure; for Europeans to imaginarily as well as physically explore the cultural Other both at home as well as in the various tourist locations on the African continent. African music is also a labor market. African musicians from the continent as well as the diaspora now frequently give performances in the countries of western Europe and North America. There are festivals and other world music events featuring African music and dance, and it is also taught in workshops and classes on all levels. In many German cities we find bars and dance clubs targeting audiences with a special preference for African musical styles.

Overall, we can identify two divergent tendencies in approaches towards the representation and performance of African music. On the one hand there is an attitude of protectionism with regard to African culture. As Agawu argues for the African perspective, "in postindependence Africa, one frequently encounters the most self-conscious attempts to hold up certain cultural products as quintessentially 'African'" (Agawu 2003:17). It is in this context that we have to consider what Agawu calls the "invention" of traditional music in post-independence Africa (ibid.:17ff). Traditionalist perspectives are, on the other hand, opposed by modernist visions of African culture that stress transformation and change. This perspective also finds its expression in numerous musical styles, be it Nigerian Afrobeat, Ghanaian highlife, or Zimbabwean chimurenga, to name but a few examples. These versions of African music are mostly not, or only marginally, included in representations of Africa as we encountered them in the cases of the zoo. And also in Africa itself the inherent and explicitly stressed hybridity of styles like these is often ambivalently tied to stigmatizations of "inauthenticity," sometimes labeled "acculturation," sometimes "Westernization," or whatever euphemism is used.

Considering the place(s) of African music in the global cultural economy, then, we see that the inherent ambivalence of this category continues to have a strong impact on the constitution of discursive and performative spaces. Meanwhile, the history of this ambivalence is long and leads over the discovery of "primitive peoples" in the course of European expansionism to the appropriation of African music as an emblem of the racially Other.

Discovering the Primitive

The African continent has for long caught the attention of Europeans. For travelers in Africa, the music of the people they encountered has always been a subject of great fascination. As early as in the sixth century BCE, in what is one of the earliest accounts of African music in European literature, the Greek chronicler Herodotus mentions songs of "Libyan" women. We also find detailed descriptions of music in later reports written by Arab travelers. The earliest of these stem from the seventh century. From the sixteenth century onward then, in the wake of the so-called "age of exploration," it is predominantly European sources that deal with African music (cf. Kubik 2001). Written in the seventeenth century, we have for example descriptions of xylophone and lamellophone music in the southern parts of Africa by the Portuguese missionary João dos Santos (Kubik 1998:75ff). A detailed account of the music of the Khoi people in South Africa by the German scholar Peter Kolb stems from the eighteenth century (Mugglestone 1982).

In the encounter between Europeans and Africans music has always played a vital role. And African musical practices were not always necessarily an index emblematically representing difference and otherness. If we consider, for example, the encounter between Vasco da Gama's crew and indigenous people at the Cape of Good Hope in the late fifteenth century — maybe the earliest encounter between Europeans and Africans in this part of the world — we see that music can actually also be an indicator of sameness and common humanity. The description of this encounter reads:

> On Saturday [December 2, 1497] came approximately two hundred Blacks, tall and short, and they brought twelve pieces of cattle, oxen and cows, and four or five wethers. When we saw them, we immediately went on land. And they instantly began to play four or five flutes, and some played high and the others low, that together it sounded very beautiful for Negroes of which one wouldn't expect music, and they also performed a Negro dance with it. And the commander let the trumpets blow, and we danced in our boats, and the commander also danced with us.[4]

---

[4] "Am Samstag [den 2. Dezember 1497] kamen ungefähr zweihundert Schwarze, groß und klein, und brachten zwölf Stück Vieh mit, Ochsen und Kühe, und vier oder fünf Hammel, und wir gingen, als wir sie kommen sahen, sofort an Land. Und sogleich fingen sie an, vier oder fünf Flöten zu spielen, und die einen spielten hoch und die anderen tief, so daß es sehr schön zusammenklang für Neger, von denen man keine Musik erwartet, und dazu führten

Bearing all qualities of the "first encounter" classically featured in ethno-graphic literature, music and dance in the situation described here function like a mirror through which identity and alterity are reflected. The account illustrates well how mimesis comes into play in the encounter between Self and Other. In his analysis of *Mimesis and Alterity* Michael Taussig describes the "mimetic faculty" as "the nature that culture uses to create second nature, the faculty to copy, imitate, make models, explore difference, yield into and be-come Other" (Taussig 1993:xiii). Music and all the more collective musical performance is undoubtedly a very effective means in such a transformation; the immediacy of sound often forbids any strict delineation between Self and Other. Taussig considers the mimetic faculty equally important for "the very process of knowing as it is to the construction and subsequent naturalization of identities" (ibid.). What seems remarkable in the encounter between the Por-tuguese and the South Africans as described above is the fact that it is rather the former mimicking the latter. Especially if we consider later descriptions of encounters between Europeans and Africans such a constellation is clearly ex-ceptional. The situation seems overall fairly balanced.[5]

Over the course of many centuries Europeans did not know much about Africa apart from its coastal areas, which is where most of the early encounters with Africans took place. The production of myths about strange creatures, half human, half beast, and other uncanny beings inhabiting the interior of the continent was therefore flourishing already in the Middle Ages (Herkenhoff 1990). The lack of factual knowledge about Africa also contributed considera-bly to the image of the "dark continent," not only in the popular imagination, but also in academic accounts. This becomes clear if we consider Hegel's de-scription of the continent, for example (cf. Hegel [1822-28] 1986:120f). Though at the beginning of the nineteenth century there were already some substantial accounts available, in his *Lectures on the Philosophy of History* Hegel uses a highly stylized image of the unknown Africa to corroborate his argu-ment about the rise of the *Weltgeist*, or, "world spirit" — which, hardly surpris-ing, has not touched Africa yet. Africa, for Hegel, was a continent without his-tory, its inhabitants inevitably caught in a pre-historic, pre-conscious — and

---

sie einen Negertanz auf. Und der Kommandant ließ die Trompeten blasen, und wir tanz-ten in den Booten, und der Kommandant tanzte auch mit uns" (quoted in Keller 2000:15).
[5] We shouldn't forget that the Portuguese's mission was, of course, the breakage of the Arab trade monopoly in the Indian Ocean, and that this encounter, at the same time, marks the beginning of several centuries of exploitation of South African peoples. In this regard the situation is not balanced at all. My comments here concern the politics of representation in the description of the instance and not the wider implications of the historical moment de-scribed.

that also means: pre-human — state. The image of the "dark continent" with all its metaphorical and ethical implications was, after all, also used to legitimize the transatlantic slave trade for several centuries. Comparing the writings about Africa stemming from Greek antiquity to those of Enlightenment philosophers, Eze comes to conclude:

> [I]n both the realms of philosophy and politics, the major thinkers of Greek antiquity articulated social and human geographical differences on the basis of the opposition between the "cultured" and the "barbaric." [...] European Enlightenment thinkers retained the Greek ideal of reason, as well as this reason's categorical function of discriminating between the cultured (now called "civilized") and the "barbarian" (the "savage" or the "primitive"). It can be argued, in fact, that the Enlightenment's declaration of itself as "the Age of Reason" was predicated upon precisely the assumption that reason could historically only come to maturity in modern Europe, while the inhabitants of areas outside Europe, who were considered to be of non-European racial and cultural origins, were consistently described and theorized as rationally inferior and savage. (Eze 2000:4)

Paradigmatically marked by Mungo Park's *Travels in the Interior Districts of Africa* ([1799] 2000), the nineteenth century, then, became the century of travels into, and the systematic exploration of, the interior of the African continent (Rotberg 1970). This phase of European conquest cumulated in what has come to be known as the "scramble for Africa," that is, the competition among European powers in the colonial acquisition of virtually the whole continent, with the exception of only Ethiopia and Liberia. Among the explorers of the African interior were also many German travelers such as Heinrich Barth, Gerhard Rohlfs, Gustav Nachtigal, or Georg Schweinfurth, to name but a few.

With the intensification in travel traffic the literature on African music grew immensely, particularly after the European occupation of Africa in the 1870s. The accounts of these travelers, in contrast to those of former centuries, are clearly in the spirit of a colonial ideology, which in its most extreme form hardly saw Africans as full human beings. Accordingly, African music was often depicted as noise rather than humanly organized sound, and travelers were frequently and quite literally robbed of their sleep by it (Carl 2004:25ff). The racial thinking of the time, put in scientific terms by Enlightenment intellectuals such as Kant, Blumenthal, or Hegel (cf. Eze 2000), and then developed further by physical anthropologists such as Eugen Fischer (cf. Roller 2002b), undermined the inferior status of Blacks. And this thinking is, after all, also prevalent in accounts of African music.

Like music from other parts of the world newly "discovered" by Europeans, African music was categorized as "primitive." While this meant "less elaborated" and inferior vis-à-vis the European tradition of art music, primitivity implied at the same time "prior" in a temporal sense. In African music Europeans thought they had discovered their own musical origins. The construction of the Other in the nineteenth century was based on what Fabian called the "denial of coevalness," that is, "a persistent and systematic tendency to place the referent(s) of anthropology in a time other than the present of the producer of anthropological discourse" (Fabian 1983:30). Additionally, in the course of the nineteenth century primitivity became more and more equated with mimesis, understood as an instinctive, animalistic form with aping. This discursive trope found its expression in the ascription of an extraordinary musical faculty to Africans in a somewhat paradoxical manner. Though regarded as inferior human (or, at times, pre-human) expression, the fascination with African music by no means ceased in the nineteenth century. As Bohlman and Radano argue:

> This contradictory discourse of discipline and desire appears consistent with the rhetoric of masculinized conquest that narrated modernity's colonial mapping. Yet the intrusion of a Rousseavian conception of "natural ability" into a prior discourse of heathenish, black "noise" made for a peculiarly schizophrenic projection when attention focused increasingly on African and African American musical practices [...]. In "Negro music" Europeans identified a kind of mimetic genius: despite their intellectual limits, blacks produced imitations of European singing that seemed to exceed the value of the "original." (Bohlman & Radano 2000:18)

Aestheticians of the nineteenth century conceptualized African music, or "primitive music" more generally, as non-music. On the other hand, an extraordinary rhythmic faculty was ascribed to "primitives." Ranking as "natural music," the musical forms Europeans encountered throughout the world ultimately served to undermine the superior status of European art music with its emphasis on melodic and harmonic development. Rhythm and dance, that is, music as a bodily expression, was detested as a pathological state of the primitive (Carl 2004:83ff). Eduard Hanslick, for example, reasoned about the assumed strong effect that particularly rhythmic music would have on "savages." He argued that in contrast to harmony and melody, rhythm would already exist outside human nature, since many sounds that nature produces are rhythmic (as for example the heartbeat). Therefore, if non-European peoples would produce rhythms and utter their "incomprehensible howling," this could at best be considered "natural music," but not music proper (Hanslick [1854] 1902:183f).

Especially in the last quarter of the nineteenth century, non-European musics were rethought in the context of Darwin's general theory on evolution and Social Darwinist thinking. Already Darwin himself had speculated about the origin and function of music. He saw particularly Africans equipped with a highly developed musical talent. As he writes in *The Descent of Man*:

> We see that the musical faculties, which are not wholly deficient in any race, are capable of prompt and high development, for Hottentotts [sic] and Negroes have become excellent musicians, although in their native countries they rarely practice anything that we consider music. (Darwin [1871] 1998:591)

For Darwin the emergence of human musicality could be explained by natural selection, and he was convinced that the musician "uses the same means by which his half-human ancestors long ago aroused each other's ardent passion, during their courtship and rivalry" (ibid.:594). "Primitive music" served to prove this argument. Other theories on the origin of music follow Darwin's basic line of reasoning. For Richard Wallaschek, for example, African music paradigmatically marked the beginnings of human musicality, as he explicates in *Primitive Music* (1893). In his book he enfolds a panorama of the musics of the world that represents, at the same time, the evolutionary hierarchy. Departing from Africa and leading us through all continents, Wallaschek's narrative finally arrives in Europe and cumulates in the musical "genius" of Richard Wagner — the end of history, as it were (cf. Bohlman & Radano 2000:18 and Carl 2004:98ff).

The Appropriation of African music

The nineteenth century brought an enormous increase in the traffic of goods and people between Europe and Africa. While Africa provided labor in the form of millions of slaves for the plantation economies of the New World in the preceding centuries, with the colonial conquest of the continent it became a huge reservoir of raw materials for Europe's rapidly growing industries. At the end of the nineteenth century particularly the Congo basin with its rich natural resources such as latex came into focus (cf. Hochschild 1998). Travelers, adventurers, missionaries, colonial officers, and business people went to Africa, while Africans increasingly started to travel to the colonial metropoles, in search of education and other things. We can say that in the wake of these developments and in contrast to former descriptions in travel accounts and other literature, African music became a more physical reality in Europe towards the end of the nineteenth century. Around the turn of the century African music moved from an imaginary space — from the mythical space of primordial origins — to the Lacanian space of the Real.

There were the *Völkerschauen*, the popular ethnographic shows in which supposedly "primitive" people put up staged performances of their customs, including music and dance. For European audiences these exotic plays had, as we have seen in the previous chapter, a great appeal. Apart from representational modes that reinforced primitivist fantasies about the "savage" African, the major difference to literary accounts was the fact that ethnographic shows actually included real movement and sound. For the first time Europeans could really hear African music performed by real people, howsoever orchestrated these staged performances might have been. Moreover, alongside the shows an interaction between Europeans and Africans took place that often contradicted existing representational patterns.

In the German Empire this social reality became an issue particularly after the major colonial exhibitions at the end of the nineteenth century, namely the colonial exhibition in 1896 and the *Deutsch-Ostafrikanische Ausstellung* as well as the *Transvaal-Ausstellung* in 1897 (cf. van der Heyden 2002b). Perceived as highly scandalous in conservative circles, alongside these events "white women and girls ran after the Negroes and proposed to them" (quoted in Roller 2002a:79), as a German parliamentarian observed to his dismay. The growing number of romantic relationships between Africans and Germans, due to an increasing African presence in Europe, became a hotly debated topic in public discourse, and in Germany the issue was discussed up to the level of the *Reichstag*. Such relationships undermined the dominant racial logic and, therefore, touched the heart of racial sensitivities. But German-African relationships also caused judicial problems concerning the legal status of people from the German colonies and the offspring of German-African couples. As a consequence, authorities prohibited the recruitment of Africans from Germany's protectorates for ethnographic shows in 1901 (Thode-Arora 2002).

Apart from such undesired "side effects" ethnographic shows also raised the interest of the scholarly community, and researchers took them as opportunity to study non-European peoples and their cultural expressions "on their doorstep" (Carl 2004:121ff). These encounters changed the image and perception of "primitive music" in significant ways. We have for example a detailed description by Carl Stumpf (1886), an experimental psychologist and one of the founding fathers of comparative musicology in Germany, how he analyses songs of Native Americans from Vancouver with the help of one member of an ethnographic show that was organized by Hagenbeck in 1885 (cf. Haberland 1988). In the same manner Stumpf had transcribed Zulu music during a performance he witnessed in Germany earlier that year, aiming with his transcriptions, as he writes, at exact "phonographic replicas" of the songs he heard (Stumpf 1886:424). Scholars now started to scrutinize the structural aspects of musical expressions that had been considered mere noise until then.

"Exact replicas" of performances had indeed become possible with Edison's invention of the cylinder phonograph in 1877. From the turn of the century, with the foundation of the Berlin Phonogram Archive in 1900, Stumpf and his colleagues made extensive use of this technology (cf. Simon 2000). While ethnographic shows made music from Africa audible in Europe for the first time, the phonograph eventually made possible its physical storage and therefore its appropriation in a physical sense. The end of the nineteenth century was marked by a media revolution that had a fundamental impact on the perception of music; a revolution that changed patterns of music's production and circulation as well as processes of its commodification and consumption in significant ways (Connell & Gibson 2003:45ff). As Erika Brady remarked, the phonograph was not just "another ingenious invention to exclaim over; its reproduction of sound experientially challenged fundamental universal expectations concerning the nature of hearing in a profound and disturbing fashion" (Brady 1999:32). The invention of the technology of mechanical sound reproduction marks the birth of a new *Aufschreibesystem*, a new "writing system," to use a term coined by Kittler (1995). It not only enabled a new perspective on an already existing phenomenon, but reproduced sound constitutes a new type of object, it constitutes a new reality. "Media define what is real," as Kittler writes, "they are all along beyond aesthetics" (1986:10).

Led by Erich M. von Hornbostel who became its director in 1905, the phonogram archive in Berlin became the most extensive archive for non-European music in the world until the beginning of World War II. With 3281 wax cylinders in 1933, recordings of music from Africa represented the largest portion of its inventory (Ziegler 1998). The predominance of African recordings is no coincidence, but reflects the intertwinement of the emergence of a discipline like comparative musicology with politics. Germany played, after all, a crucial role in the history of European colonialism, hosting the International West Africa Conference (Congo Conference) 1884/85 in Berlin — an event that represents the most drastic turning points in Africa's geopolitical history

(Gründer 2002). It facilitated the expansion of European markets and the economic exploitation of the African continent, and eventually led to some of the
bloodiest military conflicts the world had seen thus far.

The German empire acquired its colonial possessions in Africa in the
same years as the Congo Conference was held. To administer the colonies in
Africa effectively, more systematic knowledge about the occupied territories
was required. At subsequent colonial congresses in 1902 and 1905 academic
disciplines like geography, anthropology, ethnology, linguistics and also comparative musicology demanded more public funds to meet this requirement.
This led to the installation of the "Commission for the Geographical Exploration of the German Colonies" (*Kommission für die landeskundliche Erforschung der
deutschen Kolonien*), which was attached to the Colonial Office (*Kolonialamt*) at the
Ministry of Foreign Affairs (cf. Weule 1908:18). If the image of the "explorer
hero" in the style of Mungo Park, selflessly risking his life while traversing the
African continent from north to south and from east to west, had been the
dominant type of traveler and literary figure in the nineteenth century, at the
beginning of the twentieth century we witness the emergence of a new, more
sober type of traveler, scrutinizing a limited colonial territory on short infor-
mative trips (Essner 1985). With the help of mimetic machines such as the
phonograph and the cinematograph — which, in a way, became bodily exten-
sions, the sense organs through which sound and motion was captured —
travelers of this type had also a more sober and controlled approach to African
music and dance.

African music in the Age of Mechanical Reproduction

Following an official directive, from the beginning of the twentieth century
every scientific expedition leaving Germany was equipped with a phonograph
and copies of the thus recorded material were incorporated into the Berlin archive. Recordings from Germany's African protectorates Togo, Cameroon,
German East Africa and German South West Africa are therefore clearly
overrepresented. "Only by means of the phonograph," Hornbostel wrote,
"can we get the 'real thing'" (1928:5). It was through the phonograph that
comparative musicologists in Berlin eventually got to know "not only how exotic music [...] looks like, but how it really sounds" (Hornbostel 1921:178). To
make sure that recordings met a certain standard required for their analysis,
Hornbostel and his colleague Otto Abraham published instructions for travelers and missionaries how to handle the technology of the phonograph (cf.

Abraham & Hornbostel [1904] 1975:200ff). And they developed a general methodology for the analysis of "exotic" music (cf. Abraham & Hornbostel 1909/10), which Hornbostel applied to a number of recordings from Africa (cf. Hornbostel 1909, 1910, 1913 and 1917). On the basis of these analyses, which became an influential model for future research, Hornbostel developed one of the first academic theories of African music (Hornbostel 1928).

In his attempts to transcribe the phonograms recorded in Africa Hornbostel was struggling with the rhythmic organization of the music. At times, he was "disoriented" within a piece; he found the rhythms "very intricate" or "refractory." African rhythms would often show "a level of development Europeans are completely unprepared for," making it "impossible to comprehend the rhythmic complications only by ear" (1913:356). Fortunately, recording technology makes possible what Kittler (1986) calls the "manipulation of the Real." Throughout the nineteenth century time was conceptualized as history — an extended space imbued by a spirit (*Geist*) that continually developed through time, from some mythical, primordial origin up to its perfection. The "primitive" as the mythical place of this primordial origin was the identical yet non-identical reflected image in which the Western subject discovered itself (Carl 2004:98ff; cf. Foucault 1973). With the technology of mechanical sound reproduction, then, time was demystified. The "authenticity" or what Walter Benjamin (1969) has called the "aura" of an object, formerly grounded in the mythic origins of time-space, disappeared in favor of its "realness." There is no temporal distance to an object in the space of the Real.

In contrast to historical time, real time can be manipulated: it can be stopped, rewound, forwarded, slowed down, speeded up, or completely cut into the smallest pieces. In this manipulative process lay the advantage of the phonograph as an analytical device. As Abraham and Hornbostel write:

> With the phonograph one can record a piece of music and study it at leisure in the studio, where attention is not so much distracted visually as it is at performances by exotic peoples. Moreover, the phonograph has special advantages. It can be adjusted to run fast or slow at will, and thus one can bring within the ear's comprehension pieces of music whose tempo was too quick to be analyzed at its original speed, by playing them at a slower tempo, in corresponding transposition. Furthermore one can split up the piece of music into small fragments, play back single measures, even single notes, and make precise annotations and measurements in conjunction with them. (Abraham & Hornbostel [1904] 1975:195f)

In this way, the phonograph constitutes what we might call the "musical unconscious," to borrow from Walter Benjamin, who in his study of *The Work of
Art in the Age of Mechanical Reproduction* (1969) speaks of the "optical unconscious"
with regard to the reproductive technologies of film and photography. At the
end of the nineteenth century, the phonograph became a model for "primitive
memory," a means to study the "musical unconscious" of "primitives" by way
of its dissection. This becomes evident, for example, in a study of musical
memory by Wallaschek (1892). Discussing a number of clinical studies on the
effects of acoustic stimuli on mentally handicapped patients and people under
the influence of narcotic drugs, Wallaschek compares these findings to descriptions of non-European music. Principally he conceptualizes memory as a
"restrained mimetic reflex"; every learning process, for him, can be traced
back to the effects of such imitative reflexes. The primitive, in such a view, becomes a pathological mimetic state. As Wallaschek writes:

> [T]he musical memory of Hottentots is surprisingly great, but we
> forget that the imitative reflex is overall greater on a primitive level
> than it is with cultivated man; and it is indeed only a reflex — even
> if a highly developed one — when music is reproduced together
> with lyrics that are not understood, as it happens sometimes on
> primitive levels of culture. We find other cases of merely reflective
> reproduction, hence memory in a lower sense, in idiots.[6]

At the end of his essay, Wallaschek concludes that such pathological states of
mind are principally comparable to the processes in the mind of an artistic
"genius." But the musical unconscious on the primitive level, for him, is an
obsessive, mechanical urge to imitate, a "dead" repetitive mechanism. It is
therefore a pathological state rather than an ingenious one. In the encounter
with the primitive, Wallaschek writes, the unconscious "speaks to us like a living phonograph" (Wallaschek 1892:250) — just as the African unconscious
spoke to Hornbostel in the encounter with the phonograph. As Hornbostel
explicates:

> In the life of so-called primitive man, and especially of the African

---

[6] "[D]as musikalische Gedächtniß der Hottentotten [ist] ein erstaunlich großes, aber wir
vergessen, daß der Imitationsreflex auf primitiver Stufe überhaupt größer ist als beim Kul-
tur-Menschen, und ein — wenn auch hochentwickelter — Reflex ist es doch nur, wenn
Musik sammt einem Text reproduciert wird, den man nicht versteht, wie das auf primitiven
Kulturstufen wohl vorkommt. Andere Fälle von rein reflektiver Reproduktion, also Gedächtnis im niederen Sinne, finden wir bei Idioten" (Wallaschek 1892:207).

Negroes, music and dance have a quite different and incomparably greater significance than with us. One does not give them their due in classifying them, as authors of ethnographical works mostly do, under the general headings of Art or Games. They serve neither as mere pastimes nor recreations. They are not meant to edify the mind aesthetically; nor can they be regarded as a brilliant decoration on festive occasions, or as a means of effectively staging ceremonies. They rely ultimately on psycho-physical conditions. Bodily motion is freed from effort by repetitions. It is molded into a precise shape, and proceeds in accordance with its own laws and seemingly by itself. Along with it, and as a part only of the whole movement, speech forms itself rhythmically and tonally. Thus vitality is heightened above its normal state. Music is neither reproduction (of a 'piece of music' as an existing object) nor production (of a new object): it is the life of a living spirit working within those who dance and sing. Of this they are conscious. (Hornbostel 1928:32)

African music is, in other words, *wirklich*, that is, effectively real. Though now considered music proper, in the early twentieth century we are confronted with a fundamental difference between African and European music, which "are constructed on entirely different principles and […] cannot be fused into one" (Hornbostel 1928:3). Ultimately based on "psychophysical" conditions African music is not connected to European music by a common origin anymore, however remote in time-space this primordial origin might be imagined. For Hornbostel African music is the body and European music the mind. Both are expressions of an unbridgeable gap between two "races," between Blacks and Whites, and only by giving up their racial identity Africans could appropriate European musical forms. Such an act of "impurity" would inevitably lead to a musical "bastardization process" as Hornbostel saw it taking place in African American music (cf. Hornbostel 1911 and 1921) or in the "conditions among the Zulus, who have hardly preserved any African characteristics even in their melodies" (Hornbostel 1928:15). While the European mind was able to appropriate African music and conquest the world without loosing its innate characteristics, the reverse process seemed impossible. This is, after all, the structural superiority of the "universal subject" over the "racial subject."

Music and the Production of Space

For travelers in Africa in the nineteenth century the music they encountered often appeared as an annoying, sometimes mysterious, uncanny, even threatening, and ultimately uncontrollable "noise." In contrast to that, with the advent of the reproduction of sound and motion questions of how to discipline and manipulate music and performance practices for specific ends become predominant (Carl 2004). The media revolution at the end of the nineteenth century marks the beginning of what Foucault (1986) has called the "epoch of space." One of the prime concerns of this era is what he identified as "siting" or "placement," which becomes apparent also with regard to recording technology. As we indicated in the previous sections the phonograph became an instrument in various projects of colonial mapping. Not only did this device facilitate the drawing of ethnic maps, but it ultimately also served to map what we called the "musical unconscious," that is, the colonial subject's mind. While "[t]he great obsession of the nineteenth century was [...] history," Foucault writes in his seminal text *Of Other Spaces*, "[t]he present epoch will perhaps be above all the epoch of space" (1986:22). And he continues:

> We are in the epoch of simultaneity; we are in the epoch of juxtaposition, the epoch of the near and far, of the side-by-side, of the dispersed. We are at a moment, I believe, when our experience of the world is less that of a long life developing through time than that of a network that connects points and intersects with its own skein. One could perhaps say that certain ideological conflicts animating present-day polemics oppose the pious descendants of time and the determined inhabitants of space. (Foucault 1986:22)

This is not to say that time, which in the nineteenth century was thought of as history, disappeared altogether. Rather the way time is conceptualized changed. Subordinated to space time constitutes one possible way among others how points in space are connected. The problem of siting in what Foucault calls the epoch of space concerns, then, more than only recording technology. It generally concerns the distribution of elements in space and the relation among sites in an age when, as Marc Augé (1995) has put it, time and space have become "excessive." A number of authors have identified a fundamental transformation of time and space, that is, drastic changes in speed and scale, as the characteristic of the present age.[7] For Augé one outcome of these developments is the multiplication of what he calls "non-places," that is, sites he defines

> in opposition to the sociological notion of place, associated [...] with the idea of a culture localized in time and space. The installations needed for the accelerated circulation of passengers and goods (high-speed roads and railways, interchanges, airports) are just as much non-places as the means of transport themselves, or the great commercial centres, or the extended transit camps where the planet's refugees are parked. (Augé 1995:34)

Foucault has also noted that demography, which basically means "knowing what relations of propinquity, what type of storage, circulation, marking, and classification of human elements should be adopted in a given situation in order to achieve a given end" (Foucault 1986:24), is one of the very concrete forms in which the problem of siting arises. Related questions fueled, as we have seen, the debates about German-African relationships in the metropole, and issues of how to deal with "foreigners" or "migrants," that is, the increasing number of "determined inhabitants of space," as Foucault calls them, still dominates political debates in the "Fortress Europe" of today. We are dealing with problems of migration and citizenship here, with questions of ethnic and cultural identity, as they arise with the intensification and acceleration of the movement of people, objects, and ideas.

This process, mostly subsumed under the header of "globalization" (cf. Inda & Rosaldo 2002), which is evident as early as in the nineteenth century, has increased drastically in the twentieth century. More and more people cross national borders and the massive migration movements of the last decades as well as the development of electronic communication technologies have lead to the establishment of transnational social spaces in which the most diverse cultural formations meet (Castles & Miller 1993). The dynamics unfolding within these spaces goes well beyond our classical understanding of concepts like "culture" and "nation." In a highly critical essay Gupta and Ferguson (1997) challenge the way ethnographic maps have been drawn since the emergence of ethnology in the nineteenth century. In the majority of cases, they write, it is either the nation-state, which is chosen as the premier analytical entity, or smaller ethnic territories. They argue that

---

[7] See for example Giddens' (1990) or Harvey's (1989) analyses of late modernity or post-modernity respectively.

in all these cases, space itself becomes a kind of neutral grid on which cultural difference, historical memory, and societal organization is inscribed. It is in this way that space functions as a central organizing principle in the social sciences at the same time that it disappears from analytical purview. (Gupta & Ferguson 1997:34)

Producing what they refer to as the isomorphism of space, place, and culture, that is, assuming that social spaces are naturally disconnected rather than hierarchically interconnected, the analytical denial of space veils geopolitical power relations and spatial mechanisms of control, it makes it impossible to account for processes of social and cultural exchange and transformation. Denying space means to keep things in place. The notion of culture on which this isomorphism is based can easily be identified as a racialized concept. The terms "culture" and "race" were indeed often used interchangeably in the nineteenth and early twentieth century (cf. Stocking 1982). Based on such conceptual grounds musical mapping has always been a central concern in comparative musicology and ethnomusicology, from the diffusionist models of the early twentieth century to later attempts such as Lomax's "cantometrics" project.[8] The inscription of music in space coincides with Europe's racial or ethnic maps, creating isolated entities without any connection. There is no place for hybridity — or "musical bastards," as Hornbostel had it — in these models.

To overcome the shortcomings of these center-periphery-models and account for the complex interrelations, overlappings, and contradictions in sociocultural space current theorists have developed different models. Appadurai (1996), for example, has suggested thinking the global cultural economy in terms of a variety of cultural landscapes such as "ethnoscapes" and "mediascapes." Holding that culture, today, is basically in a state of "deterritorialization," he focuses on the global flow of cultural elements as well as on processes of their "reterritorialization." Due to the dominance of rapidly expanding media networks across the planet, for Appadurai it is the imagination that plays the most vital role in current cultural processes and the production of sociocultural spaces. In accordance with Appadurai's model, other authors have also stressed the "fluidity" of modernity (Bauman 2000). Hannerz describes the cultural complexity of modern "habitats of meaning" as "moving interconnectedness" (Hannerz 1992:167), holding that culture is "a thing of

---

[8] For examples of diffusionist models of the early twentieth century such as the so-called *Kulturkreislehre*, developed largely on the basis of material culture such as musical instruments, see Ankermann ([1901] 1976) and Sachs (1929). An example for a later attempt at musical mapping on a global scale is the cantometrics project (Lomax 1976), which was based on the analysis of song styles.

relationships rather than of territory" (ibid.:232).

Although anxieties about the cultural homogenization, or, as Adorno (1941) had it, the standardization of cultural artifacts, on a global scale might not be completely unjustified,[9] most authors agree that within what Hannerz (1996) calls the "global ecumene" modern life takes quite different shapes in different locales around the world. Commodities themselves develop a social life of their own, as Appadurai ([1986] 2003) has argued; their sociocultural identity changes over time and with the movement in space. The global cultural economy can overall be described as a political economy of cultural difference. Homogenizing processes are, in this view, juxtaposed with the multiplication of cultural differences, and this dialectical process of differentiation and identification can be traced down to the level of the individual. Cultural difference is more and more economized, politicized, and, to not a small extent, individualized (Bauman 2000). While the accumulation of capital and knowledge occurs on a global scale, the sheer unlimited number of forms contrasts these totalizing tendencies. Hybrid, fragmentary, and contradictory identities have become not the exception but rather the rule (Hall 1992). As one consequence, in the age of what Bauman (2000) has coined "liquid modernity," power is hardly localizable any more.

In recent literature the mobility of music, the geographical distribution of soundscapes as well music's role in processes of cultural reterritorialization, has come into focus (cf. Connell & Gibson 2003 and Stokes 1994). With the principal detachment of identities from territories, musical identities have also become highly mobile. Media technologies — from mechanical apparatuses such as the phonograph to electronic devices such as the Walkman and digital gadgets like the iPod we are used to today — are a precondition for this musical deterritorialization. And technologies have become important means in processes of reterritorialization and the "reembedding" (Giddens 1990:88) of social relationships in temporal and spatial contexts. As Martin Stokes has argued:

> Music is clearly very much part of modern life and our understanding of it, articulating our knowledge of other people, places, times and things, and ourselves in relation to them. [...] Amongst the

---

[9] These debates are, as we have seen in our discussion of Hornbostel's accounts of African music, as old as ethnomusicology or comparative musicology, respectively. Particularly in later studies of popular music and then also in discussions world music in the 1980s and 1990s, the issue of commercialization and homogenization was taken up again in debates about "cultural imperialism." See for example Erlmann (1993), Garofalo (1993), Guilbault (1993 and 1997), or Taylor (1997).

countless ways in which we 'relocate' ourselves, music undoubtedly
has a vital role to play. The musical event, from collective dances to
the act of putting a cassette or CD into a machine, evokes and or-
ganises collective memories and present experiences of place with an
intensity, power, and simplicity unmatched by any other social activity. The 'places' constructed through music involve notions of difference and social boundary. They also organise hierarchies of
moral and political order. (Stokes 1994:3)

Music is therefore not just an expression of some prefabricated or "standardized" identities floating in space. There is no simple homology between particular musics and sociocultural identities of groups of people, and neither can
we expect any fixed musical subjectivity that inhabits individuals. As Born and
Hesmondhalgh have noted,

> music "reflects" nothing; rather music has a formative role in the
> construction, negotiation, and transformation of sociocultural iden-
> tities. In this view, music engenders communities or "scenes"; it al-
> lows a play with, a performance of, and an imaginary exploration of
> identities. Its aesthetic pleasure has much to do with this vicarious
> exploration of identities. (Born & Hesmondhalgh 2000:31)

Music, then, plays a significant role in the political economy of space. It is constitutive in the production of space itself, as it engenders concrete communities
and scenes as well as imaginary musical landscapes — what Hesmondhalgh
calls "musically-imagined communities" (Born & Hesmondhalgh 2000:35).
This is, after all, what becomes clear from the debates on African music, as we
have outlined them thus far. The articulation and negotiation of identities
through music as part of the production of space can be self-empowered as
well as ascribed from outside. As for the colonial discourse on African music,
African voices and subject positions were clearly silenced. Yet African music
was also re-appropriated by Africans in a number of ways. Unveiling the
strategies of siting and the role of music in processes of identity construction is
therefore one of our major concerns. The representation and performance of
music engenders places. Musical terminology, events, and performances always imply relations; they articulate, reinforce and transform identities and
differences. Musical performance is indeed itself a way to use and transform
space, and musical events leave their marks and traces in space. Music is, after
all, a bodily experience, and it is "by means of the body that space is perceived, lived — and produced" (Lefebvre [1991] 2004:162).

When we consider the significance of the representation, performance and appropriation of "Africanness" in popular culture, and the place or the places of African music in a sociocultural space that geographically expands between Africa, Europe, and the Americas, music's constructive role as a means of siting becomes apparent. The musical encounters we are dealing with take place in a border zone between Self and Other, a zone Taussig (1993) describes as "space between," where boundaries are sometimes blurred, relations confounded and dislocated, and the "microphysics of power" (Foucault 1979) is at work. Disclosing music's constitutive role in processes of identity formation and the production of space must therefore be the aim of any musical geography.

4 Approaching Urban Space

Welcome to the Bronx of Berlin

Why not Berlin? — It must have been such a rather simple thought that stood at the beginning of this project. Thinking back to the time when I finished school, I remember it was many of my classmates' desire to move to Germany's reunited capital. Berlin was "hip," at least in an average, mid-sized West German city such as Osnabrück, where I grew up, and among people of my age, whose political consciousness was just about to arise at the end of the Cold War. In our imagination, which is to say, the imagination of those who sought to move beyond the city borders, Berlin meant metropolis, while Osnabrück was regarded part of the provinces. We had gone on a school trip to Berlin once. I also visited Berlin with my family, not long after the fall of the Wall. My parents, I think, wanted to be a part of this historical moment, while I could not really comprehend the significance of events. All I remember are the pictures that reappeared over and over again on television and imprinted themselves in the collective memory.

That was in the nineties, after the so-called *Wende*, when there was no other city in the country that altered its appearance at such a fast pace. The "New Berlin," as it was now promoted, became the largest construction area in Europe. Vast empty spaces, cutting right through the center of the city, waited to be filled. For the most part capitalism took over. But the wastelands left behind also promised a certain freedom: room for appropriation, even subversion, room for urban adventure. Emerging subcultural formations took hold of some of the void spaces, always on the move, in search of new locations to fit their needs before authorities would chase them out.[1] Especially for younger people and subculturalists of all sorts it was trendy to move to one of the city's eastern quarters such as Mitte or Prenzlauer Berg, later also Friedrichshain, from then on open to anyone from East and West, where apart-

---

[1] See Schwanhäußer (2005) for a personal account of how the techno scene appropriated urban space in Berlin in the 1990s. Another example is the illegal occupation of houses in the eastern districts of Berlin after 1989/90, reminiscent of the alternative scene in Kreuzberg in the 1980s (cf. Diehl et al. 2002).

ments were still inexpensive. With the collapse of the socialist system in Eastern Europe, Berlin, it seems, regained some of its mythical qualities.

Once a symbol of separation, Berlin, now, stood for the crossing of borders, for national unity, a new historical era. Encouraged by the initial success
of the so-called New Economy in the 1990s there was, on the whole, an atmosphere of change in Germany — and Berlin, for many, embodied that
change. In political discourse terms like *Aufschwung* were employed to evoke
economic upswing particularly in the eastern parts of the country, where the
then chancellor Helmut Kohl saw "flourishing landscapes" (*blühende Landschaf-
ten*) arising. The social climate, however, has changed over the course of the
last fifteen years and the boom is said to be over. With one of the highest un-
employment rates, Berlin belongs to Germany's economically weaker regions
these days. Nevertheless, its appeal as the country's largest metropolis with all
its contrasts and rich cultural life is still strong. Be that as it may, eventually all
these images of the "bright lights" of the city might have played a role in my
decision to move from Cologne, where I had just graduated, to Neukölln, literally "New Cologne," which seemed to make sense in a way. That was in
spring 2004.

"Why Neukölln?!" — When you mention that you live in Berlin-Neu-
kölln, the city's largest district, most people react with a mixture of skepticism
and pity (and I'm only slightly exaggerating for rhetorical purposes here).
What they really mean to ask is whether you were not able to find something
better in their eyes, which is unlikely since there is basically an oversupply of
vacant housing space. While living in Berlin was, and in many respects still is,
fashionable, living in Neukölln is not, no matter how often residents stress that
it is possible to live there (though it has to be added that they would preferably
not raise their children there if they had the choice). Neukölln is generally considered one of the more "problematic" areas in Berlin — in fact, in Germany
as a whole. It has no glamorous nightlife with fancy cafés, bars, and clubs as
we find in Mitte and Prenzlauer Berg, no leftist radicals as there are (or, at
least, were) in Kreuzberg, or, for that matter, impressive tourist attractions and
sites of national prestige. Neukölln, in a sense, is pretty normal. There is no
social or cultural capital attached to the quarter, on the contrary. There is, as
someone noted, "no myth that could be criticized. Kreuzberg in the nineteen-
eighties stood for a dream of a better life, Mitte in the nineteen-nineties stood
for a dream of the most beautiful capitalism. Both dreams failed. Neukölln has
no dream" (Diehl et al. 2003:3).

As early as the 1920s Franz Hessel, who explored the city as a *flâneur*,
commented that

visiting Neukölln for its own sake is not really advisable to anyone. It
might be that behind the gigantic scaffoldings currently towering
above Hermannsplatz, where this quarter approximately begins,
nice new architecture is in the making. Yet, the proper Neukölln is
one of those suburbs, which had hardly ten thousand inhabitants in
the [eighteen-]seventies, whereby now, they have between two- and
three-hundred thousand. […] A sad area. At the time it was still
called Rixdorf and had been a destination for short trips, it might
have been more interesting. There is no more music [»*Musike*«] in
Neukölln, as there was, according to that popular song, in Rixdorf.[2]

Hence, Hessel only passed through these, at that time, poor and overpopu-
lated working-class neighborhoods, where one could see, as he writes, "many
beggarly children roaming the streets" ([1929] 1984:193). Formerly just some
small villages at the southern border of the city, which in 1920 became incorporated into Greater Berlin, the area which is now known as Neukölln witnessed an enormous population explosion with the advent of industrialization
in the late nineteenth century. In 1890 it had a population of some eighty
thousand people; until the early twenties the populace increased to over two-
hundred-fifty thousand. Large multi-story dwelling blocks where put up where
rooms were crowded and hygienic conditions poor.
    While circumstances have surely changed since then, the quarter's status
as a "sad area," as Hessel had it, at least in connection with its socio-economic
problems, persists up to this day. It is rather associated with social decay than
improvement. In the north of Neukölln, where one finds the neighborhoods
that are considered most problematic, many people are affected by unem-
ployment and depend on social aid to make a living. In these areas, about forty
percent of the population are immigrants, the group among which the unem-
ployment rate and the number of those receiving social aid is particularly high.
In Neukölln's north it is not unlikely that you see people drinking on the street
in the early morning, and even at a first glance it is not difficult to detect the
overall desolate economic situation. Strolling along Karl-Marx-Straße, the

---

[2] "Um seiner selbst willen Neukölln aufzusuchen, dazu kann man eigentlich niemandem
raten. Vielleicht entsteht hinter den Riesengerüsten, die zur Zeit den Hermannsplatz, mit
dem dieser Stadtteil ungefähr beginnt, überragen, schöne neue Architektur. Aber das ei-
gentliche Neukölln ist eine der Vorstädte, die in den siebziger Jahren kaum zehntausend
Einwohner hatten und jetzt zwischen zwei- und dreihunderttausend haben. [...] Eine trau-
rige Gegend. Als sie noch Rixdorf hieß und Ausflugsort war, mag sie interessanter gewesen
sein. »Musike« ist nicht mehr in Neukölln, wie sie, nach dem bekannten Liede zu schließen,
in Rixdorf gewesen ist" (Hessel [1929] 1984:193).

major shopping street of the quarter (which in the 1950s, it is said, had better days as one of Berlin's more prestigious sites for consumption), you see many shops empty. Apart from the larger department stores, those small-scale dealers who somehow survive sell either poor-quality articles at low prices, *Schnäppchen* made in China and other "developing" parts of the world where labor is cheap, or they deal in second-hand goods such as used refrigerators, washing machines, mobile phones, and the like. If nothing else, in Neukölln one can still get the cheapest *Döner Kebab* in the whole country.

The economy in the area, which includes the bordering Kreuzberg, is to a considerable portion a market run by and used by immigrants. As for the most numerous group, the Turkish community, we find an infrastructure covering most sectors of daily life, such as housing, banking, recreation, shopping, and religion; there are Turkish supermarkets, cafés, restaurants, undertakers, doctors, lawyers, clubs, associations, and mosques. If you walk the streets around northern Sonnenallee, for example, where I used to live, Arab-speaking people from North Africa and the Middle East are the keepers of most shops. There are barbershops, groceries, and stores renting Arab movies, and you pass cafés where the scent of water pipes fills the air. Inside these shops usually exclusively men are seen, playing cards in the glaring lights of fluorescent tubes. Omnipresent are so-called call shops and communication centers, offering low-rate international calls that give a hint about the overall makeup of the population in the quarter and the transnational connections that link it with the world at large: Turkey 0.05 € per minute, Lebanon 0.19 €, Algeria 0.22 €, Palestine 0.10 €, Vietnam 0.45 €, Ghana 0.16 €, Nigeria 0.16 €, Slovenia 0.15 €, Poland 0.07 €, Russia 0.10 €, Kosovo 0.19 €, and so on.

Particularly for the youth, those teenagers roaming the streets of the quarter today, the situation is acute. The violence in schools is increasing and quite a number of young people from immigrant families in Neukölln's north are school dropouts with only little chances of finding a job on the regular labor market.[3] What follows is therefore also a common picture of Neukölln: If you leave the subway at Hermannplatz, one of the liveliest parts of the city in the daytime, you might probably notice some young men who seek to attract potential buyers, whispering: "Hashish? Want Hashish?" The public park Ha-

---

[3] A widely discussed case in point that also found its way into the national mediascape was that of the so-called Rütli-Schule. About one third of the students in this school comes from Arab families, roughly a quarter have a Turkish family background. Overall, more than eighty percent of the students are of non-German descent, and ethnic conflicts are on the increase. In February 2006 the teaching staff, unable to control the situation and resolve internal conflicts, sent out a cry for help in form of an open letter that brought Neukölln to the center of national attention.

senheide in Neukölln has also been known for years to be a territory for dealers in marihuana, divided between Turkish and Arab gangs and dealers from sub-Saharan Africa. Police raids take place quite often here, though it never takes long until everything is back to its "normal" state, and you see the same people standing at the corners, waiting for customers. Harder drugs are dealt with at Kottbusser Tor, two subway stations north in the center of what some people refer to as "Little Istanbul," that is, the Turkish dominated part of Kreuzberg.[4]

For this and other reasons, Neukölln, together with supposedly "bad" neighborhoods in districts like Wedding and Kreuzberg, has gained some prominence in German debates of late, though its reputation is not exactly a glorious one, ranking rather as the "Bronx of Berlin." In political discussions, Neukölln often stands as a worst-case scenario, an example par excellence for the failed "integration" of immigrants into society at large. Particularly after the events of 9/11 politicians employed catch words like *Überfremdung* (foreign infiltration or control) and *Parallelgesellschaften*, that is, "parallel societies" detached from the overall social order, which are often represented as menacing and uncontrollable, to make their point (cf. Vogels 2005). "We don't want parallel worlds in the midst of Germany," exclaimed for example Bavarian state minister Edmund Stoiber, "where all kinds of languages are spoken except German" (Stoiber 2006). Neukölln, it is said, hosts many of such "parallel worlds." In the same vein, some of Stoiber's colleagues were warning against an imminent "Kreuzbergization" of the whole country. A case in point was a so-called "honor killing" of a young Kurdish woman that was taken as evidence for the "Muslim village morality" of immigrants "in Berlin's modernity" (Bullion 2005). And whenever social rumor in other European cities is discussed in the German public — burning cars and raging youths in the *banlieues* of Paris or the assassination of the Dutch director Theo van Gogh in Amsterdam being recent examples — it is said that similar incidents, if they were to happen somewhere in Germany, could most likely occur in Neukölln (am Orde 2004).

Difficulties and conflicts undoubtedly exist. But social tensions as we face them in Neukölln are not an exclusive feature of the quarter alone; they are evident in many urban areas throughout Germany. Whatever one can say about Neukölln, with regard to Berlin's ill-reputed neighborhoods we are neither dealing with ghettos in the sense of no-go areas as parts of New York's Bronx might be (or might have been in the 1980s), nor in the sense of ethnic

---

[4] For reports on the quarter's drug market, an issue discussed in the print media for at least a decade now, see for example Kunzemann (2002) or Miller (1998).

enclaves. What can be observed in areas like these are the workings of social segregation in Germany, which manifests itself, to be sure, to not an insignificant degree along ethnic lines, though this is only one factor among others. Districts like Neukölln are, first of all, highly heterogeneous, they are multiethnic and characterized by diversity. This diversity is clearly part of the social reality in contemporary Germany. As for "no-go areas" and ethnic segregation, we find it rather in the eastern suburbs of Berlin where virtually no "people of color" live. Due to the risk of violent racist attacks, which took place there recurrently, it is not advisable for foreigners — or for those who are conceived of as such — to enter these districts.[5] This, after all, is also part of the social reality in contemporary Germany.

Nights in Kreuzberg Are Long

"These Asante people! These Asante people!" Kay said amused, laughing and shaking his head, while we were dancing in the midst of the crowd to the blaring sounds of highlife music somewhere in Kreuzberg. The place was sultry and much too small for so many people, sweat running over their faces as they were dancing or pushing each other through the narrow corridor on the way down to the street to get some fresh air. Looking at all these formally dressed Ghanaians, the men in their heavy suits, definitely too thick for such a warm summer night, and the women in their long evening dresses, we didn't really fit into the overall picture in our jeans and T-shirts. The contrast made the situation only more absurd. I was the only White, anyway, and together with the African American woman who accompanied us probably the only non-Ghanaian at the occasion. "These Asante people," as Kay identified them, obviously (and quite literally) liked to lay it on thick, wearing their best suits no matter whether they were appropriate for the weather or not. So, finally Maggie, Kay, Yeboah, Kofi, and I had ended up at a Ghanaian outdooring (a naming ceremony for newborn babies) in Berlin-Kreuzberg, among people who matched quite well the social type they refer to as *burger* in Ghana.

---

[5] This was actually a hotly debated issue before the soccer world cup started in Germany in 2006. Due to racist attacks in parts of Brandenburg, particularly a homicide in Potsdam, several immigrant associations and left-wing political groups declared parts of Berlin and areas in eastern Germany to be "no-go areas," intended as a guideline for foreign visitors during the world cup. Since conservative government officials wanted to promote Germany as an open, tolerant nation, they strongly opposed these guidelines as a threat to the country's image.

Popular etymology has it that the term *burger* derives from the name of the city of Hamburg. As we have already mentioned, Hamburg hosts the largest Ghanaian community in Germany. Yet, the concept of the *burger* more generally refers to all Ghanaians who have spent some time in Germany or elsewhere abroad, particularly in Europe and North America, that is, the countries of the so-called West. The term thus matches what is referred to as *beento* in Nigeria and implies a "general sophistication [...] acquired abroad, a savoir-faire with regard to the way of life of the metropolis, and an intimate appreciation of its finer points" (Hannerz 1992:228f). *Burger* signifies a distinctive style associated with Western modernity that is marked by wealth and mobility. As someone commented in an interview, a *burger* is someone who has the means to "move freely" — the unfulfilled dream of many Ghanaians. As a social type and popular character, then, the *burger* embodies cosmopolitanism and openness to the world, which is expressed in a particular clothing style and habitus. London, New York, or Paris are today clearly parts of West African culture, as Hannerz remarked, "if not as situated experiences, then at least as vibrant images" (Hannerz 1992:229). *Burger* and *beento* respectively represent the "figure of a migrant returning home laden with cultural capital" (ibid.) and they nurture the "myth of migration," the story of the ultimately successful migrant.

The term and its implications became also associated with a musical style, the so-called burger highlife, initiated in the 1980s by musicians like George Darko who with his band Cantata introduced a more synthesizer-based form of highlife music (Collins 1992b:323f). Darko lived in Berlin at that time and produced a number of records in Germany that became very popular in Ghana. Other musicians in the diaspora followed Darkos example and made burger highlife the most popular dance music in Ghana and its diaspora in the 1980s and 1990s. Burger highlife music also popularized the *burger* style, though this style changed somewhat over the decades and has by now become more diversified.[6] Some of today's most popular Ghanaian musicians associated with burger highlife such as Daddy Lumba, Amakye Dede, or Ofori Amponsah still produce in Germany, and particularly the Rheinklang Studio in Düsseldorf run by Bodo Staiger had a profound impact on the "Ghanaian

---

[6] One of the typical haircuts of the 1980s, for example, that Darko and others wore is what people in Ghana refer to as "back bush," that is, long hair only in the neck and the rest cut short. Today, we also find Americanized versions of the *burger*, some reminiscent of the typical cowboy image, others more associated with hip hop music and its Ghanaian variant hiplife.

sound" of the 1990s.[7] Since the massive emigration of Ghanaians in the 1980s, which included many of Ghana's professional musicians, the diaspora has more generally become an important market and place of production for Ghanaian popular music. Apart from occasional performances in Ghana, concerts of the above mentioned musicians attract thousands of enthusiastic fans in the diaspora, and their largest shows take place rather in Hamburg, London, or Toronto than in Accra or Kumasi (cf. Carl et al. forthcoming).

It was the close of a strange day. Dances like *adowa* or *kete*, which Adikanfo had performed in the zoo of Leipzig in the afternoon, are actually considered part the cultural heritage of the Asante. In the process of nation building after independence in 1957, these were standardized and integrated into a transethnic canon of traditional music and dance in Ghana (Agawu 2003:17-20), what is known as "cultural music" or just "culture." The Asante are the most numerous ethnic group in Ghana and there is some rivalry between Kumasi, Ghana's second-largest city and seat of the *Asantehene*, the king of Asante, and the capital Accra, traditionally a territory of the Ga, but today a conglomerate of people from all over the country. The Asante's language Twi has become the country's most widely spoken lingua franca and there are attempts to make it an official language in Ghana in addition to English. The Asante also form the majority in the Ghanaian diaspora. It has been noted that the Ghanaian society undergoes a process of Akanization, manifest in the dissemination of Twi as well as the cultural and political dominance of the Akan. This dominance is also evident in the networks of the diaspora, particularly where larger communities have established themselves.

Kay, who is from Accra, with his dread locks and casual style is not exactly the type who normally goes to outdoorings and similar social events within the Ghanaian community. In terms of social dance he clearly prefers the Afro and reggae parties in Berlin's clubs, where many of the younger and more secular oriented Africans in the city go. Apart from that, "if you want the real Accra feeling" (which includes drinking Guinness, watching the Premier League, and, above all, conversing in Ga, the predominant language of Greater Accra), he once told me, "you have to go to the Afro shop in Moabit." Afro shops — stores selling African food stuffs, hair care products and cosmetics, sometimes also DVDs and music CDs — serve as meeting points for

---

[7] See the webpage of the Rheinklang Studio at http://www.rheinklang-studio.de (accessed on April 23, 2007). In a personal conversation with Martin Ziegler, Staiger confirmed that Ghanaian musicians regularly approach him for a particular sound. The view that only Staiger could produce the 1990s sound was also expressed in a meeting with burger highlife musicians at the Goethe Institute in Accra in March 2006, among them George Darko as well as Charles Amoah, who worked with Staiger before.

fellow country men and women in the city, and parties like the one we attended that night are publicly announced in these stores.[8] While in the zoo internal ethnic differences didn't really matter, in the interaction among Ghanaians in Berlin they surely did. As one Ghanaian interview partner commented: "Among Ghanaians here it's horrible. One says: 'I'm Ashanti, I'm a real human being.' Another one is Ewe, and so on. […] There are more Ghanaians in Berlin than Africans from any other country and they are totally grouped."

Be that as it may, the dances Adikanfo had performed in the zoo had, after all, little to do with this social occasion. Maggie had suggested coming here. She liked these Ghanaian parties and I had attended several funeral celebrations and outdoorings with her in Berlin. Events like these do usually not start before midnight. Many Ghanaians consider these occasions a good opportunity to meet people and, of course, to dance to the latest hits of Ghanaian music, that is, highlife, hiplife (the Ghanaian variant of hip hop), and above all gospel. Outdoorings and funerals are of course also about see and be seen. Besides, food and drinks are for free — a question of honor and prestige for the hosts who in their announcements would normally invite "all friends and well-wishers." When we arrived at this outdooring, coming from the rehearsal room where we had unpacked the drums after the gig in Leipzig, it was already way past midnight. We had missed the official part of the ceremony and now everyone was dancing. When we entered the scene the DJ played some gospel highlife songs and Yeboah told me that this would actually be the kind of music they play in church.[9] On Sundays, when he was not performing with Adikanfo, he played the drum set in one of the Ghanaian churches in Berlin.

As a matter of fact, the majority of guests at this occasion met in the various charismatic Ghanaian churches every Sunday. Apart from Afro shops, which can be found in every major German city, churches are important nodes in the networks of the African diaspora in Western Europe and North America. Not only do churches provide expressive spaces for an otherwise marginalized group, but they also offer practical support in legal matters, communication with bureaucracy, and the organization of everyday life. As Akyeampong notes:

---

[8] For a classified directory of Afro shops in Germany see http://www.afrika-start.de (accessed on March 12, 2007), an Africa-related website in German which lists 38 stores in Berlin alone.

[9] Gospel, which in the Ghanaian usage can be any music with Christian content, represents the largest portion of the Ghanaian music market nowadays. While US-American gospel music is very popular, there are also local variants such as gospel highlife, mostly sung in Twi. On the significance of gospel music in Ghana see Collins (1997).

Membership of African churches provides some security in racially hostile European cities. Ghanaian churches serve as information networks for jobs and housing, and these established channels of communication with officialdom assist illegal Ghanaians in securing legal status. African churches are thus an important substitute for kinship and family networks, while extending the emotive religious experience initiated by Pentecostal churches in the homeland. (Akyeampong 2000:99)

In Berlin Ghanaians founded their first church in Wedding in 1988. Since then, it seems, more and more people have started their own church, which reflects the growing number of Ghanaians in the city, but which also follows a more general trend in Ghana where churches are mushrooming on virtually every corner. By now there are at least a dozen Christian churches in Berlin where mainly Ghanaians come together for worship. Among these are the Church of the Pentecost International, the Bethel Faith Church, the Gospel Believers Center, and others, most of them charismatic in orientation. The larger churches among these have put up branches in many cities in Europe and North America and they operate not unlike transnational corporations.[10] Services take place mostly on Sunday afternoons, since these parishes usually rent church buildings that are used by German congregations in the morning. Some smaller congregations just rent rooms such as in schools, which are not used otherwise at weekends.

Yeboah was now a little worried that he would be too tired for church the next morning since it was getting very late, and he doubted whether it was a good decision to come with us. This was all the more true for the African American woman we had met earlier on the street and who had spontaneously decided to join us. We were just coming from the gig and took a drink on a bench somewhere in Kreuzberg. Nobody knew her, but apparently she found it interesting to meet Africans. "Oh, you're from Africa! Musicians? That's interesting!" she excitedly said when she approached us on the street. She claimed that she was African as well. From her accent it was easy to tell that she was socialized in North America, so Kofi wanted to know were exactly in Africa she was from. She tried to think of some place, but obviously none came to her mind. Now at the outdooring the woman seemed confused. The setting was not exactly what she had expected when we told her we would go to an "African" party. "This is the strangest thing I've ever seen," she repeat-

---

[10] On the significance of charismatic churches in West Africa and its diaspora see Adogame (1997), Coleman (2000), Ter Haar (1998), or Van Dijk (1997).

edly told me while I tried to explain to her what the event was all about, "I've never seen something like this." After a while she just left, and not even Kofi's constant affirmations how much he loved her could convince her to stay. As for the rest of us, we danced until six in the morning, until the drinks were finished and the party was over.

From Kreuzberg I finally went home to Neukölln. Kreuzberg, Neukölln, Wedding — these are the parts of the city where most Ghanaians reside and where events like this mostly take place. The northern neighborhoods of Neukölln are not only the territory of Turkish and Arab youth gangs, but also one of the centers of the African community in Berlin (cf. Adesiyan 2006, Kessen 2001, and Trüper 2000). Ghanaians refer to these areas as "Nima." As one of Accra's most densely populated quarters with only narrow alleys between houses and mosques built wall to wall, from a romanticist point of view Nima has something of the quality of an old Arab medina. Many Muslims from Ghana's northern regions live in Nima and the vernacular is rather Hausa than Twi or Ga. The reputation of Nima, associated with roughness, poverty, and criminality, pretty much matches that of Neukölln and Berlin's other ill-reputed neighborhoods. "Well, it's the ghetto," people laconically explained to me when I asked them why they call Neukölln or Kreuzberg Nima.

Reading the Streets

In Berlin's district Mitte, not far from the Brandenburg Gate, there is a street called Mohrenstraße branching off from Friedrichstraße. In the "roaring twenties" the Friedrichstraße was one of the centers for amusements in the city. Apart from ethnographic shows,[11] taking place in the Hasenheide or in establishments like the Passage-Panoptikum, another "exotic" form of entertainment was the Kolonialpanorama on Friedrichstraße that opened its premises in December 1885 for the general public (Zeller 2002). A fashionable mass entertainment in end-nineteenth-century Europe, so-called panoramas were fixed buildings, rotundas with large wall paintings showing battle scenes and other popular events. The Berlin Kolonialpanorama, a twelve-cornered rotunda with a diameter of more than thirty meters, featured paintings of scenes of the German-African colonial encounter on two floors, for example a 115 meters long portrayal of the German occupation of African territories and the conquest of African peoples. There were also rooms in which ethnographic

---

[11] On ethnographic shows in Berlin see Reed-Anderson (2000:16) and Thode-Arora (2002).

objects from Germany's newly acquired colonies were exhibited. The rooms were fitted out with palm trees and other exotic plants. Artificial fog and a special lighting system were meant to create a "tropical atmosphere."

Mohrenstraße, which got its name around 1700, points to German colonial endeavors in Africa long before the formation of the German Empire in 1871 (van der Heyden 2002c; Reed-Anderson 2000:12). In the seventeenth and eighteenth century Blacks were generally referred to as *Mohren*, that is, "Moors," whose presence in Germany has been recorded from the first half of the sixteenth century. Most of these were African slaves who were brought to Europe to work as domestic servants for the nobility (Kleßmann 1987). In the seventeenth century it also became fashionable to employ Africans as musicians in court and military bands (Firla & Forkl 1995). In the Prussian army Africans served as military musicians until 1918. But the name of Mohrenstraße actually refers to the presence of some Africans who came as a political delegation to Berlin.

It was in 1681, in the wake of attempts made by Prussia to become a colonial power and to benefit from the transatlantic slave trade, that ships from Brandenburg reached the West African "Gold Coast" at the Gulf of Guinea (van der Heyden 2002a). The Prussians managed to sign trade and protection treaties with some local African rulers, and one of the two ships sent out eventually returned with 100 pounds of gold and 10,000 pounds of ivory. In 1682, then, the trading society *Brandenburg-Africanische Compagnie* was founded and the first slaves from West Africa were brought to Hamburg — a business that turned out to be more profitable. To secure German interests in West Africa the fortress Großfriedrichsburg was built, located on the coast of present-day Ghana at what is now Prince's Town. It ranges among a number of fortresses built by Europeans along the West African coast, which played a crucial part in the transatlantic slave trade.

An African delegation from Prussia's colony in West Africa came to Berlin in 1684 and stayed there for four months to pay their respect to Brandenburg's elector Prince Friedrich Wilhelm. The presence of these Africans called forth so much attention among the local population in Berlin that the street where the delegation was accommodated was later named Mohrenstraße. In 1717 Brandenburg's trading company and its possessions in West Africa as well as the Caribbean island St. Thomas were sold to the Dutch West Indian Company by Friedrich Wilhelm I. It is estimated that by then Prussia had brought between ten and thirty thousand Africans as slaves to the New World. The early presence of Africans in the service of Europe's royal courts and armed forces is, at the same time, the beginning of the formation of an African diaspora in Europe.

Apart from Mohrenstraße there is Groebenufer, named after the first commander of Großfriedrichsburg, Otto Friedrich von der Groeben, which is reminiscent of Brandenburg's colonial past. We also find a Guineastraße in Berlin. And in the district Wedding is the so-called African Quarter, which is not another center of the African community in the city, but yet another trace of Germany's colonial past to be found on present maps of Berlin (van der Heyden 2002d). Following a directive of the German emperor Wilhelm II the first two streets in the African Quarter were given their current names in 1899 for Germany's West African protectorates, namely Kameruner Straße and Togostraße. Other streets bear names like Sansibarstraße, Usambarastraße, Tangastraße, or Ugandastraße, reminiscent of Germany's colonial presence in East Africa; Lüderitzstraße was named after Adolf Lüderitz who in 1883 signed protection treaties in South West Africa, present-day Namibia, which was the only colony in Africa where significant numbers of Germans settled.[12] Other streets like Dualastraße are named for ethnic groups that were colonized by the Germans, in this case the Douala of Cameroon. Moreover, names like Transvaalstraße give a hint to the euphoric sentiments of the colonial movement in favor of the Boer population in South Africa, which arose after the Boer Wars from 1899 to 1902 and were based on a felt blood relation with the descendants of Dutch settlers in South Africa.

The African Quarter goes back to an original plan of Carl Hagenbeck, who had the intention to construct an African animal enclosure in this part of Germany's capital. The space for the project was already included in the city maps when World War I prevented these plans being implemented. It is interesting to note that many of the streets in the African Quarter were given their current names after the end of World War I in 1918, when Germany had already lost all its colonial territories. The names of Uganda- or Sambesistraße, for example, were not introduced before 1927 (van der Heyden 2002d:262). Though Germany lost all its colonies in the course of World War I, the colonial discourse and imagination by no means ended in 1918/19. Germany's

---

[12] The presence of German settlers in German South West Africa lead to conflicts with the largest ethnic groups in the colony, the Herero, Nama and Ovambo. These confrontations were largely about the distribution of pastureland. Starting in the 1890s, the Nama were involved in an ongoing guerilla war and Germany increased its military presence. In 1904 the Herero started a revolt against German settlers, which eventually lead to the most brutal war in German colonial history. Under the command of general Lothar von Trotha whose aim was the total annihilation of the Herero, tens of thousands were killed (Gründer 1995:111-127; Smith 1978:51-65). The war lasted until 1907, and the Namibian government demands compensation from Germany up to this date. This part of German colonial history was focused on particularly in 2004, a hundred years after the Herero war broke out.

colonial "heroes" were still celebrated with enthusiasm. In the 1920s and then especially under the Nazi regime, the colonial revisionist movement gained in strength. After all, slogans like "What was German, has to become German again!" matched perfectly with the debates of the National Socialists about "a people without space" (*Volk ohne Raum*). Under Hitler's leadership this movement cumulated in plans for a large German colonial empire, a German *Mittelafrika*, stretching across the African continent from east to west (Pogge von Strandmann 2002).

Reconsidering the history of the African Quarter after World War II a great uneasiness in how Germany's colonial past is dealt with becomes apparent. Overshadowed by National Socialism and the feeling of collective shame, this part of German history has been largely forgotten in public consciousness. There were actually efforts to rename streets in the African Quarter as early as 1946. Attempts to rename Togostraße, for example, in honor of a woman active in the anti-fascist movement who formerly lived in that street and who was killed in the concentration camp Sachsenhausen remained unsuccessful. A more scandalous example of dealing with colonial history is the political fights over so-called Petersallee. The National Socialists renamed this street, formerly Londoner Straße, in 1939 after Carl Peters, one of the most brutal colonial activists in Germany (van der Heyden 2002d).

In the last quarter of the nineteenth century, Peters became one of Germany's most prominent figures in the colonial movement. He obtained huge territories for the German Empire in East Africa largely by deception and force. Taking action mostly on his own account, he nearly provoked a military conflict with the British Empire. From 1891 to 1893 he was commissioner for the German Empire in the area around Mount Kilimanjaro. Initiated by a speech given in 1896 by the parliamentarian August Bebel of the Social Democrats who accused Peters of inhumanity, disciplinary proceedings were instituted against him. Peters was alleged to have unlawfully executed Africans while in state service in German East Africa, among them a woman who was probably his mistress. Due to Peter's prominence the case eventually became a media event, and people sarcastically called him *Hänge-Peters* ("string-up-Peters"). He was found guilty, discharged from state service and deprived of all his ranks. It was only later, after his death, that the National Socialists formally rehabilitated Peters. They made extensive use of his image in their colonial propaganda (Wieben 2000).

Irrespective of this inglorious history, when in 1984 it was suggested to rename the Petersallee in the African Quarter and to choose instead the name of an African personality of the past or present for the street (Samuel Maharero who lead the Herero against the German colonial masters in the Herero war and Nelson Mandela were brought into discussion, for example), it seemed politically impossible to get the required majority of votes in the city council. Conservatives wanted to keep to the alley named for Carl Peters. As a matter of fact, we find the Petersallee in Berlin's African Quarter up to this day, and it was only because of public pressure that an additional plate has been installed, stating that the street is rather named after "Hans Peters, city councilor from 1896-1966" — a largely unknown politician of the conservative party CDU (van der Heyden 2002d:263).[13]

The Near and the Far

"Fieldwork distinguishes ethnomusicology and ethnographically based disciplines from other social sciences, and ethnographers derive from fieldwork their most significant contributions to the humanities in general" (Cooley 1997:4), writes Timothy Cooley in his introduction to one of the surprisingly few full-length collections of essays on this method (Barz & Cooley 1997), considered the most central to our field. And he continues:

> By ethnography, we mean the observation and description (or representation) of culture; for ethnomusicologists the focus is on music-culture. Fieldwork is the observational and experiential portion of the ethnographic process during which the ethnomusicologist engages living individuals in order to learn about music-culture. (Cooley 1997:4)

While most ethnomusicologists will agree that having been to "the field" constitutes an essential part of their academic as well as personal identity (just listen to the stories ethnomusicologists tell each other when they sit leisurely together), doing fieldwork, or, as some prefer, field research, is an often mythologized process that at least since the days of Bronislaw Malinowski takes the character of a scholarly rite of passage. We can think of Nigel Barley's "traumatic" experiences in Cameroon (Barley 1983), for example, familiar to probably most students of anthropology as some kind of proto-account of the realities of fieldwork, though in this case an admittedly amusing one. If you have not suffered, lost consciousness, or, at least a tooth somewhere "out

---

[13] There were similar fights over the names of streets and public places in other German cities, for example, the Petersplatz in Hanover (cf. Wieben 2000).

there," such stories seem to suggest, you have not experienced the "real" thing (I left one of my wisdom teeth in a quite unspectacular way at La Polyclinic in Accra — I wonder whether that counts). Even if we are aware that an account like Barley's is a rhetorical exaggeration, the imagery it evokes is nonetheless powerful and pervasive.[14]

Taking processes of globalization into account and considering that music and culture today are, as we elaborated on in the previous chapter, in a state of deterritorialization, contradicts older images of "fieldwork" where the ethnographer travels to some far place and immerses him- or herself in a different cultural world, aiming to experience this foreign world "from within."[15] Such a perspective reinforces highly problematic conceptions of cultures as distinct and hermetic entities in space, as self-maintaining systems embodied by a particular group of people. As we have seen earlier in this chapter, the culturalist assumption of such isolated "parallel worlds" is also a prominent feature of political discourse on immigration, where cultural difference is often represented as a threat to "mainstream" society. And even the most well-meant cultural relativism which considers the cultural other as a unique reality in its own right is nevertheless based on the claim that "they" fundamentally differ from an assumed "us."[16] As Hannerz notes, "[i]t should not [...] be only the shifting relations between culture and territory that bothers us. No less at issue is the assumption that the carrier of 'a culture' is 'a people'" (Hannerz 1996:22).

Dealing with cultural processes in an increasingly globalized and, all the more, rapidly urbanizing world, it is not only the culture concept that has to be rethought, but also the notion of the "field." Where is "the field" — a territorial concept, indeed — when culture, as we argued, has become deterritorialized? What does "field research" mean within the framework of a musical geography as we outlined it earlier? For an approach attempting not just to

---

[14] It could be argued, in fact, that the mythologization of fieldwork goes back to older images of the "explorer hero" as we encounter him in nineteenth-century travel literature (Fabian 2000). These accounts feature discussions on methodology and claim to be scientific in a positivistic manner. While fieldwork is mostly considered an invention of the twentieth century, the methodological discussions around travel as a way of acquiring knowledge are evident already in the "age of exploration," paradigmatically represented by Alexander von Humboldt, and in classical conceptions of the *Bildungsreise*, that is, the grand tour (cf. Essner 1985).

[15] Such a perspective has been conceptualized in cultural anthropology in the distinction between "emic" and "etic" perspectives, for example — a debate which was also taken up by ethnomusicologists (cf. Alvarez-Pereyre & Arom 1993).

[16] In German political debates such a view was often promoted by leftist groups, which sometimes celebrated a "happy" and unquestioned multiculturalism over the course of the last decades, and is today rather pejoratively referred to as *Multikulti*.

map presupposed cultures in space, but one that focuses on the production of space and processes of mapping as integral parts of the cultural process, the notion of "the field" becomes problematic. How, then, do we approach the city or urban space, where music-culture often, if not mostly, takes place today?

Urbanization is a far-reaching and pervasive process, which, as Lefebvre (2003) notes, tends to absorb other forms of social organization. Rather than thinking of urban space as a bounded geographical territory in opposition to rural space, he therefore employs the term "urban society" to refer to "the society that results from industrialization, which is a process of domination that absorbs agricultural production" (Lefebvre 2003:2). To speak of urban society does not concern life in the city alone. Urbanization is a social transformation that affects "entire territories, regions, nations, and continents" (ibid.:3), a processes that creates complex and multiple dependencies between villages, towns, small and mid-sized cities and metropolitan centers, and one that is characterized, first of all, by a particular mode of production. We could argue that if we travel from any small town in southern Ghana, today, via Kotoka International Airport in Accra to any destination in Germany we are moving entirely within urban space. The space we are dealing with here has indeed "been completely urbanized" (ibid.:1).

Urban space is, however, as Low (1996) has argued for the anthropological disciplines more generally, a highly undertheorized terrain. The city, as Hannerz describes it, "is a place of discoveries and surprises, whether pleasant or unpleasant; a place where it is likely that you see things today that you did not see yesterday, and encounter people who are not like yourself" (Hannerz 1992:173). Urban space, in other words, "makes people more accessible to one another" (Hannerz 1980:243) and the encounter with the cultural Other more likely. As nodes in global networks, particularly the large metropolitan conglomerates are the epicenters of the "excesses" in speed and scale that characterize today's cultural flows. The urban is, to paraphrase Foucault (1986), the space of the near and the far and the side-by-side (temporarily as well as spatially), a contradictory space he calls heterotopia. Such spaces "are linked with all the others," but at the same time, "contradict all the other sites" (Foucault 1986:23). The contradictions of urban society also penetrate rural areas today, which have mostly become "partial colonies of the metropolis" (Lefebvre 2003:4). How then, can we locate our "field" within this "moving interconnectedness" (Hannerz 1992:167), as Hannerz characterizes the cultural landscape of urban space?

James Clifford, in his suggestive essay on *Traveling Cultures* (1992), noted that there has always been a strong tendency within the anthropological disciplines that the concept of culture is confounded with the "field." We should therefore consider them separately. I assume that culture generally refers to processes of the social organization of meaning (Hannerz 1992), that is, the dialectical process of the internalization and externalization of meaningful forms, or, knowledge that is translated into practical knowledge (Bourdieu 1977; de Certeau 1984). As such, there can be no stasis but only a cultural "flow" which constantly redefines itself. All cultural knowledge is embodied in (social) space; at the same time it enables social practices occurring in and producing space (Lefebvre [1991] 2004). We have argued that music as social practice — the practice Christopher Small (1998) has coined "musicking" — is a crucial factor in the production of space. Yet we should be aware that, as Lefebvre has noted, "[s]pace is never produced in the sense that a kilogram of sugar or a yard of cloth is produced. […] It would be more accurate to say that is at once a precondition and a result of social superstructures" ([1991] 2001:85).

Ethnography is basically a modern travel practice. It constitutes therefore a movement in space. As such it is itself a social practice that contributes to the production of space. The discourse on ethnography, however, understood mostly as a form of "being there," has often been separated from discourses on travel, which is rather a way of "getting there," as Clifford (1992) remarks. Moreover, ethnographies that focus on travel itself, that is, not so much on culture in its localized form, but rather on cultural traffic that connects different locales and sites within space, are still rather the exception. As Hannerz notes: "People, meanings, and meaningful forms which travel fit badly with what have been conventional units of social and cultural thought" (1996:20). Similarly, Paulla Ebron has argued that "[m]ost literature on culture and travel assumes that travel traffic is a disruption of the cultural assumptions of ordinary life" (Ebron 2002:172). In contrast to that she suggests, "that global traffic is one aspect of culture-making" (ibid.). Consequently, travel — understood in the widest sense as the movement of people, meanings, and objects (and including, therefore, imaginary movements) in time-space — "offers a way of understanding the spatial intermeshing of relationships. Culture is a dynamic process; there is no 'once upon a time' when places were enclosed and bounded systems" (ibid.).

In a deterritorialized world the object of ethnography is "ultimately mobile and multiply situated" (Marcus 1995:102). As an account not of, but one which is consciously embedded in, the "world system," Marcus consequently calls for an ethnography which is likewise mobile, an ethnography that focuses on "multiple sites of observation and participation that cross-cut dichotomies such as the 'local' and the 'global', the 'lifeworld' and the 'system'" (ibid.:95).

As he continues:

> Multi-sited ethnographies define their object of study through several different modes or techniques. These techniques might be understood as practices of construction through (preplanned or opportunistic) movement and of tracing within different settings of a complex cultural phenomenon given an initial, baseline conceptual identity that turns out to be contingent and malleable as one traces it. (Marcus 1995:106)

Marcus summarizes the tracking strategies of multi-sited ethnography under headers such as "follow the people," "follow the thing," or "follow the metaphor," which means for us that we will have try to track the movements of meanings and meaningful forms as well as that of people as the carriers of these meanings within space. The very logic of any ethnographic approach rests on its "situatedness," that is, many of its methods demand face-to-face contact, participation, and personal experience. While this holds true for any ethnographic project, the "most important form of local knowledge in which the multi-sited ethnographer is interested is what parallels the ethnographer's own interest — in mapping itself" (Marcus 1995:112). We are, in other words, concerned with uncovering strategies of siting as we have already discussed it in the preceding chapter in connection to the characteristics of what Foucault calls the epoch of space. As Marcus explicates:

> Sorting out the relationships of the local to the global is a salient and pervasive form of local knowledge that remains to be recognized and discovered in the embedded idioms and discourses of any contemporary site that can be defined by its relationship to the world system. […] In contemporary multi-sited research projects, moving between public and private spheres of activity, from official to subaltern contexts, the ethnographer is bound to encounter discourses that overlap with his or her own. In any contemporary field of work, there is always others within who know (or want to know) what the ethnographer knows, albeit from a different subject position, or who want to know what the ethnographer wants to know. Such ambivalent identifications, or perceived identifications, immediately locate the ethnographer within the terrain being mapped and reconfigure any kind of methodological discussions that presumes a perspective from above or "nowhere." (Marcus 1995:112)

Far beyond questions about ethnography "at home" or "abroad," "insider" or "outsider," and also beyond a distinction between diachronic and synchronic perspectives, ethnography understood as a multi-sited endeavor can therefore serve as a means to bring "globalization [...] down to earth" (Hannerz 1996:19) and to give up the ahistoricity of the "ethnographic present" in favor of a "heterochronic" perspective (cf. Foucault 1986). As we discussed in the previous chapter and tried to demonstrate in a more practical fashion above in our attempt to "read" the streets of Berlin, time is one parameter how sites are situated in space. Our "field," then, is not "the world," "history," or "social space," and certainly not "a culture." It is rather a conceptual zone that follows the spatial (and this, we have argued, encompasses the temporal realm) movements of people, objects, and meanings between sites; the "field" is itself a movement that describes the relation among sites and structures; it is a strategy. The field is thus theoretical and practical at the same time, since theory goes, as Geertz once noted, "all the way down to the most immediate observational level" (Geertz 1973:28).

The field, which is to say, the space of ethnography, is eventually united by the ethnographer's own movements, by our movements, by my movements. This space is neither exhaustive nor does it constitute a coherent whole, it is fragmentary and rhizomorph in its form (cf. Deleuze & Guattari 1987). But we should be careful not to confuse ethnographic space with sociocultural space. While the former is a practico-theoretical construction, "there is nothing imagined, unreal or 'ideal' about [(social) space] as compared [...] with science, representations, ideas or dreams" (Lefebvre [1991] 2004:73). Ethnography describes ruptures and contradictions; it explores the boundaries and margins of the space we inhabit. Ethnography and therefore our field are kept together by (self-)reflection and not least the two covers of a book. There is, after all, "no definable border between the field and the space of writing" (Kisliuk 1997:41).

5 Black Atlantic Worlds

Germany and the African Diaspora

In 1877 the Fisk Jubilee Singers, a gospel choir from Fisk University in Tennessee, went on tour in Europe and also gave a concert at the Choral Society in Berlin. The African American choir was the first performing group familiarizing Germans with spirituals and the song traditions of African slaves in North America (Gilroy 1993:87ff; Reed-Anderson 2000:22). Gilroy has argued for the "profound historical importance" of the Fisk Jubilee Singers "because they were the first group to perform spirituals on a public platform, offering this form of black music as popular culture" (Gilroy 1993:88). Around the turn of the nineteenth to twentieth century spirituals were available as sheet music on the German market. On a more general level, Gilroy sees in the story of this choir a model for the "cross-cultural circulation" of music "on which the rise of more recent phenomena like Africentric rap has relied" (ibid.). After all, spirituals and gospel are not the only black musical styles that were appropriated in German popular culture. In the aftermath of World War I a vivid jazz scene evolved in Germany, and composers such as Kurt Weil also adapted jazz music. The first jazz records were on sale in Germany in 1921, and the first public radio program featuring jazz music was launched in Berlin in 1925.

While jazz as a black musical style found fans and followers among the youth of the Weimar Republic, the situation for persons of African descent living in the country became actually more difficult with the massive political and social changes after World War I, which ended in the collapse of the German, Russian, Austrian-Hungarian and Ottoman empires. Though in total numbers still a rather small minority, colonial migration from Africa to the metropole had further contributed to the formation of a black community in Germany. Some people came as participants of ethnographic shows and stayed in the country afterwards; others came within the framework of educational programs initiated by mission schools and handicraft enterprises. There were also students from African upper class families studying at German universities in the early twentieth century as well as African Americans who stayed in the country for different periods of time and for different purposes

(Bechhaus-Gerst 2004; Grosse 2002; Oguntoye 2004; Reed-Anderson 2000).

As long as the German colonial empire existed Africans from the German territories were identified as "members of the German protectorates." Generally speaking, authorities tried to prevent "colonial subjects" to travel to the "mother country" and issued papers only in exceptional cases. Africans found their ways nonetheless. When the German colonies were taken over by France and Britain according to the peace treaty of Versailles in 1919, the status of Africans who were still in the metropole became unclear. German authorities wanted to deport these individuals, but the mandate powers France and Britain refused to issue entry visa for the former German territories in Africa until 1927. On the other hand German authorities were also interested in good relations with Africans from the former protectorates, since there were plans to regain the colonies. This led to an overall paradoxical situation. Particularly for African-German couples the ambivalent legal status became problematic. Barred from traveling back to Africa together with their German wives, the predominantly male Africans in Germany were at the same time denied basic civil rights other Germans were granted (Möhle 2002:244f). Additionally, a racist climate was fostered in post-World War I Germany by the fact that France employed African troops in the occupation of the Rhineland in 1920. These stationed Africans of the Allied troops were considered an enormous insult by most Germans, and what came to be known as the *schwarze Schmach*, that is, the "black disgrace" in the Rhineland, fueled polemics and political debates (Bechhaus-Gerst 2004:25-27).

As a matter of fact, up to the middle of the 1920s most of the Blacks who stayed in the Weimar Republic found work as "artists" in the entertainment industry, where they were welcome as an "exotic touch" and to add "color" to programs. For well-educated Africans it was difficult to find jobs in their professions due to racist sentiments in society. In the larger cities some found employment as bellhops in hotels. After all, the entertainment industry offered job opportunities Blacks were otherwise denied. They thus worked in circuses and cabarets, or as "noise makers," that is, drummers in the evolving jazz scene of the 1920s. In the mid-1920s, the first guest performances by African American revue groups like the "Chocolate Kiddies" took also place in Berlin, popularizing vaudeville as a form of entertainment in Germany (Bechhaus-Gerst 2004:25f; Möhle 2002:245; Reed-Anderson 2000:42-44). We can only speculate in how far the image of Blacks as the "happy" entertainer — a figure that in post-World-War-II Germany is most prominently embodied by the singer and actor Roberto Blanco — has its roots in this time (cf. Mendívil 2006). But fact is that with the beginning of the twentieth century working as an "artist" was often the only way to make a living for Africans and people of African descent in Germany.

As the successor of the *Gesellschaft für Eingeborenenschutz* (Society for the Protection of Natives), the so-called *Gesellschaft für Eingeborenenkunde* (Society for Native Studies) had already been responsible for the "welfare" of Blacks in Germany in the 1920s, and it continued its work in the 1930s. This society eventually became an instrument for the control of "Coloreds" in the country. Apart from that, the problems black people faced due to an increasing racism also stimulated their political self-organization; in 1929 a German section of the League for the Defense of the Black Race (*Liga zur Verteidigung der Negerrasse*), first founded in France in 1924, was formed. This organization was part of the growing international movement fighting for the rights of Blacks in Africa, Europe and the Americas. In 1914 the Universal Negro Improvement Association (UNIA) had been founded in Jamaica. After the first pan-African congress was held in Paris in 1919, in the 1920s and the subsequent decades several pan-African congresses took place throughout Europe and the United States. These played an important part in the formation of the African independence movements. While Africans and African Americans organized themselves nationally and internationally, the racist climate got, at the same time, more violent in many parts of the industrialized world. After World War I racial unrest and riots shook Great Britain and many places in North America, as for example during the so-called Red Summer of 1919, which in the United States left hundreds of people dead (Reed-Anderson 2000:40-52).

Under the Nazi dictatorship, then, black musical expressions like jazz were considered "degenerate art" (*entartete Kunst*) and were therefore proscribed in Germany. Records were only available on the black market. Radio transmissions of foreign stations featuring swing music that could be received in Germany and which were popular among Germans, were often jammed by the National Socialist regime. As a musical style which was considered essentially African and, all the more, which highlighted ideas such as individualism and free expression, jazz obviously contradicted the ideology of National Socialism. While in other European countries fanzines and so-called "hot clubs" for jazz sprang up, Germany was more or less disconnected from the developments of the international scene until 1945. Nonetheless, the Nazis also appropriated African American musics such as swing, and they copied radio programs produced by the Allies during the war years. The musical pieces in these shows, officially promoted by the *Reichsmusikkammer*, were often replicas of American originals, reproduced with propaganda lyrics in German (Knauer 1996).

In 1933 when Hitler took over, the situation for Blacks living in Germany became worst than ever. Their passports were seized and they were declared stateless. It is known that the Nazis executed forced sterilizations of Blacks, particularly of the so-called *Rheinlandbastarde*, that is, children from liaisons between German women and French soldiers stationed in the Rhineland. An unknown number of Blacks was killed in concentration camps. But in contrast to other groups identified by the Nazis as "non-Aryan," such as Jews or Sinti and Roma, there was no systematic persecution of Blacks, as one might expect. The colonial desires of the National Socialists might explain this ambivalent relation to people of African descent (Bechhaus-Gerst 2004:27ff). As a part of the colonial revisionist movement and in order to keep the few former "colonial subjects" who were left in the country under control, in 1936/37 the *Gesellschaft für Eingeborenenkunde* suggested initiating the so-called *Deutsche Afrika-Schau* (Möhle 2002). As there was, because of the racist regime, no other legal source of income for black people, it was argued that in this way

> the Negroes are withdrawn from idleness, which bears the risk of a
> forbidden livelihood, and are given an occupation to feed themselves
> and their families. They are not a burden for the social welfare; the
> money drawn from public funds for their support will be saved. By
> their concentration and through the organizer's duty for supervision,
> a much better control than hitherto possible can be exercised, to
> prevent racial offenses more easily this way.[1]

In 1940 then the "German Africa Show" was finally stopped by direction of the authorities while the troupe was giving performances in the area around Vienna. The show and its members increasingly faced harassments. At the end of 1940, then, performances by "Coloreds" (*Farbige*) were completely banned in Germany.

After World War II the situation for Blacks in Germany changed, and their number increased constantly in the following decades. In addition to those who survived the war years, there were the so-called *Besatzungskinder* ("occupation children"), children of American GIs and German women. In the 1950s and 1960s these individuals actually attracted the attention of the federal government, and the way they were discussed reveals the kind of racial

---

[1] "Die Neger werden dem Müßiggang entzogen, der die Gefahr eines unerlaubten Lebensunterhalts in sich birgt, und erhalten eine Beschäftigung, um sich und ihre Familie ernähren zu können. Sie fallen nicht der öffentlichen Fürsorge zur Last; die aus Reichsmitteln zu ihrer Unterstützung zur Verfügung gestellten Gelder werden erspart. Durch ihre Zusammenziehung und die den Unternehmern auferlegte Beaufsichtigungspflicht kann eine weit bessere Kontrolle, als bisher möglich gewesen, ausgeübt werden, um auf diese Weise Rassevergehen leichter unterbinden zu können" (quoted in Möhle 2002:249f).

thinking prevalent in the postwar years: we are confronted with a mixture of racism, paternalism, and pity. An official study about the so-called *Besatzungs-kinder* carried out in 1951 came to the conclusion that the best would be to "reunite them with their fathers because of the 'unsuitability' of Germany's climate" (Hopkins 1999:9). This absurd recommendation clearly links up with notions of racial difference as we find them in the eighteenth century, when climate was thought to be one of the major factors in the constitution of a "human race" (cf. Eze 2000). Overall, Hopkins, in his study of Afro-German history and the representation of Blacks in German popular culture, comes to the conclusion that, "[i]n the early years of the Federal Republic, the problem of race was defused by relegating it to the realm of *Kitsch*, the banal, and the melodramatic" (Hopkins 1999:10).

Starting in the 1960s and growing in numbers by the late 1970s, Africans came again to Germany for educational purposes, studying at German universities and other educational institutions. Particularly in East Germany there were also significant numbers of contract workers who came on the basis of intergovernmental agreements between the GDR and African states with a more or less socialist orientation such as Angola or Mozambique.[2] As for these workers, their situation resembled that of guest workers in the early FRG, as they were accommodated in barracks and kept under a strict regime of control (cf. Ha 2003). Though the official ideology in the GDR was that African socialist countries were "brother states," the reality of African workers in East Germany was rather that authorities tried to physically separate them from the local population. The administration wanted to limit the possibility of contact to Germans to make sure that the workers would return to their home countries when their contracts ended. A similar politics of separation was pursued in the case of guest workers in the West. As for West Germany, in the 1970s and 1980s we find an increasing number of political refugees and economic migrants from Africa. The 1980s were also the time when most Ghanaians came to the country.

In the mid-1980s two publications focused attention on the everyday racism Blacks were confronted with in German society. These represent the first attempts of Germany's black minority, especially of black women in Germany, to publicly define their own identity in contrast to the stereotypes impressed upon them. Both, Gisela Fremgen's *...und wenn du dazu noch schwarz bist* (1984) as well as the collection of essays *Farbe bekennen* (Oguntoye et al. 1986) document the life histories of women and their experiences with racial discrimina-

---

[2] On the history of African immigrants and the small but vivid African music scene in the German Democratic Republic see Eger (2005).

tion in Germany. *Farbe bekennen* was at the same time part of a broader initiative to establish a new, racialized German identity, namely that of Afro-Germans. These political efforts eventually led to the creation of the *Initiative Schwarze Deutsche* (ISD) and other Afro-German political organizations (Hopkins 1999:12-15; Wiedenroth-Coulibaly & Zinflou 2004).

In the realm of popular culture there was a steady influx of black musics into Germany after World War II, the strongest influence being the US-American culture industry. As a surrogate of African American music, rock 'n' roll became highly popular in the 1950s. A German jazz scene was also reestablished in the aftermath of World War II. The country was touched by the waves of Latin American musics circulating in the global cultural economy, such as rumba in the 1950s, bossa nova in the 1960s, and, more recently, salsa and samba. Particularly in recent years the Brazilian practice of capoeira, combining music-making and physical exercise, has become highly popular in Germany (just as caipirinha has become a fashionable drink these days). Since the political upheavals of the 1960s and the subsequent liberalization of European societies distinctive black European musical forms evolved, and today we find German varieties of hip hop, rap, reggae and other styles (cf. Hopkins 1999:23ff). Another development that has its roots in the late 1960s is the emergence of a workshop scene where African drumming and dancing is taught. This development clearly precedes the world music boom in the early 1990s. Initiated by individual Africans who traveled to Germany in the sixties and seventies, with the growing number of Africans who immigrated in the 1980s and 1990s, scenes for African drumming and dancing have now been established in many parts of Germany.

Of Spaces and Counter-Spaces

Music is one of the most important media within what Paul Gilroy labeled *The Black Atlantic* (1993). He understands the Black Atlantic as a "transcultural, international formation" and describes its structures as "rhizomorphic" and "fractal" (Gilroy 1993:4). Somewhere else Gilroy characterizes the Black Atlantic as a "negative continent," a "hidden space" (Gilroy 2004) that emerged with the dispersion of Africans around the Atlantic world. The emergence of this transcultural space as Gilroy depicts it has its roots in the transatlantic slave trade and found its continuations in colonialism as well as today's migrational flows. The Black Atlantic, therefore, stretches across "the spaces between Europe, America, Africa, and the Caribbean" (Gilroy 1993:4); it encompasses the African continent as well as its diaspora, and particularly concerns the cultural forms that result from the movements of people, ideas, and objects within this space. We can identify specific types of music that evolved within this complex network of interrelations, exchange, and cross-fertilization, and these Black Atlantic musics arguably dominate today's global soundscapes (cf. Barber 1997; Béhague 1994; Erlmann 1999; Monson 2000).

Gilroy chooses the ship as the central symbol of this transcultural space. "Ships," he writes, "immediately focus attention on the middle passage, on the various projects for redemptive return to an African homeland, on the circulation of ideas and activists as well as the movement of key cultural artifacts: tracts, books, gramophone records, and choirs" (Gilroy 1993:4). As a "floating piece of space, a place without a place" that connects a variety of spaces and other places, the ship is at the same time, as Foucault writes, "the heterotopia par excellence. In civilizations without boats, dreams dry up, espionage takes the place of adventure, and the police takes the place of pirates" (Foucault 1986:27).

As a space of movement, exchange, and connectedness, but also of contradictoriness, Gilroy conceptualizes the Black Atlantic as a counter-space, and argues, "that black musical expression has played a role in reproducing" a "distinctive counterculture of modernity" (Gilroy 1993:36). In the twentieth century the dialectics of modernity has particularly come to the fore under the impression of fascism and other forms of totalitarianism (Adorno & Horkheimer 1972). As a counter-space the Black Atlantic contradicts totalizing tendencies and modern regimes of discipline, control, and subjugation, which in the case of the dispersion of Africans around the Atlantic are intimately tied to slavery and the experience of racial terror. For Gilroy the codes of the "hidden space" of the Black Atlantic therefore bear the peculiar answers to modernity and modernism. He writes that the

> vitality and complexity of [black] musical culture offers a means to get beyond the related opposition between essentialists and pseudo-pluralists on the one hand and between totalizing conceptions of tradition, modernity, and post-modernity on the other. It also provides a model of performance which can supplement and partially displace concern with textuality. (Gilroy 1993:36)

For the slaves who were brought to the New World the written word was prohibited on pain of death. Drumming was also banned. Gilroy thus points out the high importance of song, music, and performance, that is, "the pre- and anti-discursive constituents of black metacommunication" (Gilroy 1993:75), and argues that the "topos of unsayability produced from the slaves' experiences of racial terror" (ibid.:74) has been cultivated in black musical expressions and performance culture in a ritualized form. Black expressive culture therefore serves as a means to produce counter-hegemonic structures. This counter-hegemonic quality of music also becomes obvious in the colonial encounter, where African performances often undermined commonly assumed power structures within colonial space, which was overall dominated by a regime of discipline and control (Carl 2004).

The collective power of African performance has, as we have already indicated earlier, fascinated travelers for long. Performativity and collectivity have in fact themselves become perpetual metaphors for African music. Scenes of dancing masses are, for example, a prominent feature of nineteenth-century travel accounts. Due to a substantial lack of understanding of the meaning of performances on the side of Europeans, these musical events were often pictured as some kind of natural force, like a thunderstorm or a natural disaster. The felt powerlessness under the impression of African music and dance was a source of uneasiness, even fear, for Europeans, and nineteenth-century descriptions of dance scenes make it sometimes appear as if the white body would disappear, as it were, by way of an anthropophagous act of incorporation within the African collective, an overwhelming black mass. In the colonial encounter African performances were conceived as an expression of uncontrollable "ecstasy," a form of anti-discipline to European regimes of power (Carl 2004:36ff and Carl 2006; Fabian 2000). It is no coincidence that the performance of music and dance, in fact, the celebration of performance itself (cf. Gilroy 1993:200f), eventually played a crucial role in the emergence of separatist churches in Africa as well as in the mobilization of African resistance movements against European domination. These processes took place as early as the nineteenth century, and they were intensified in the twentieth century when African musics became incorporated into the various nationalist projects (Collins 1992a).

Another concrete example for the workings of a "microphysics of power" (Foucault 1979) in the creation of performative counter-spaces are so-called "talking drums." These are also an ambivalent topos of fascination and anxiety, and an important means of identification in Africa, since drumming languages are associated with power and leadership. Travelers in Africa frequently reported on drum languages that made it possible to spread messages over wide distances (Carl 2004:28ff).[3] This is part of the reason why drumming

---

[3] A close relation between speech and instrumental patterns is a widespread phenomenon on the African continent and does not only concern drumming (cf. Vogels 2001).

was banned by the slaveholders in the New World. In contrast to "ordinary" musical performances, in the case of drums that talk we additionally have to consider a semantic level. Not capable of being read, or, rather heard, the issue of talking drums illustrates well the colonialists fear of what Gilroy calls the anti-discursive constituents of black metacommunication. At times, every African drum was suspected of speaking.

As we know from the report of an inner-African expedition that was lead by Hermann von Wissmann (Wissmann et al. 1891),[4] so-called "talking drums" also played their part in the German-African colonial encounter. Wissmann was an important figure in German colonial history. As an imperial envoy he was mainly responsible for the suppression of the so-called Abushiri Revolt in German East Africa where he was governor from 1895 to 1896. In his report on the Kasai expedition, after he describes an instance in Central Africa where the German research team witnessed the use of drums as a means of communication, he mentions with regard to East Africa that the "drum language later caused manifold difficulties for our navy, because as soon as a boat went on land or any maneuver was performed by the ships, this was immediately made known by drumming signals in the farthest distance."[5]

Ludwig Wolf, a companion of Wissmann, mentions the "drum language" in the same report at a later point. As the expedition was passing through the Kasai region, Wolf had been send out to establish friendly relationships with the Kuba people in whose territory they traveled. He had to convince them that the Europeans came with peaceful intentions. After he negotiated with a leader of the Kuba the message of the expedition's presence in the area was spread. The way Wolf describes this nightly scene gives us at least an impression of the uncanniness Europeans felt while encountering sounds and musics they couldn't comprehend.

> In the still of the following night the chief informed the surrounding villages about what I had told him. This conversation lasted for hours, and, judging from the strength with which the single beats were led, it seemed to take on a vivid character at times. During the

---

[4] This expedition was sent to out by the Brussels committee of the International African Association to explore the Kasai region in the Congo basin between 1883 and 1885 (cf. Fabian 2000). This region became part of the "private" colony of the Belgian king Leopold II, the Congo Free State, after the Berlin Congo Conference in 1885, and then part of the Belgian Congo in 1908 (cf. Hochschild 1998).

[5] "Diese Trommelsprache hat nachher unserer Marine vielfache Schwierigkeiten bereitet, da, sobald ein Boot an Land ging oder irgendein Manöver von den Schiffen ausgeführt wurde, dies durch Trommelsignale sofort in der weitesten Ferne bekannt gemacht wurde" (Wissmann et. al 1891:4).

pauses one could hear the sound of the answering drum from afar. Apart from Cameroon I had not had the opportunity to hear such a sophistication in the drum language, which, by the way, less developed or only as a signal system, was known to all African tribes I had contact with until now.[6]

Many other examples of music's (real as well as imagined) subversive nature as described in nineteenth-century travel literature could be cited. But Europeans also conquered such performative and acoustic counter-spaces. At the end of the nineteenth century, with the colonial occupation of African territories, we can observe that African music is appropriated in a variety of ways. If it had often been seen as an incomprehensible, "ecstatic," undisciplined and uncontrollable force, Europeans by and by discovered the disciplining power of African rhythm. Put in scientific terms by the economist Karl Bücher, who in 1896 published a book on *Arbeit und Rhythmus* ([1896] 1924), that is, "labor and rhythm," colonialists in Africa actually started to use African music to organize African work force and to increase working efficiency in the colonial territories (Carl 2004:53ff). Bücher gives the example of the French who used African musicians to accompany railway construction works in their colonial possessions (Bücher [1896] 1924:277). Expeditions used rhythmic music to make their African carriers march faster. And the German colonialist Carl Peters on his so-called "Emin Pascha expedition" even used Ugandan "war drums" to scare Arabic expeditions away that were also operating in the East African hinterland at the end of the nineteenth century (Peters [1891] 1907:305). The following statement by Karl Weule, director of the ethnological museum in Leipzig, who traveled to German East Africa at the beginning of the twentieth century, is very typical as to how the relation between rhythm and work was conceptualized with regard to Africans. He writes:

I believe that the Negro cannot carry out the slightest thing without accompanying his work with an instantly improvised song; even the heavily chained captives at the coast [of East Africa] push their bar-

---

[6] "In der Stille der folgenden Nacht theilte der Häuptling durch Trommelsprache den umliegenden Ortschaften mit, was ich ihm gesagt hatte. Stundenlang dauerte diese Unterhaltung, die zuweilen nach der Heftigkeit, mit welcher die einzelnen Schläge geführt wurden, zu urtheilen, einen lebhaften Charakter anzunehmen schien. Während der Pausen hörte man aus weiter Ferne den Schall der Antwort gebenden Trommel. Außer in Kamerun hatte ich bisjetzt [sic] noch keine Gelegenheit gehabt, eine solche Fertigkeit in der Trommelsprache zu hören, die übrigens, weniger ausgebildet oder nur als Signalsystem, allen von mir bisjetzt [sic] berührten afrikanischen Völkerstämmen bekannt war" (Wissmann et al. 1891:231).

row or pull their cart under constant call-and-response singing. Thus is the hoeing of the field actually also more a game, to which the whole body is set into the rhythmic motion of dance all by itself.[7]

Black Music and the Post-Colony

Leaving colonial space and entering the post-colony, we see that the topos of domination and resistance, of the appropriation and counter-appropriation of space and the subversion of modernity's "grand narratives" by way of musical performance, is also a recurrent theme in more recent literature not only on African music, but actually on popular music more generally (cf. Hamm 1995). Many authors in the field of cultural studies, for example, have stressed the resistant and counter-hegemonic nature of musical scenes and subcultures (Gelder & Thornton 1997). As Frith has pointed out, the fact that music, by way of embodying a "rhetorical truth" which connects performer and audience, serves as a means of empowerment and self-identification, is by no means restricted to black popular culture, though some of its worldwide popularity could perhaps be explained by this fact (Frith 1996:117f).

Musical forms are, after all, appropriated and re-appropriated, and the production, consumption, and appreciation of what is considered "black" musical expressions is by no means restricted to either black performers or black audiences. As Steven Feld in his *Notes on 'World Beat'* has remarked with regard to musical appropriation more generally:

> Musical appropriation sings a double line with one voice. It is a melody of admiration, even homage and respect, a fundamental source of connectedness, creativity, and innovation [...]. Yet this voice is harmonized by a countermelody of power, even control and domination, a fundamental source of asymmetry in ownership and commodification of musical works. [...] Appropriation means that the question "Whose music?" is submerged, supplanted, and subverted by the assertion "Our/my music." (Feld 1994a:238)

---

[7] "Ich glaube, der Neger kann nicht das geringste ausführen, ohne seine Arbeit mit einem schnell improvisierten Liede zu begleiten; selbst die schwerstgefesselten Kettengefangenen der Küste schieben ihre Karre oder ziehen ihren Wagen unter stetem Wechselgesang. So ist denn auch das Hacken des Feldes eigentlich mehr ein Spiel, zu dem der Körper ganz von selbst in die rhythmische Bewegung des Tanzes verfällt" (Weule 1908:472).

Particularly in the realm of so-called world music the image of resistance is also extensively used by the music industry to market African popular musics and to create an aura of "authenticity" around non-European styles that are, at the same time, commoditized as the exotic Other (Taylor 1997; Erlmann 1993). The ambivalent nature of musical appropriation, as we described it for the colonial encounter and Feld delineates it more generally, becomes also apparent in German popular culture where the styles of the Black Atlantic have since long been performed, mediated, and transformed not only by Germany's black minority, but also among white performers and audiences. Serving on the one hand as a counterpoint to official versions of culture and the nation, black musical styles are on the other hand commercialized and de-politicized, turned into consumable mass products by media networks.

An example from contemporary popular culture is German rap music. Strikingly, a subculture such as hip hop, which first emerged among African American youths and Spanish-speaking immigrants in New York, has in Germany first been appropriated by young immigrants and black Germans before it became a part of the German mainstream. The example of the hip hop trio Advanced Chemistry illustrates that upcoming groups in Germany in the late 1980s consciously saw themselves in the tradition of the pioneers of hip hop, such as Africa Bambaataa and the Zulu Nation (Yakpo 2004). Their album *Fremd im eignen Land* ("foreign in one's own country"), released in 1992, explicitly deals with the paradoxes of being black and German at the same time. In the liner notes to their 1993 published record *Welcher Pfad führt zur Geschichte*, Advanced Chemistry claim that

> [e]very activist of today's hip-hop scene, whether in Bremerhaven or Brooklyn is in the tradition of the Zulu Nation whether or not s/he acknowledges it. Therefore: respect to the pioneers of the old school, because paying respect is just as much a heritage of black culture as the painting of public property or break-dancing. (Quoted and translated in Hopkins 1999:26)

In line with Gilroy's argument concerning black musical expressions, hip hop "is presented as a counter movement to modernity, an anti-capitalistic rescue of subjectivity, and the denial of a central tenet of white culture" (Hopkins 1999:27) here. As the liner notes continue:

> Black culture also signifies openness. An openness for the mixing and adaptation of different cultural elements, as is the case in Hip-Hop. All this which is foreign to white culture we term Funk. Funk is

rebellion against society. When you scratch with papa's record-player or paint a train, that is rebellious, but it is always creative and productive. In New York the innovators of this culture were pre-dominantly African-Americans, Jamaicans, Haitians, Puerto Ri-cans... It is no accident that because of the rebellion contained in this culture, many black Germans, Turks and Kurds, Yugoslavs, Roma and Sinti are attracted to and do Hip-hop. (Quoted in ibid.)

Reggae music and culture, which has become increasingly popular since the early 1990s and now attracts many followers among urban youths, is yet an-other recent example of musical styles that originated in the Black Atlantic and were appropriated in German popular culture. With the emergence of styles like ragamuffin we see many overlappings of the reggae and hip hop scenes. In how far the subversive and countercultural potential of musical styles such as hip hop and reggae, employing techniques such as sampling, cutting, and mix-ing (cf. Hebdige 1987) that are based on black performance models, is turned into its opposite and becomes an expression of "white domination" through their appropriation by the music industry and, consequently, by the "white mainstream," is a controversial question. Such debates actually parallel more general discussions on the music industry's dominant role in popular culture (cf. Aikins 2005; El-Tayeb 2004; Hamm 1995). In the realm of world music such discussions are closely connected to what is mostly described as "cultural imperialism" (cf. Erlmann 1999; Feld 1994a, 1994b, and 1996; Frith 2000; Garofalo 1993).

    The popularity of an all-white group such as Die Fantastischen Vier, by now the best-selling German rap group, that performs a largely depoliticized form of rap music for audiences mostly outside the smaller urban hip hop scenes, is a case in point. Aikins (2005) critically questions what he thinks of as "white" appropriations of black musical styles and describes the transition from "rap in Germany" to Deutsch-Rap as a silencing of black political posi-tions, a suppression of the countercultural potential of black musical expres-sion. Another controversial example is Berlin's rap label Aggro. While the art-ists on this label such as Sido, B-Tight, or Fler are highly popular among German teenagers, their lyrics often glorify aggression and violence and are even held to be latently fascistic. Himself an Afro-German, the rapper B-Tight called wide attention in 2002 when he published his album *Der Neger in mir* ("the Negro within me"), which includes a song with the same title. A promo-tional text on the website of the label states: "The Negro within him is also the cause for his unbelievable aggressive, bloody lyrics. B-Tight is caught up in a constant fight with himself. White against Black. And he lives this fight in his music."[8] What the record label uses mainly as a marketing strategy has, in fact, called the attention of politicians, activists, concerned parents, and writers of the feuilletons in the republic.[9] Aikins comments that in this case "a racist minstrel show" has become a marketing strategy that "satisfies the demand for racist images" (2005:291). The terrains of the Black Atlantic are, after all, contested and subject to complex processes of appropriation and counter-appropriation.

Celebrating Independence Day

We are in the interior of an airplane. We see the sky and clouds through the window of the cockpit. A male voice from the intercom, speaking with an American accent, starts: "First of all, let me tell you a little bit about Ghana. That was the first country in Africa that became independent after World War II. In 1960, they broke away from the British Commonwealth and became an independent republic. The country took its name, Ghana, from a very powerful African republic…"[10] Meanwhile, we see the passengers in the plane. Most are Blacks; some are looking out of the windows, others sleep. The Afro hairstyle of a woman, smoking a cigarette, gives us a hint that the scene must have been recorded some time back in the seventies. The voice from the speakers is drowned out by another man's voice. It is Ike Turner sitting next to Tina Turner, who is sleeping, reciting from a book: "… one thing no one can control, and that's my black soul. So I keep on singing, expressing what I'm feeling inside. The one thing I will die with inside is my pride and my soul. I'm proud of what I am, as black as I may be, and all I'm looking for in life is the freedom to be free…"

---

[8] "Der Neger in ihm ist unter anderem der Auslöser seiner unglaublich aggressiven, blutigen Texte. B-Tight ist im ständigen Kampf mit sich. Weiss gegen Schwarz. Und diesen Kampf lebt er in seiner Musik aus" (Quoted from a press release published on the label's official website at http://www.aggroberlin.de, accessed on April 16, 2007).

[9] See for example a discussion of the *Aggro* rappers in the weekly newsmagazine *Der Spiegel* (Koischwitz 2005).

[10] Ghana became independent from British colonial rule in 1957 and became a republic in 1960. Ghana is still member of the Commonwealth of Nations. The name of today's Republic of Ghana was, of course, not derived from another republic but from the ancient empire of Ghana, whose origins date back to approximately the sixth century. The old empire Ghana was located around present-day Mauritania, Senegal, and Mali, and was conquered and Islamicized by the Almoravides in the eleventh century, who afterwards superseded the dynasty of the Umayyads in Spain.

The passengers are African American musicians. They were invited to perform in Ghana on its fourteenth anniversary of independence. The *Soul To Soul* concert, a massive fourteen-hours show, took place on Independence Square (Black Star Square) in Accra on March 6, 1971. Among the American musicians were Wilson Pickett, Ike and Tina Turner, Les McCann and Eddie Harris, The Staple Singers, Santana, Roberta Flack and the gospel choir The Voices of East Harlem. Ghanaian acts that were part of the concert included Guy Warren, also known as Kofi Ghanaba, the Damas Choir, soul singer Charlotte Dada, highlife pioneer Kwa Mensah, the Kumasi Drummers (a cultural troupe from the Ashanti Region), one of Ghana's best known rock band of that time, the Aliens, as well as the house band of the Ghana Arts Council, the Anansekromian Zounds, and others. Pickett, by far the most famous of the American musicians in Ghana at that time, was the headliner of the *Soul To Soul* concert. He was known as "soul brother no. 2." The number one in soul music by that time, James Brown, had given a concert in Lagos the year before, in 1970, ten years after Nigeria gained independence from British colonial rule. His show had actually given Edward and Tom Mosk, who were organizing the *Soul To Soul* concert, the idea to stage a similar event in Ghana.

Back inside the plane. People are asked about their feelings concerning the *Soul To Soul* concert and their travel to Africa. Most are excited: "Some people get offended by talking about going back home and all that, but… the way I really feel it deep inside is like… I couldn't even sleep for the whole week gettin' ready to come over here and all that." Someone else explains: "It's every black person's dream and I am no exception […]. I'm really excited because everybody is dreaming about going to the motherland at least once." Another one is primarily looking forward to "all the pretty materials" and the "pretty prints" and intends to buy "batches" of cloth to take them home to the Unites States to sow clothes out of it. Cut.

The plane arrives at Kotoka International Airport in Accra. A Ghanaian cultural troupe is performing while the American musicians and the crew members come down the stairway, getting off the plane. Many spectators have come to the airport, cheering the guests from the United States. The crowd is excited. People sing and dance. When Wilson Pickett appears in the door of the plane, choruses start praising him: "Wilson Picket oh, yeah-yeah… *akwaaba*, welcome!" Everybody wants to get close to Picket, who is surrounded by people. Meanwhile, the performance of the cultural troupe continues; they play dances from different regions of Ghana such as *adowa* from the Ashanti Region. A woman is recording the scene with a hand camera. A policeman vainly tries to keep order. Some of the American musicians start dancing to the music along with the cultural troupe. Picket is offered *akpeteshie*, local hard liquor made from sugar cane. He pretends to collapse after taking some sips of the strong drink. People laugh, rejoice. Everybody is happy. Cut.

These are some of the first scenes of a documentary film about the *Soul To Soul* tour. The documentary, directed by Denis Sanders and released in 1971, features excerpts of the main performance on Independence Square as well as scenes of the American artist's arrival and stay in Ghana before the show. For most of them it was their first visit to Africa. The guest artists witnessed a number of performances of traditional music and dance and a cultural program in the days after their arrival. They were presented the cultural traditions of different regions in Ghana, and the tour program also included a visit to one of the castles built on present-day Ghana's coast, formerly the nodes in the transatlantic slave trade.

The oldest one of these, São Jorge da Mina, was built by the Portuguese in 1482. At the end of the fifteenth century they thought that they had finally found the legendary "land of gold," known only from myths. The Portuguese named the place of their first trading base on the "gold coast" La Mina, which is today Elmina, meaning "the mine." Ten years later Christopher Columbus reached the shores of the New World. After only two and a half decades the population of Native Americans, who were initially used by the European settlers in the Americas to work on their plantations and in their mines, was decimated to such an extent that they began to ship African slaves to the New World. The slave trade dominated the movements in the Black Atlantic for more than three hundred years. From the nineteenth century onward, then, an increased reverse movement of people and cultural forms took place from the Americas back to Africa.

Efforts to link up with African Americans and particularly to bring performers for the independence celebrations were made in the time of Kwame Nkrumah. Himself one of the major exponents of pan-Africanism and well acquainted with W. E. B. Du Bois who initiated the first pan-African congress in Paris, he became familiar with African American intellectuals and their writings such as Marcus Garvey, Du Bois, or George Padmore in the 1930s and early forties when he studied in the United States. In the mid-forties Nkrumah helped organizing the fifth pan-African congress in Manchester. The ideas of pan-Africanism as they are expressed in Garvey's "back to Africa" ideology or the ideas of Négritude became major means in the political organization of Blacks in the independence movements in Africa as well as the civil rights movement in the United States.[11] In the realm of popular culture

---

[11] Gilroy reminds us that the development of the pan-Africanist movements and various ideologies of black nationalism, inspired by the biblical story of the enslavement of the peo-

Rastafarianism is today maybe the most visible and audible expression of pan-Africanist thought. Calling upon a common African heritage and destiny was an important part of processes of nation building in postindependence Africa, which had to deal with inner-ethnic tensions and "tribalisms" as national territories were rather randomly put together and borders cut through linguistic and ethnic entities. "African culture" as a canonical representation of the multitude of cultural traditions became an important means to promote, as Nkrumah coined it, "unity in diversity" within the multiethnic setting of the nation. At the time when the *Soul To Soul* concert took place, Nkrumah was, however, already in exile in Conakry. Having become more and more despotic, his government was overthrown in a military coup in 1966 while he was on a state visit in China.

Just as soul music was highly popular in Ghana in the 1970s, African musical forms inspired performers in North America and elsewhere in the African diaspora. There are many examples for the exchange of musical idioms between America and Africa. Instead of seeing these cultural flows as one-way movements in either way, we can think of them rather as processes of mutual inspiration. As Gilroy remarks,

> the circulation and mutation of music across the black Atlantic explodes the dualistic structure which puts Africa, authenticity, purity, and origin in crude opposition to the Americas, hybridity, creolisation, and rootlessness. There has been (at least) a two-way traffic between African cultural forms and the political cultures of diaspora blacks over a long period. (Gilroy 1993:199)

As early as in the years between 1890 and 1898 the Virginia Jubilee Singers, actually a spin-off from the Fisk Jubilee Singers, toured in South Africa, and from the early twentieth century onward a vivid jazz music scene developed in the townships of Johannesburg and other South African cities (Ballantine 1992; Coplan 1985). At the end of the nineteenth and the beginning of the twentieth century popular cultural forms evolved in all parts of Africa, as an increasing urban population developed distinctively urban identities (cf. Barber 1997).[12] In Ghana it was particularly the development of highlife music

---

ple of Israel in Egypt and their subsequent exodus to the promised land, are historically linked and paralleled by the formation of modern Zionism (Gilroy 1993:205ff).

[12] An early account on the development of urban identities and popular cultural forms in Africa is Mitchell's study on the *kalela* dance among migrant workers along the Zambian copper belt (Mitchell 1956). On Nigerian popular music see Waterman (1990); Turino (2000) has worked on the emergence and development of Zimbabwean popular music, and

that is connected to new forms of social dance that became popular among urban elites from the early twentieth century onward (Collins 1986 & 1994; Coplan 1978).

As an explicit expression of pan-Africanist ideas and ideals, reggae music and Rastafarianism found followers all over the African continent; Bob Marley himself gave performances on the continent, most prominently at Zimbabwe's official independence celebration in 1980.[13] His widow, Rita Marley, has been a resident of Ghana, as other African Americans such as Du Bois have been before her. More recently African American rap and R&B artists have started to travel and perform on the African continent. US-American rapper Jay-Z, for example, came to perform in a concert in Ghana in October 2006 where several local hiplife and highlife musicians such as Reggie Rockstone, Batman Samini, or Ofori Amponsah were also featured. Afterwards, he went on to perform in Lagos along with R&B star Beyoncé Knowles and other American acts such as En Vogue, Missy Elliot, Busta Rhymes, or Snoop Dogg, as well as local Nigerian performers. The show was part of Nigeria's forty-sixths anniversary independence celebrations.

The stylistic examples for the multidimensional cultural exchange between the so-called Old and New World's are manifold, and they stand against a simplified image of a one-directional movement of musics first from Africa to the Americas, and then back to the African continent. The relationship between funk and Afrobeat is a case in point. James Brown visited Nigeria in the 1960s and met Fela Ransome Kuti. He later remembered one of his concerts:

> While we were in Lagos we visited Fela Ransome Kuti's club the Afro Spot, to hear him and his band. He'd come to hear us, and we came to hear him. I think when he started as a musician he was playing a kind of music they call Highlife, but by this time was developing Afro-beat out of African music and funk. He was kind of like the African James Brown. His band had strong rhythm; I think Clyde picked up on it in his drumming, and Bootsy dug it too. Some of the ideas my band was getting from that band had come from me in the first place, but that was okay with me. It made the music that much stronger. (Quoted in Gilroy 1993:199)

Stewart (2000) on the history of popular music in the two Congos, to give but a few examples.

[13] For an account of Rastafarianism and reggae music in Ghana and other West African countries see Savishinsky (1993). The most prominent reggae musicians from the African continent are today probably Lucky Dube from South Africa, who died in 2007, and Alpha Blondy from the Ivory Coast.

Other examples for the cross-fertilization, processes of re-appropriation and blending of musical styles within the Black Atlantic is the development of Afro jazz in the 1960s and seventies which combined elements of jazz with African percussion. Today's evolving hip hop scenes in the urban centers of Africa show at times a very creative use and blending of the most diverse materials, linking African American rap, which relies itself on African-derived traditions of "signifying" and narrative performance practices, with African instrumental traditions in a variety of ways. In Ghana this has led to the creation of hiplife, a combination of digitally programmed highlife rhythms and rap verses mostly performed in Twi (cf. Klein 2004).

Less obvious examples for processes of musical bricolage, borrowing, and exchange can also be found in what is sometimes considered the most "traditional" African musics. These cases are, at the same time, reminders that oppositions such as that between tradition and modernity are rather fragile constructions. A style like kpanlogo in Ghana, today considered a "traditional" — sometimes "neo-traditional" — music and dance style of the Ga people, exemplifies well that the "sharp distinctions and boundaries between folk and classical music, traditional and modern that Westerners have created do not apply" (Collins 1992b:42) in Africa, as Collins reminds us (and we should add that these rather theoretical constructions do equally not apply in Europe, unless as a means of social distinction). Kpanlogo was actually invented in the 1960s by Otoo Lincoln, who told Collins in an interview:

> In our house our fathers were playing oge [introduced by Liberian Kru seamen and popular in Accra during the 1950s]. It's like a slow kpanlogo played on one drum, clips, and a saw and nail to scrape it. Kpanlogo is really a mixture of different dances like highlife and oge, there's even a rock and roll in it, as I used to dance rock and roll around 1960 with Frank Lane at the Black Eagles Club. (Quoted in Collins 1992b:44)

Other examples for such "invented" traditional styles in the Ghanaian national repertoire of traditional music and dance are Ewe borborbor music, which became popular in the 1950s (Collins 1992a:187), and *agbadza* dance-drumming, which, as Collins writes, "first appeared in Ghana's Volta Region between the two World Wars" (1992b:43). Interestingly, these examples also show that the mostly assumed process that "traditional" music moves to the urban centers and becomes "modernized" there, can in fact also take place in a reverse fashion, that is, that "hybrid" musics move from the city and becomes "traditional" in the hinterland.

The process of promoting a national canon of "cultural music" in post-independence Ghana has been described by Agawu:

> Beginning in the 1960s, musical tradition was invented in Ghana through the establishment of the Arts Council of Ghana, the creation of a National Dance Ensemble, and the formation across the country of many so-called cultural troupes. These associations brought together drummers, singers, and dancers from different ethnic groups to learn and perform their most popular or most prominent dances (including *Kpanlogo*, *Adowa*, *Atsiagbekor*, *Bawa*, and *Damba-Takai*). The result would be the establishment of a transethnic canon, a classic collection of cultural artifacts. Public concerts featured a selection of these dances for nonparticipating audiences. The idea was to preserve the authenticity of each dance by reifying certain dance steps, body movements, costumes, and styles of singing and drumming. (Agawu 2003:19)

Today, these dances are performed in the most diverse contexts. From official events such as Independence Day celebrations, state visits and other formal functions, over private parties, outdoorings, or funeral celebrations where cultural troupes are hired, to the typical tourist sites where "Ghanaian culture" is presented to foreign visitors — at all these occasions "culture" is performed. As for African American visitors traveling to the country like those musicians who came for the *Soul To Soul* show, the display and appreciation of African culture has additionally become an important means to link up with their African roots. Therefore, apart from the promotion of national identities through African music, for Blacks in the diaspora "traditional" African music and dance have become an important means of identification that links people with their own imagined past.

Inspired by projects such as David Haley's *Roots*, in the United States there are today organized "homeland" tours offered by travel agencies targeting an African American clientele. The voyage to Africa on these tours becomes a ritualized pilgrimage back to the "motherland" (cf. Ebron 2002:189ff). For many West African countries this form of "homeland" tourism is becoming increasingly important as an economic factor. Ghana, as one of the countries that played an important part in the history of slave trade, and also as one of West Africa's English-speaking, politically stable countries in which it is relatively easy for foreigners to travel, is one of the major destinations for black Americans to get in touch with their roots. In the context of such a commercialization of people's search for identity, Ebron asks about the significance of

"sponsored identities" in the generation of "a particular relationship to concepts of self and community and globalization" (ibid.:208). Regarded against
this background she points to the need to "consider history and memory as
themselves a transnationally circulating 'scape'" and "to think about the in-
tertwined relationships between culture and economy in the making of such
scapes" (ibid.:212).

Considering the American-African encounter, we see differences in how
Africa is envisioned through the cultural forms of the Black Atlantic. While on
the one side Africa, as the mythical site of roots and tradition, is imagined
through a reinvented past, on the other side Africa is re-envisioned through
American modernity and its popular cultural forms. But the cultural flows
within the Black Atlantic world are, as we have seen, also a means to move
beyond such clear-cut dual oppositions, and it is in this sense that Gilroy regards the Black Atlantic as a counterculture to modernity — in its resistance to
and contradiction of simple binaries that dominate Western modernity's
"grand narratives." The Black Atlantic, just as social space more generally, is a
contradictory terrain after all.

In Ghana's fiftieth year of independence, the "Golden Jubilee Year,"
which was promoted as "Ghana @ 50," some of these contradictions became
apparent at the celebrations on Independence Square. A Ghanaian journalist,
commenting on the official parade on March 6, 2007, which was broadcasted
on all (of the by then four) channels on television, remarked that the event
would illustrate well one of the main features of Ghanaian culture, namely the
ability to mix and blend the most diverse influences. But the way in which
these influences — African and Western, traditional and modern — were put
together became actually an issue in public debates the day after. Many people
articulated their concern about president John Kufuor's appearance at the
event. In contrast to honorary guest president Obasanjo from Nigeria, he wore
a simple dark suit rather than "traditional African attire," that is, *kente* cloth, as
Nkrumah and other presidents used to wear for such occasions before him. In
a reaction to the criticisms, Kufuor explained that, as "much as he appreciated
the country's traditions and culture, it was equally important to recognize the
dynamics of cultural change and identify oneself with the rapidly advancing
world" (Achiaw 2007). As we already noted: the terrains of the Black Atlantic
are a contested territory after all.

Reconsidering the Black Atlantic

A program that took place in Berlin in 2004 celebrated Germany as a part of the Black Atlantic. The program, which was hosted by the Haus der Kulturen der Welt ("House of World Cultures"), included concerts, performances, installations, movies, lectures, discussions, and workshops. During one of the performances the dub poet Linton Kwesi Johnson expressed his hope that the program would actually reflect the process "that Germany is coming to terms with the fact that it is a multicultural society." Gilroy himself, who served as curator for the "Black Atlantic" in Berlin, saw one of the key issues of the project in questions about "how the nation could imagine itself anew and include its colonial past" (Gilroy 2004). These issues are, as we have seen in our discussions above, still very much contested. Considering the ship as the central metaphor of the Black Atlantic (though the major means of transportation to cross the Atlantic nowadays is rather the airplane — maybe today's heterotopia or non-place par excellence), the freedom of movement becomes, as it were, the measure of freedom within a globalized yet racially still divided world; a world in which the self-determined crossing of (physical as well as symbolical) borders is, still, often restricted to only some privileged classes, depending on income, nationality, and also the color of the skin.

Reconsidering the program "Black Atlantic" in Berlin, we see, after all, that the event was caught up within the ambivalences of appropriation and counter-appropriation. In the case of the Berlin program this resulted not least from the paradoxes that emerged between officialdom and the essentially informal nature of what we would consider a "counterculture." Supported by leftist media as well as the *Kulturstiftung des Bundes* (Federal Foundation for Culture), the Black Atlantic as the House of World Cultures celebrated it became actually a form of highbrow cultural event. Elevating the cultural forms of the Black Atlantic into the realm of officially certified "art" and capital "C" Culture, they acquired a status which they are often denied, to be sure, but lost at the same time the peculiar qualities Gilroy considers so essential for their countercultural potential. Is it possible to state-sponsor "counterculture," after all? Nonetheless, as a means to raise public consciousness about the concerns of Blacks in Europe the program surely had its worth (though a general problem of events like this is, of course, that those who attend them are already aware of the issues at stake).

While Afro-German organizations and individual activists supported the program and were actively engaged in its realization, associations of African immigrants were not or only marginally included. Overall, African American and diasporic perspectives dominated the event, and it became clear that the whole intellectual background of the concept of the Black Atlantic is based on a diasporic experience. Contemporary Africa was included in the program mainly in the form of world music events. The event took on a highly academic character. Though united in the common interest to fight racist stereotyping and to create an atmosphere that empowers black people to unrestrictedly move within social space, the debates around the "Black Atlantic" actually showed discrepancies within the black community, particularly between first-generation African immigrants and young black Germans (cf. Wellershaus 2004). Thus, André Degbéon, initiator and chief editor of Afro-Berlin-TV, a television program made by African immigrants broadcasting weekly on Berlin's "Open Channel" (Offener Kanal), who is himself a first-generation immigrant from Ivory Coast, heavily criticized the "Black Atlantic":

> What made me so angry was that the program series made it appear as if black history wouldn't begin before the Atlantic. That made me very upset. Our children are always taken away by the Whites and alienated from us. That was already the case during colonialism. First the colonialists raped the black women, and then they took away their children. They separated the children from the black culture by privileging them. They told the children that they are worth more than their black mothers, causing of course immense conflicts by that. The children thus thought of themselves rather as Whites and not as Blacks anymore. Blacks were kept down this way. This system is reinforced by a program series such as "Black Atlantic." If black identity starts only behind Africa on the Atlantic, you are suggesting to my son that he is better than his father. Here we Africans say: Stop it! We don't want our children to sit there and talk about themselves without mentioning us anymore.[14]

_____

[14] "Was mich so erzürnt hat, ist, dass diese Veranstaltungsreihe es so dargestellt hat, als würde die Schwarze Geschichte erst auf dem Atlantik beginnen. Das hat mich sehr empört. Unsere Kinder werden uns von den Weißen stets weggenommen und von uns entfremdet. Das war bereits während des Kolonialismus so. Erst haben die Kolonialisten die schwarzen Frauen vergewaltigt, und dann haben sie ihnen ihre Kinder weggenommen. Sie haben die Kinder von der schwarzen Kultur separiert, indem sie sie privilegiert haben. Sie haben den Kindern erzählt, dass sie mehr wert sind als ihre schwarzen Mütter, und dadurch haben sie natürlich immense Konflikte produziert. Die Kinder haben sich dann eher als Weiße und nicht mehr als Schwarze verstanden. So wurden die Schwarzen am Boden gehalten. Dieses System setzt eine Veranstaltungsreihe wie 'Black Atlantic' fort. Wenn Schwarze Identität erst hinter Afrika auf dem Atlantik beginnt, suggeriert man meinem Sohn damit, dass er besser ist als sein Vater. Da sagen wir Afrikaner: Schluss damit! Wir möchten nicht mehr, dass unsere Kinder dasitzen und über sich reden, ohne uns zu erwähnen" (Degbéon 2005).

In terms of free movement we could also ask in how far Africans and Blacks in the diaspora really fight the same fight. Thus, while an Afro-German like Alexander Ngoubamdjun from the ISD can assert that the "German passport isn't worth the paper on which it is printed" (quoted in Mielke 1999:70), for someone with a West African passport trying to get an entry visa for the Schengen states in order to visit his or her family such a statement can only sound sarcastic. Privileged positions that enable Whites "to consume counter-culture [*Widerstandkultur*] from a position of power, to hide behind exactly these symbols of resistance" (Aikins 2005:284), as a common criticism goes, are not only concealed within the "white mainstream." Just as white is not always white, we should not forget that also black actually not always equals black. Power positions are also concealed in a "black" discourse appropriating the "moral authority of a black experience of injustice" (ibid.), a discourse hiding behind an image of the indiscriminately suppressed "black subject."

Coming back to the program in Berlin and Linton Kwesi Johnson's performance, in a sense the ambivalences of the Black Atlantic project were already embodied in the venue, the Haus der Kulturen der Welt. Maybe we can say that these ambivalences were pre-inscribed in space. The House of World Cultures is located right in the political power center of the country, a direct neighbor of the *Reichstag*, the ministries, and the residence of the German president. As formulated in its mission statement, the institution has set itself the task of "presenting cultures from outside Europe through their fine arts, theatre, music, literature, film and the media and engaging them in a public discourse with European cultures."[15] The institution follows, in other words, a "fine arts" approach to non-European cultures. Such an approach already contradicts performance models of black musical expressions beyond textuality or what Gilroy describes as the "ethics of antiphony," as we find it in the "ritual act of story-telling" (Gilroy 1993:200).

This contradiction also manifested itself when Linton Kwesi Johnson and his reggae band performed. The concert hall of the House of World Cultures, embodying a discourse of "disinterested" contemplation of "art for art's sake" not only in the clear separation of stage and auditorium but also in the form of fixed rows of seats that are immoveable, left little space for what Gilroy laboriously describes a as "the constituents of black metacommunication," that is, simply the audience's desire to respond to the music with dance, to identify with and become part of the performance.

---

[15] The mission statement and more information on the House of World Cultures can be found on its website at http://www.hkw.de (accessed on March 20, 2007).

6 Mapping the Scene

An International Performance

I remember a program at the Statthaus Böcklerpark, which is one of these so-cial projects in Kreuzberg around Urbanhafen at the Landwehrkanal. Nor-mally you see groups rehearsing Kurdish or Croatian folk dances, Brazilian capoeira, or African drumming here, or the youth of the quarter, which oth-erwise loiters around the premises in the afternoons, engaged in break dance and other activities. The program on April 24, 2004, went under the header "International Künstler/in Tanz Performance" [sic] and was organized by Gordon Odametey.[1] Put together in a somewhat chaotic fashion and compris-ing two major parts, the afternoon program featured a bizarre mix of perform-ances of the "for the whole family" type. For the evening, then, a group called Boba presenting "Drumming and Dancing from Ghana" was announced.

I got Gordon's contact from Ofei and we only spoke on phone before we met face-to-face that Saturday afternoon. Gordon, a drummer and percus-sionist from Ghana, came to Germany at the age of eighteen, more than twenty years ago, in 1985. Like most of his fourteen brothers and sisters as well as his numerous nephews and nieces, many of whom are based in Germany today, he was engaged in drumming and dancing since the days of his youth. It was a "family affair." Over the years he worked with many people and played in a number of different groups. His current group in Berlin was Sene-gambigha, a joint project with drummers from Senegal and The Gambia. They called their style "African trance percussion." He also did solo per-formances under the label "Spiritual Healing Drumming." When he came to Europe in the 1980s, his oldest brother Aja Addy Odametey was working with their uncle Mustapha Tettey Addy in Germany, a pioneer in the business and one of the best known drummers in Ghana today. Establishing a school for

---

[1] This program was the first occasion I met Gordon Odametey. At that time, apart from frequent public performances with a number of different groups, Gordon was teaching weekly drumming classes in different parts of the city. I started to regularly attend his Mon-day classes in Moabit. For an overview of his professional activities see Gordon's website at http://www.gordon-odametey.com (accessed on January 23, 2008).

traditional music and dance for international students like the Academy of African music and Arts (AAMA), which his uncle founded in Kokrobitey in Greater Accra, where they all come from, was one of his dreams. Teaching African drumming in workshops and classes in and around Berlin nowadays, he had also organized trips to Ghana for his German students.

The program at the Statthaus Böcklerpark was an interesting event in a number of ways, and many people involved in Berlin's Afro scene were present. One of the main reasons why I came there was because Ofei's dance class also performed in the afternoon. We had been rehearsing this choreography in the weekly dance classes at the Percussion Art Center in Kreuzberg, which I attended regularly, for a long time (though I should say that I always joined the drummers rather than the dancers). Ofei Ankrah, a Ghanaian dancer who had formerly worked with the National Dance Ensemble at the National Theatre in Accra, and who came to Germany in the year 2000, was in fact my first contact in the scene. I came across a flyer advertising his dance classes on my mission to find "Ghana in Berlin" through a friend of a friend, who happened to be a colleague of Ofei's German wife. Through him I got to know Mark Kofi Asamoah, one of the "pioneers" in Berlin's Afro scene. Ofei was performing with Asamoah's group Adikanfo and I therefore also attended their weekly rehearsals regularly. Though they now rather avoided each other, Asamoah and Gordon had actually also worked together in a group called Bibiba. That was back in the eighties.

Other acts of the "international" performance Gordon had organized included a German *kora* player accompanied by an African drummer, a classical clown's show for the children, and two African women dancing to a recorded tape of African popular music, a style which sounded like soukous. One of them afterwards performed a solo dance in some sort of grass skirt. I encountered her quite often later as she also performed with Gordon's group Senegambigha. Her name was Bijou and she was from Congo, people told me. A German woman called Carmen Issler, who might have been in her mid-forties, wearing long blonde dreadlocks and a wide, flowing dress, presented an eccentric dance that seemed somehow improvised. She was, as I found out, a teacher for "African dance" herself. And someone everybody referred to as "Patrick from Congo" presented a strange mixture of acrobatics, dance, and slapstick, which gave the overall impression that he did not really have a concept what to do on stage.

In the evening Boba, a group based in Düsseldorf in which a number of Gordon's brothers were involved, gave a performance of Ghanaian drumming and dancing, that is, "culture." Since Ofei had worked with them before, he also joined the dancers on stage. Later that year Nii Ammah, one of the dancers from Boba and a younger brother of Gordon, joined Ofei's weekly dance classes occasionally and helped him teaching his students. Involved in the afternoon performances were also Kofi and Yeboah who otherwise played with Adikanfo, as well as Abdul Aziz, a drummer from Burkina Faso who played with a number of groups, among them Adikanfo, Badenya, and the Mano River Multi Cultural Band, a project initiated by drummers and dancers from Guinea, Sierra Leone, and Liberia. All of them, Kofi, Yeboah, and Abdul, worked for Ofei as drummers in his weekly dance classes at times. Abdul, moreover, organized workshops and also trips for his drumming students to Burkina Faso together with his brother, who was also based in Berlin.

Alongside the show on stage I noticed a squat Rastaman who helped Gordon setting up equipment on stage and the chairs in the auditorium. That was Jonathan, also a Ghanaian who has lived in Berlin since the 1980s, and whom everybody in the scene knew as "Shaka." I later became acquainted with him in Gordon's weekly drumming classes in Moabit, which we both attended, though his job focused not so much on the advancement of his own drumming skills, but rather on the entertainment of the rest of the class. Jonathan regarded Gordon as his master. I remember that before I went to Ghana in November 2004, he insisted that I would have to meet his sister in Accra and marry her, so that she could also live in Germany. Together with Steffi, also a drumming student of Gordon, and occasionally with Gordon himself, we met to cook and eat *banku* and tilapia a few times after I came back from Ghana in February 2005. We also went out to Afro events and reggae parties all together.

While the program took its course, someone called Freeman was offering African drums, clothes, figurines, and other "African art" for sale in the entrance area, where a sister and a niece of Gordon were selling "African food" (which in Germany mostly involves rice). When Freeman had arrived at the venue around noon and greeted everyone, he told us that he returned from a trip to Ghana just recently — he would be "back from the jungle," as he humorously put it. Organizing events and workshops himself, and being involved in different drumming groups in the city, he owns a shop called "African Village" in Prenzlauer Berg where he sells "African music and art." I met him frequently at events and parties afterwards. In some years Freeman also rented a stand at the *Karneval der Kulturen* ("Carnival of Cultures"), Berlin's great multicultural street festival, which attracts thousands of visitors every year, to sell his products and advertise his shop.

In the evening Lina, who was one of Ofei's dance students and who became a good friend of mine, introduced me to Kay, another Ghanaian drummer present at the event. In the course of the two following years Lina and I explored the Afro scene together on many occasions and discussed our views and observations. Kay and Lina got to know each other in Ghana, where Lina stayed for overall almost two years, studying at the University of Ghana in Legon and taking dance classes with different teachers at the School of Performing Arts as well as the privately owned Odehe Cultural Centre in Teshie. Kay again was also a friend of Ofei. They had performed together already in Accra, where Kay had been working at the Centre for National Arts and Culture among other things. Though Kay left Adikanfo after performing with the group for a while, he still sporadically helped out when they were in need of a drummer. And he had also performed with Gordon before, in a group called Ogidigidi. When I first met Kay he was working with Alpha Oularé, a drummer from Guinea, who offered workshops and had a group called Sugé, as well as with an African American jazz singer in Berlin for whom he played percussion. But he tried to establish himself outside Berlin, organizing drumming workshops in the small town of Goslar in the Harz Mountains. In the provinces, he explained to me, African music would still be perceived as something "authentic." People were more enthusiastic about what he did, because they were not confronted with such an oversupply of cultural activities as in Berlin.

Moving in Networks

In most of the larger urban centers in Germany we find a terrain of musical activity centering on styles that are held to have some innate African characteristics. We can think of this cultural formation as the Afro scene, a designation that is, in fact, commonly employed by people moving within the territories of the scene themselves. In conversations people told me about their former experience in other musical scenes such as the techno, hip hop, even the punk scene, and how they got involved in the Afro scene. There is, then, what I would call a pronounced "sense of scene" among "scenesters," a consciousness I consider crucial to the very logic of musical scenes. In this regard the German term *Szenegänger*, which can be translated as "scenester," but which literally refers to somebody who is "walking" or moving within a scene, is revealing. It touches a central aspect of what musical scenes are all about, namely the movement within a particular terrain of musical activity and within a particular social network. The movement of people in particular networks, we could say, constitutes the space of a scene.

It is for reasons we discussed above that I prefer the much more open term "scene" to other concepts such as "subculture," which tends to suggest an isomorphism of place, space, and culture as we criticized it in chapter three. However, both terms are often used interchangeably. Generally, when I speak of a musical scene here, I use the term in Will Straw's sense, distinguishing between musical communities and musical scenes. A musical community, he writes

> presumes a population group whose composition is relatively stable — according to a wide range of sociological variables — and whose involvement in music takes the form of an ongoing exploration of one or more musical idioms said to be rooted within a geographically specific historical heritage. A musical scene, in contrast, is that cultural space in which a range of musical practices coexist, interacting with each other within a variety of processes of differentiation, and according to widely varying trajectories of change and cross-fertilization. The sense of purpose articulated within a musical community normally depends on an affective link between two terms: contemporary musical practices, on the one hand, and the musical heritage which is seen to render this contemporary activity appropriate to a given context, on the other. Within a musical scene, that same sense of purpose is articulated within those forms of communication through which the building of musical alliances and the drawing of musical boundaries take place. The manner in which musical practices within a scene tie themselves to processes of historical change occurring within a larger international music culture will also be a significant basis of the way in which such forms are positioned within that scene at the local level. (Straw [1991] 1997:494)

As a particular segment within social space, or, better said, as one of the factors in the production of social space, a musical scene is, first of all, constituted by and constitutes itself as a network of people as well as of places or "locations," both of which are connected by particular musical practices and musical alliances. Far from any objective coherence, the networks of people, places, and musical practices that constitute the scene are usually united in the name of style. These go along with specific symbolic economies that make styles recognizable as such. In the symbolic economy of the Afro scene (which we will consider in more detail in the next chapter) representations of blackness or the colors red, yellow, and green are certainly among the most common features indicating "Afro-ness."

Musical scenes are urban phenomena. Many researchers working in the city have stressed the importance of social networks in the production of urban space. The city itself has actually been described as a "network of networks," and the role of "world cities" as nodes within transnational networks and global cultural flows has particularly been highlighted (Hannerz 1996:127ff). Following the basic idea of a network, we have pointed out culture's relational nature in earlier chapters and suggested thinking of urban space as "moving interconnectedness," as Hannerz (1992:167) put it. In line with this argument, then, a musical scene represents a paradigmatic example for how social inter-action is shaped in urban society. It is certainly no accident that early network analyses, as developed in studies of social anthropologists of the so-called Man-chester School in the 1950s, have focused on processes of urbanization in con-nection to performance culture, particularly along the Copper Belt in southern Africa (cf. Hannerz 1980:119ff and Mitchell 1956).

In order to grasp the complexity of interaction of individuals and collec-tivities in urban space, we can principally distinguish between a number of so-cial domains such as kinship, provisioning, recreation, neighboring, and traffic (Hannerz 1980:244ff). Each of such domains has a particular inventory of roles attached to it, according to which individuals are enabled to act in a meaningful way in a given social situation. Regarded from this perspective ur-ban society can be seen as

a collection of individuals who exist as social beings primarily through their roles, setting up relations to one another through these. Urban lives, then, are shaped as people join a number of roles together in a role repertoire and probably to some degree adjust them to each other. The social structure of the city consists of the re-lationships by which people are linked through various components of their role repertoire. (Hannerz 1980:249)

As a particular social network where people set up relationships through vari-ous components of their role repertoire, a musical scene does not fall into any single social domain. Within the terrains of a musical scene a number of do-mains can overlap, most commonly those of recreation and provisioning. In extreme cases individuals can be immersed more or less completely within the networks of a musical scene, which then encompass almost all domains of their social life and which can even become a substitute for kinship.

The roles employed by people in social interaction depend not solely on the domains within which such interaction takes place, but on a variety of fac-tors. We have to consider the overall role people play: in musical scenes we find DJs, musicians, students of African dance, or event organizers, for example; there are also drumming teachers, "scenesters" who just like "partying," and sometimes we may find an ethnomusicologist who claims to be studying Ghanaian music. The social role somebody plays goes along with a specific function, and it will also depend on who interacts with whom. Roles performed in interaction with others therefore always embody a social relationship. As far as musical scenes are concerned we can think of constellations such as teacher/student, DJ/dancers, performer/event organizer, musicians/audience, call/response, scenester/scenester, and so on.

Social interaction is also determined by factors such as class, gender, ethnicity, and age. While many musical scenes have been described as decisive "youth cultures," the age structure in the Afro scene is more heterogeneous. We find teenagers as well as people in their twenties, thirties, forties, and fifties (the oldest person I met, a student of African drumming attending weekly classes, was already in her sixties). Quite a number of occasions within the scene are explicitly "family friendly," and a common picture at many events are parents who bring their children along. Ethnicity, race, and gender are obviously also very important social factors on which interaction in the Afro scene is based. Straw has suggested that these might actually be the central aspects on which the logics of musical scenes are based. His argument opposes other accounts of popular culture, which regard music's "countercultural" potential and the role of the music industry the most crucial factors, and which mostly debate issues of appropriation and counter-appropriation, or, hegemony and counter-hegemony, as we outlined them in the previous chapter. Thus, with respect to the politics of space within musical scenes Straw writes:

> What these logics invite [...] is a reading of the politics of popular music that locates the crucial site of these politics neither in the transgressive or oppositional quality of musical practices and their consumption, nor uniformly within the modes of operation of the international music industries. The important processes, I would argue, are those through which particular social differences (most notably those of gender and race) are articulated within the building of audiences around particular coalitions of musical form. These processes are not inevitably positive or disruptive of existing social diversions, nor are they shaped to any significant extent by solidarity, wilful acts of realignment. Typically, the character of particular audiences is determined by the interlocking operation of the various institutions and sites within which musics are disseminated [...]. These sites, themselves shaped by their place within the contemporary metropolis and aligned with populations along the lines of class and

taste, provide the conditions of possibility of alliance between musical styles and affective links between dispersed geographical places.
(Straw [1991] 1997:504)

While the discourse on popular music often focuses on a superstructural realm,
engaging ourselves in the networks of musical scenes might therefore help us
reconsidering abstract and rather theoretical constructions of popular or public culture in their relation to the concrete level of social interaction. Thinking
about while moving within musical scenes calls, in other words, for a "theory
of practice" (Bourdieu 1977). As a sociocultural terrain located rather in the
periphery of the global cultural economy, considering the logics of Berlin's
Afro scene sheds also a different light on discussions of what is commonly referred to as world music. While many of the styles featured in the Afro scene
fall into this category, what we mostly find in the literature on world music are
discussions of widely recognized performers and the politics of representation
of the international music industry. Musical mediation, as we encounter it for
example in workshop situations, and performance practices that make the
drawing of boundaries between audiences and performers often difficult, are
seldom included in discussions of world music. Talking about the Afro scene
means to consider world music (or whatever label one might prefer) at a "mi-
cromusical" level, to use a term coined by Slobin ([1993] 2000), that is, as a
localizing and localizable musical practice.

   Conceptualized as concrete social networks that are locally situated and,
at the same time, translocally interlinked, a consideration of musical scenes
might additionally help us "[s]orting out the relationships of the local to the
global" (Marcus 1995:112). This, we have said in chapter four, is one of the
main tasks of multi-sited ethnography. As a matter of fact, the spaces of musical scenes coincide with the fields of multi-sited ethnography in that they constitute themselves a multi-sited territory in which connections between sites are
established through social actors, musical practices, and styles and their respective interactive dynamics. Reconsidering Marcus' characterization of the
position of the ethnographer within multi-sited cultural terrains, it comes with
little surprise that in a musical scene "there is always others within who know
(or want to know) what the ethnographer knows, [...] or who want to know
what the ethnographer wants to know" (ibid.). This became apparent to me
when I found out that I was not the only person collecting flyers advertising
events, compiling lists with Afro shops in the city, and systematically scouring
all sorts of media for information on upcoming events. As a matter of fact,
these are common activities in the scene.

   It should be clear at this point that the cultural space of a musical scene is highly dynamic. The networks of places and people, just as the media- and ideoscapes of musical scenes, are in a state of constant reconfiguration. This dynamism is driven by musical practices and social interaction on the local level and their relation to transformations within the larger cultural economy. The dynamics of musical scenes are determined, as Straw notes, by "two sorts of directionality," one which concerns the local production of styles, and one "which articulates these styles elsewhere" ([1991] 1997:501). A musical scene has no clear boundaries and we hardly find stylistic stability, though there are some stylistic features that are more persistent than others. What holds the Afro scene together is a specific cultural product, namely "Africa" or "Afroness," which we have to regard as a particular style. It is a specific preoccupation with "things African" and blackness around which performances, events, and the symbolic economy of the Afro scene are organized. A "sense of scene" is established among "scenesters" through the movement in concrete social networks, common musical practices, the face-to-face interaction of individuals and groups, and the resulting experience that if you go to particular places at particular times, you will always meet familiar people.

There are, after all, different strategies how people approach and link up with the networks of a musical scene, based on their strategic interests (which, in turn, have much to do with the overall roles people play within the scene). As far as I myself am concerned, I played the roles of an apprentice, a student of African drumming, a camera man, a performer, a researcher, a dancer, a tourist, an organizer, a colleague, a friend, a potential promoter, a workshop participant, and many more. Like anyone else in the scene I pursued my interests by employing different "tracking strategies" as Marcus (1995) has described them for the movement in multi-sited terrains — which is to say, I followed things, people, sounds, metaphors, stories, biographies, conflicts, and allegories.

Metropolitanism and Expressive Specialists

On March 21, 2004, a concert entitled "Afrika Mma Cross Over Berlin Vibes: traditional African music, Afro Reggae, AfroPop" took place at the Werkstatt der Kulturen ("Workshop of Cultures"), a venue in Berlin's district Neukölln. The event promised, as the anonymous author of the program notes wrote, to become "a firework of Berlin's African music styles from Afro Beat, Hip Hop, Dancehall, Abdjiben, and Highlife to Susu and Jibaas." As one of the institutions hosting Afro events in the city, the Werkstatt der Kulturen is located in an old building on Wissmannstraße, which was formerly a brewery, right next to the public park Hasenheide. The institution is in the middle of the so-called Rollbergviertel, which is considered to be the most "problematic" neighborhood in Neukölln. While some of the problems of urban society, personified in Turkish, Arab, and African drug dealers and their German customers, can be observed in the park next door, the Werkstatt der Kulturen devoted itself to the promotion of the aesthetically more pleasant sides of "multiculturalism" in the city. Founded in 1993 and supported by public funds, the institution offers space for performances, exhibitions, symposia, and other events, and is also the official organizer of the widely recognized Karneval der Kulturen.

The performance in early spring 2004 started with a group of young drummers, all of its members Senegalese. They were announced as newcomers in the scene. Thereafter came a local reggae band, the Berlin Vibes, which claims to be the first exclusively female reggae formation in the city. The group closing the evening was Afrika Mma, a name that translates as "the children of Africa." We were informed that the five members of Afrika Mma are from Ghana, Nigeria, and Senegal. While the Berlin Vibes played more or less "classical" roots reggae without any stylistic surprises, the music of Afrika Mma was percussion-oriented and featured a number of different types of West African drums. To the rhythms and songs an acoustic guitar was occasionally added. Some of the lyrics were in English; other, more "traditional," pieces were sung in African languages. I remember one song accompanied by guitar only, which called for peace in the world and condemned the war in Iraq (a fashionable activity in Germany those days), but the rest of the program was not explicitly political. Judging from the interaction that took place between the stage and the auditorium one could tell that the group was well known. The program notes actually asserted that Afrika Mma would be a "legend" in Berlin's music scene.

At one side of the concert room two African women were selling drinks as well as "African food" (again, basically rice). As the evening proceeded, a number of people started dancing in front of the stage. I particularly noticed three or four white women who apparently had some training in the performance of African dance styles, and who expressively threw their bodies around to the drumming of Afrika Mma. Other people danced in a less obtrusive fashion, and yet others were sitting in groups of two or more around the small tables that surrounded the dance floor, chatting, eating, drinking, smoking, or just listening to the music and watching the dancers. There were some Blacks among the audience, maybe a dozen out of a hundred and fifty or so, but the majority of people seemed to be Germans. All in all my impression of the eve-

ning was that of a rather unspecific "Africanness," both as far as the performance on stage as well as that in front of the stage are concerned. In any case,
the audience quite obviously enjoyed the evening.

In its mission statement the Werkstatt der Kulturen defines its goals as
providing a stage for the cultural diversity of the city and serving as a forum
for intercultural encounters and political dialogue. The Werkstatt intends to
represent Berlin as an international, open, and creative metropolis. "Almost
half a million people," its mission statement reads, "from more than 180 nations, among them many artists and intellectuals, form with their culture, religion and language, their aesthetic ideas and their arts the international Berlin
— a changing world city."[2] A newspaper article on the occasion of the institution's tenth anniversary celebrated the Werkstatt der Kulturen as "tour guide
to the world city" (Schröter 2003). As such it fits well into the overall city marketing as it was designed after the reunification of the two Germanys, which
tries to (re)establish an image of Berlin as a "world city."[3] As Hannerz notes,
"[w]orld cities are places in themselves, and also nodes in networks; their cultural organization involves local as well as transnational relationships" (Hannerz 1996:128). And this is exactly the image which the Werkstatt der Kulturen promotes: on the one hand we have Berlin as a geographically, historically,
and culturally distinctive place, on the other hand its connectedness to other
places and cultures around the world is stressed. We find a similar representational strategy at work in the reference to "Berlin's African music styles" used
in the program notes to the above outlined event. Such a practice of siting
strategically positions the event on a local and non-local level at the same time.
Whether the non-local component of the site is really a concrete and identifi-
able place or just some vague cultural elsewhere seems to be of little relevance
in this context.

The logic of multiculturalism is guided by two opposing tendencies: universalism and at the same time a "politics of difference" (cf. Taylor 1992).
While universalism claims that we are all the same, the other ideological tendency of multiculturalism claims that we are all different. It is interesting to
note that the same statistical facts — for example: Neukölln hosts immigrants
from 163 nations; or: people from 180 nations live in Berlin — are employed
by the advocates as well as the opponents of multiculturalism, by people both

---

[2] See the official website of the Werkstatt der Kulturen at http://www.wdk.de (accessed on
June 23, 2005).
[3] Though irrelevant for my own argument, the question whether Berlin is really a "world
city" or not is the subject to some controversy. Most people agree that at its current state
the city is not a "world city" in the sense as are New York, London, or Paris. See Frei
(2003:62ff) for a review of some of these discussions.

arguing that foreigners are a "menace" to society as well as by multiculturalists who stress the riches of "cultural diversity."[4] For the proponents of multiculturalism, transnational connectedness and internationalism are matters of prestige and symbolic capital. The more a place is interlinked, the more symbolic capital is presumably attached to it. But the notion of "culture," which is at the heart of this form of, as we might say, positive multiculturalism, is also based on an equation of culture and the nation. In this regard the politics of multiculturalism somewhat paradoxically coincide with nationalistic ideologies and culturalist ideas about the fixed and static relation between culture and territory. As Lefebvre writes in *The Production of Space*:

> The ideology of culture or culturalism supports the unsteady theory of the coherence and singleness of culture, which is the official theory; but, in fact, culture is atomized and sub-cultures of various denominations are no novelty: country life, city life, aristocracy, proletariat, bourgeoisie, 'underdeveloped countries', culture of the masses, etc.; but so many 'sub-cultures' […] do not make a culture; the fragmentation of specialized knowledge and labour is not conductive to unity. Culture is not a myth, it is worse: it is a state ideology. (Lefebvre [1991] 2004:96)

As we have seen above in the outline of the event at the Werkstatt der Kulturen, it is significant to name the origin of performers (whether they have lived in Germany for twenty years or not): they come from Senegal, from Ghana, and Nigeria. In the case of the Berlin Vibes, where all the members are Germans, this information is withheld from us. While "they" have particular and distinguishable "cultures," "we" have a rather unspecific, absorbent multiculture. We remember that internationalism has also been stressed in the program organized by Gordon outlined in the first section of this chapter. Such a politics of representation is extensively used at world music events. World exhibitions are likewise based on this logic and we could in fact argue that the great colonial exhibitions at the end of the nineteenth century also employed such a "revalorization of place," as we might call it, by representing, in this case, the metropole's connectedness with territories all over the world (though here, of course, rather than being culturally enriched, control over the cultural elsewhere was stressed).

---

[4] Compare for example the newspaper articles by Plarre (2004) and Schirmeyer (2002) on the social situation in Neukölln. For a more general discussion of multiculturalism and the history of this concept see also Frei (2003:99ff).

The city is not only the space of a symbolic juxtaposition of places. Urban society, we have said earlier with Hannerz, "makes people more accessible to one another, in more or less shared, limited space" (Hannerz 1980:243). The city is a space where strangers potentially meet, where it is likely to "encounter people who are not like yourself" (Hannerz 1992:173). Considering this characteristic of urban society, there are individuals who are principally better prepared to navigate the sometimes "chaotic surface of space" (Lefebvre [1991] 2004:366) than others. This category of people has been described as cosmopolitans, that is, people who "are presumably actively engaged in the transnational flow of culture by being mobile themselves" (Hannerz 1996:131). Rather than generally referring to "the global," which tends to the suggestion that cultural forms are evenly diffused throughout the world, the concept of cosmopolitanism refers to "objects, ideas, and cultural positions that are widely diffused throughout the world and yet are specific only to certain portions of the populations within given countries" (Turino 2000:7). Cosmopolitanism reminds us that globalization is an uneven process and often a matter of degree. The concept presumes a certain awareness of processes of globalization. Cosmopolitanism can be seen as a conscious, indeed an often profitable, way of dealing with globalization.

Hannerz identifies four different groups of people who are involved in the transnational flows of culture by being mobile themselves. These "four social categories of people [...] play major parts in the making of contemporary world cities" (Hannerz 1996:129), and are represented by "transnational business people," the "various Third World populations" present in the large cities of the West, tourists, and finally people Hannerz calls "expressive specialists," that is, "people concerned with culture in a narrower sense, people specializing in expressive activities" (ibid.:130). As far as international migrants or, as he writes, "Third World populations" are concerned, Hannerz reminds us that in "the age of jet planes, people can move over great distances, back and forth almost in a shuttle fashion, in ways which our more timeworn understandings of migrants and migration hardly account for very satisfactorily" (ibid.:131). While migrants can of course be cosmopolitans at the same time, for Hannerz "most of them are not."

> For them going away may be, ideally, home plus higher income; often the involvement with another culture is not a fringe benefit but rather a necessary cost, to be kept as low as possible. A surrogate home is again created with the help of compatriots, in whose circle one becomes encapsulated. (Hannerz 1996:106)

Most of today's transnational tourists have a similar "home plus" attitude with regard to traveling abroad and can therefore not be regarded as cosmopolitans. Encapsulated together with like-minded people in hotels and beach resorts, for many tourists going away might simply be home plus sunshine and beach. Contacts with natives can be restricted to "exotic" entertainment, and might sometimes also take place in the form of sexual adventure.

In contrast to such tendencies of encapsulation the networks of a musical scene are characteristically open. Some individuals within these networks are more exposed or expose themselves more than others, which is particularly true for expressive specialists. These are important nodes within the network of a scene, since for them being highly connected is an economic necessity. It is in this sense that Hannerz remarks that "[t]ransnational cultures today tend to be more or less clear-cut occupational cultures (and are often tied to transnational job markets)" (Hannerz 1996:106). Expressive specialists are by definition cosmopolitans. Revealing in connection to this is the fact that most Ghanaians I met in Berlin, who were professionally involved in the Afro scene, were actually not very much involved in the migrant networks as they have been established around diasporic churches. This fact illustrates the distinction we made between communities and scenes quite well. Many Africans in Berlin's multicultural scene complained to me about the way some of their compatriots isolated themselves; comments like "they hide at home" were very common.

Images of cosmopolitanism and metropolitanism are perhaps the most vivid images associated with musical scenes. At the same time, urban subcultural life considerably contributes to the "bright lights" image of large cities (cf. Brettell 2000). Particularly for musicians or performers who seek to be successful on the music market, knowing what different audiences want and being able to adjust to the needs of the market in different locales is highly important. For expressive specialists, cosmopolitanism and a broad, flexible role repertoire is indispensable. As we have seen, internationalism, multiculturalism, and metropolitanism are important images promoted by institutions like the Werkstatt der Kulturen. Moreover, for "scenesters" and expressive specialists alike, cosmopolitanism is a significant aspect of self-identification. For people moving within the networks of the scene, speaking English (which is often the case in the territories of the Afro scene) and calling people "who are not like yourself" friends (which in the case of white German *Szenegänger* most obviously applies to black performers), are important means to demonstrate one's (imagined and real) cultural openness and devotion to cosmopolitanism.

As cultural brokers and professional dealers in cultural difference, the role of expressive specialists is often not unlike that of "professional friends" (we will discuss this category of people in more detail in chapter eight). Their task is to mediate different cultural positions, to give people access to different experiential worlds, to make them "feel" metropolitan. In this regard, as "guides to the world city," their role coincides with that of institutions like the Werkstatt der Kulturen. We can say that their role includes a performative embodiment of the metropolis and cosmopolitanism; they stand as living examples for the cultural openness and diversity of the city, which they impart on others by way of contact, interaction, and musical performance.

The Geography of Afro Clubs

Clubbing and social dance are important musical practices within musical scenes. Apart from our considerations so far, the Afro scene is also a dance scene. In a city like Berlin we find a host of clubs targeting the specific audiences of the Afro scene, some exclusively, others with specific events in their weekly programs. Social dance is also an important element during and after concerts. We find specialized Afro clubs as well as venues that have built up a reputation as locations for regularly occurring Afro events and parties. As Straw has argued, we can delineate a particular geography of dance clubs in cities, in which each club is

> positioned relative to others, not only along the predictable lines of musical style, age, sexual orientation and ethnicity, but in terms of a variety of less frequently acknowledged criteria: the explicitness of sexual interaction within them, the manner in which their DJ handles the tension between playing requests and retaining prestige within his peer community, the level of tolerance of deviations from expected behavioural norms and so on. […] Most importantly, the composition of audiences at dance clubs is likely to reflect and actualize a particular state of relations between various populations and social groups, as these coalesce around specific coalitions of musical style. (Straw [1991] 1997:499f)

Among Berlin's Afro clubs are the Lumumba in Mitte, the Tam-Tam, the Mandingo, or the Lagos Club in Kreuzberg, and the so-called Bantu Bar. Other locations like the YAAM at Ostbahnhof or the Hoppetosse in Treptow are also important places within the networks of the Afro scene. In terms of dance music the most popular styles in the scene are reggae and dancehall as they are featured in countless clubs throughout the city. In specialized Afro clubs we might additionally hear styles like soukous, zouk, salsa, black American styles such as soul or funk, and a number of other styles commonly subsumed under the label of world music. Most of the Afro clubs happen to be owned by Africans and also exemplify the overlappings between the multiculturally oriented Afro scene and the various African immigrant communities in the city. The Tam-Tam, for example, tried to establish a "Special Senegalese Night" as well as a "Special Ghana Night" in 2004, highlighting styles like mbalax, or highlife and hiplife respectively, thereby specifically aiming at Ghanaian and Senegalese immigrants in the city. It seems, however, that the critical mass of people interested in such specialized offers was lacking. People rather prefer a general "Afro Cocktail" of musical styles as featured, for example, at the Lumumba at weekends.

As far as musical style is concerned there are overlappings between the different dance music scenes in the city. The Lagos Club, for example, which labels itself "Afro-Cuban Tanzbar," features also a "house electro minimal" party on Tuesdays. While electronic dance music is particularly in the United States associated with black as well as gay urban dance culture (cf. Fikentscher 2000), the attraction of black audiences to styles like techno and house in Germany is less obvious. Whereas there are strong affinities of the gay community to techno, in the Afro scene homosexuality is clearly out of the picture, even tabooed. Especially recent Jamaican dance music has often been explicitly homophobic. In fact, quite contrary to homosexuality, the form of sexuality celebrated in the Afro scene strongly reinforces heterosexual female-male role models. In this respect clubs like the Lumumba or the Tam-Tam have built up a reputation as centers of African-German romantic affairs in the nightlife of Berlin.

Particularly the Lumumba positions itself as a club of explicit sexual interaction. Male-female interaction of a more or less explicit nature is generally a feature of the Afro scene, and it is expressed in the way social dance events are shaped. While dance rituals in other scenes are often based on solitariness or, for that matter, involve groups of friends (often of the same sex) dancing in enclosed circles, thereby excluding other dancers on the floor, dancing styles in the Afro scene often involve active communication between dancers on the floor and particularly a playful interaction between the sexes. Couple dance is additionally encouraged in clubs like the Lumumba by formal instructions to styles such as salsa. The "Old African Juke-Box" parties in the Lumumba on Sundays are particularly recommended "for singles (especially women) and couples over thirty" by their organizers. Summing up the role of dance clubs, Straw writes:

Bringing together the activities of dance and musical consumption, the dance club articulates the sense of social identity as embodied in the conspicuous and differential display of taste. As such, it serves to render explicit the distribution of knowledge and forms of cultural capital across the vectors of gender, race and class. (Straw [1991] 1997:500)

Within the Afro scene explicit sexual interaction takes predominantly place between Whites and Blacks. This interaction reflects the composition of audiences of clubs and also the overall social structure in the scene. While on the male side we see mostly Blacks, the majority of women in Afro clubs are white. This applies, as a general tendency, also to the relation between expressive specialists and participants in workshops and to other Afro events. While migration from Africa has long been an almost exclusively male affair, unmarried African women coming to Europe are still rather the exception. Moreover, cultural performance as a migrational strategy is also rather a male than a female affair. Most of the Africans in the scene are therefore men.

At the Lumumba male club goers are also almost exclusively Blacks, while the women are almost exclusively white Germans. In other clubs like the Tam-Tam, there tend to be more African women, though still much fewer as their male counterparts; therefore we see mid-aged German men who potentially meet these women. As a matter of fact, the explicitness of interaction between Germans and Africans is not only, and often not even in the first place, based on a particularly strong erotic affinity between these two groups, but has much to do with the German legislation and immigration politics, an aspect which should not be underestimated. For younger Africans the terrains of the Afro scene and particularly dance clubs, which allow for a more explicit intersexual communication than other locations, are a territory for finding potential German marriage partners, which is for many the only way to obtain or maintain a legal residence status in the country. But irrespective of these aspects, for Germans as well as Africans, women as well as men, Afro clubs are also potentially the gateway to a more or less "exotic" sexual experience.

The City as Festival

There is another important aspect about the practice of clubbing, which has been stressed, for example, by Schwanhäußer (2005). In her account of the techno scene in Berlin she highlights a particular way of the exploration of urban space through what she calls a "culture of drifting," which describes a movement in space without any particular destination. The terrains of a scene constitute themselves in this way as a space that is not permanently devoted to any particular location or place. The German expression "um die Häuser zie-hen," roughly, "to roam around the houses," used as a synonym for "going out," describes this practice quite well. There are popular songs that celebrate the city as the territory of such nightly roaming, such as the German dancehall hit "Dickes B" by the group Seeed. As Schwanhäußer writes, "subcultural ac-tors practice a kind of collective sauntering [*Flanieren*], the circling, searching travel through urban space" (2005:167).

This practice is also evident in the Afro scene; particularly in the summer months many people move from event to event, from party to party, or club to club. As long as you move within the space of the scene, you will always meet some people somewhere, and somebody has always heard of some other event elsewhere to which one can move on to. It is not too late to go to a club like the Lumumba around four or five o'clock in the morning, where quite a lot of people end their nightly journey through the city at weekends. There are also locations that somewhat paradoxically celebrate the practice of drifting, as for example the YAAM. The YAAM ("Young African Arts Market") was founded in 1994 as a private initiative, and offers a multicultural market as well as par-ties, sport and deejaying competitions, concerts, and other events. At its cur-rent location at Ostbahnhof the premises of the YAAM include an artificial beach directly at the Spree River, as there are now a number of "beach bars" in Berlin. The club hosts parties such as "Black Atlantic Vibes," "Bass Radio," or the "Barney Millah Night." Live concerts featuring German artists such as the dancehall act Culcha Candela or international artists such as Cutty Ranks from Jamaica or the group Black Positive Soul from Senegal take also place at the YAAM. In 2005 the Senegalese community in Berlin celebrated its inde-pendence day at the YAAM, and programs for children or workshops in Afri-can drumming take place here also.

In contrast to officially sponsored multicultural institutions such as the Werkstatt der Kulturen or the Haus der Kulturen der Welt, aiming at the "in-tegration" of foreigners through the representation of "their culture," the YAAM's approach focuses largely on urban youths and their self-representation. The project promotes "street culture" rather than multiculture and claims therefore to have more "street credibility" than other institutions (cf. Frei 2003:119f). In the course of its history the YAAM moved several times from one location to the other, depending on the temporary use (*Zwischennut-zung*) of plots of land in the inner city, the final usage of which has not been determined by the administrative authorities yet. As a way of "developing and

celebrating a lifestyle" for which "movement is better than stasis," out of the
necessity to move the YAAM has eventually made an integral part of its philosophy.[5]

The ultimate embodiment and musical celebration of the movement
through urban space is the music festival. In Berlin a host of larger and smaller
festivals and open-air events take place every year. Most prominently among
these are the Loveparade, the Karneval der Kulturen, or the festivities on May
Day in Kreuzberg. The Loveparade was initiated in 1989 as the countries
largest techno festival, but has now been stopped due to organizational problems. The Karneval der Kulturen, organized by the Werkstatt der Kulturen,
was initiated in 1996 and is by now Berlin's largest open-air music festival, at-
tracting over a million visitors every year (Frei 2003; Knecht & Soysal 2005).
The multicultural festival was modeled after similar events such as the Notting
Hill Carnival in London or the Zomercarnaval in Rotterdam, and it is also a
platform for many groups within Berlin's Afro scene to present themselves.
Featuring a four-days program that cumulates every year in a large multicultural street parade through Neukölln and Kreuzberg, the politics of the Karneval follows a similar multicultural logic as we described it for the Werkstatt
der Kulturen. This form of multiculturalism is also prevalent at Kreuzberg's
"Mayday," though here the festival takes on a more violent form in the night,
when leftist groups, joined by the youth of the quarter, fight with the police in
a yearly recurring ritual (nowadays mostly for old times' rather than for revolution's sake, it seems).

There is a general association of communal musical events and social
dance with a festival atmosphere, which in the case of the Afro scene, I would
argue, is intensified by the tendency to produce events as a "holistic" sensual
experience (most events include African food, for example). As Stokes has
pointed out:

> The parallel association of music and dance with social licence, sex-
> ual adventure, drink and drugs establishes [...] communal musical
> events as a vital and pleasurable part of life. The fact that pleasure is
> involved is immensely important. As Foucault repeatedly pointed
> out, pleasure becomes a significant arena of political experience and
> a focus of control, through the definition of what pleasures "are"
> and whether or not they are permitted, and, conversely, through re-
> sistance to that control. The association of pleasure, licence and a

festival atmosphere with music and dance makes them experiences which are distinctly "out of the ordinary." (Stokes 1994:12f)

Festivals in this sense, as experiences "out of the ordinary," can also be spontaneous, improvised and of an informal nature. This could include private parties and gatherings in public parks, as they are very common not only in Berlin. With regard to the Afro scene we can make out particular locations where such gatherings preferably take place: the Mauerpark in Prenzlauer Berg where people frequently meet for drumming sessions, for example, or, Görlitzer Park in "SO 36," where Africans and Germans meet to enjoy and relax alongside Turkish families. Through all these places urban space and the movement through the city is celebrated in a stylized form, and all these occasions establish the city itself as an experience "out of the ordinary." Many places can be part of what Schwanhäußer calls "collective sauntering." A day in the scene might look like this: people might meet at Görlitzer Park in Kreuzberg, for example, and some took drums along for a jam session; they later move on to Oranienstraße to get some food (most likely Turkish fast food); there they (intentionally or coincidentally) meet some other people, and all collectively move on to the YAAM to spent some time dancing and drinking there. From the YAAM they might go to a different club and maybe even another club afterwards. The whole city becomes the space of the festival, and the movement through the urban landscape — most commonly by bicycle or public transport — an important aspect of the overall musical experience.

Informal musical gatherings are an integral part of collective movement. These are also a characteristic feature of larger festivals such as the Karneval der Kulturen, where people spontaneously gather for drumming and dancing sessions alongside other events. These occasions illustrate the importance of collective forms of "musicking" within the Afro scene. Social dance in clubs is one example. Similarly, "African dance" is not only practiced in dance workshops, but is an integral part of other events. Likewise, African drumming does not only take place in classes and workshops but is practiced in a variety of contexts. Enthusiasts gather spontaneously in public parks for sessions, and many concerts in the Afro scene take on the character of jam sessions toward their end, where people jump on the stage to join the performers. In addition to professional bands we find many more or less fixed drumming and dancing groups. Some of these group are held together by a drumming teacher who functions as the master drummer; there are other amateur groups which meet on different occasions and combine the most diverse stylistic elements in their music.

There is, as some authors have stressed, generally a tendency towards a "festivalization" of urban society (Frei 2003:110ff). "To festivalize culture," Barbara Kirshenblatt-Gimblett commented, "is to make every day a holiday" (1991:420). The YAAM is a case in point here. Through its inclusion of a beach, the location is already constructed as a place out of the "ordinary" space of the city — not unlike a beach resort. On Sunday afternoons people come here to relax, to enjoy drinks, play beach volleyball and other games, listen to reggae and dancehall music, to meet other people and to dance. The Hoppetosse, where many continue their party on Sundays after relaxing on the YAAM's beach, also establishes itself as an extraordinary place. It is a scrapped boat on the Spree in Treptow. Parties take place on the inner decks, and when it gets to hot and crowded inside, people relax on the open top deck and enjoy the view of the illuminated Oberbaumbrücke with the Fernsehturm, Berlin's prominent landmark, in the background.

The festival as an "experience out of the ordinary" is then a particular way of experiencing and appropriating urban space. It is an aestheticization of urban space and a way of contemplating the city, a way of encountering the city as a sensual experience. Just as expressive specialists, as we have argued, embody and mediate a particular experience of place — of the metropolis as a non-local local site, a heterotopia, and therefore an extraordinary place —, so do locations like the YAAM and the Hoppetosse. In a portrait of the YAAM its initiators ask:

> What is the YAAM? A Club? — Yes, and yet much more. The YAAM is a special place that cannot be described, but has to be ex-perienced, a place like no other in this country. YAAM is many: Every Sunday more than 1500 people who couldn't be more diverse come, as if a New York subway had fastened on the river banks of the Spree.[6]

Considered this way, the YAAM is indeed a heterotopia, an embodiment of the metropolis in miniature.

---

[6] "Was ist das YAAM? Ein Club? — Ja, und doch viel mehr. Das YAAM ist ein besonderer Ort, der sich nicht beschreiben läßt, den man erleben muß, ein Ort wie kein anderer in diesem Land. YAAM ist viele: An jedem Sonntag kommen über 1500 Menschen wie sie unterschiedlicher nicht sein können, als hätte gerade eine New Yorker U-Bahn am Spree-ufer festgemacht" (see self-description at http://www.yaam.de, accessed April 10, 2007).

7 Symbolic Economies

The Politics of Style

While we explored networks of people and places in the previous chapter and considered some of the musical practices that are significant within these networks, in the following we will scrutinize the symbolic economy of the Afro scene. We have said that the networks of people, places, and musical practices as the constituent elements of this sociocultural formation are united in the name of style. Styles, we have further said, are based on symbolic economies that produce a certain stylistic coherence, and that position each style relative to others within the larger cultural economy. Thus, while people move in social networks and between particular sites both of which are connected by musical practices, the symbolic economies of styles are important means of orientation within these networks. In times when culture is, as Appadurai put it, basically in a deterritorialized state, styles are therefore a means of structuring cultural practices and putting things "in place." This is not to say that styles form coherent wholes or that they exist next to each other as clear-cut and distinguishable entities. Following the essentially relational logic of cultural processes in favor of which we argued in the proceeding chapters, styles should in the first place be regarded as an expression of relations in space. Styles situate sites relative to each other in social space. Style is, after all, a practice of siting; it is a strategic moment in the production of space.

Stylistic variation positions every element within the cultural economy relative to others. Since there are no clear-cut boundaries, it is impossible to define styles from their outer margins; we can think of them better as being arranged around specific gravitational centers. As we suggested earlier, some elements within stylistic formations are more persistent than others. From such focal symbolical positions, as we might call them, connections are drawn to various stylistic elements. At least theoretically any combination of symbols available in the cultural economy is possible. In chapter five, in connection with the debates around German rap music, we mentioned some of the cruder stylistic bricolages, where black musical forms are even combined with elements borrowed from fascistic symbolic regimes. The National Socialists' propaganda in the form of swing music is an equally crude, and in the first place probably unexpected, stylistic mixture. The workings of style as an economic and ideological strategy become obvious here.

Some of the issues that are involved in how sites establish themselves relative to one another in terms of style and stylistic nuances were part of our discussion in the previous chapter. As constituent elements of the symbolic economy of the Afro scene multiculturalism, internationalism, and cosmopolitanism are, for example, strategic practices of siting. Through the promotion of multiculturalism and metropolitanism as discussed above, a city like Berlin strategically positions itself as a cultural product on the market, competing with other cities for tourists, visitors, and investors. Combined with other attributes such as its particular history, architecture, geographical location, and so on, the city as a whole is stylistically put into place in relation to other cities around the globe. From a local perspective styles are a means of navigating the cultural landscape of urban space and, therefore, also a means of navigating musical scenes. We discussed, for example, how dance clubs position themselves relative to other clubs on the basis of stylistic variation. Styles symbolically mark territories; they draw boundaries as well as they show pathways and form transitions. It is not least through the politics of style that musical alliances and coalitions, but also oppositions and discrepancies are expressed, reproduced, negotiated, and transformed.

In the realm of popular culture, symbolic economies and the meaning of style have prominently been analyzed by Dick Hebdige (1979). He speaks of "sign communities" with regard to subcultures. In Hebdige's reading of subcultural practices the politics of style turns out to be mainly guided by a dialectics of appropriation and counter-appropriation. For Hebdige, style represents a constant struggle between subcultures and a "dominant culture" over processes of signification. Paraphrasing this line of argument, Stokes writes:

> Subcultures borrow from the dominant culture, inflecting and inverting its signs to create a bricolage in which the signs of the dominant culture are 'there' and just recognizable as such, but constituting a quite different, subversive whole. [...] The dominant culture, through the music industry and media, attempts to reappropriate the space for its own purposes. The moment it does this, new stylistic criteria for articulating an inflected 'difference' vis-à-vis the dominant culture are found by the subcultural group. (Stokes 1994:19)

Considering the politics of style within the world music economy, we often find similar interpretations of the meaning of stylistic inventories, that is, readings that also assume a basic dualism of domination and subordination govern-ing symbolic regimes. Whereas the "dominant culture," in Hebdige's analysis represented by the dominant social class, in interpretations of world music is mostly conceptualized as the "Western world," its subordinated counterpart often appears in the form of a culturally exploited "rest," paradigmatically embodied by the "Third World." World music constructs, it is held, by way of its representational practices, an exoticized Other; through a fetishization of ethnicity and locality the styles of world music become a "cradle of authentic-ity," as Connell and Gibson argue for example. They write:

> More generally world music exemplifies a "fetishization of margin-ality" and an essentialist identification of cultural practices in devel-oping countries with otherness itself [...]. This fetishization is part of a broader trend to seek out cultures that are relatively untouched by processes of commodification, most evident in some forms of tour-ism, which exaggerate, reify and romanticise the extent to which any culture, and place, is isolated from others. Exceptionally this is part of a tendency to eulogise Africa, and African 'roots', above and be-yond that of other non-white people, such as Asians, let alone mi-nority white groups; racism has often resulted in blacks being seen as more 'authentic' in terms of musical (and sexual and sporting) ex-pressions of the body, whereas Europeans have often been associ-ated more with the mind and less spontaneous types of musical per-formances. (Connell & Gibson 2003:157)

In our discussion of Afro events taking place in the zoo we have seen how a specific politics of representation puts images of a naturalized and authentic Africa into play, thereby fostering processes of racialization. As Connell and Gibson continue, such a politics of representation has also "resulted in the dis-covery of the 'healing' sounds of particular kinds of (usually drum or ambient) music, the 'primitivist fantasy' that resulted in Western musicians adopting the music of central African pygmy peoples" (ibid.). Modes of representation as outlined here — and the quotation specifically refers to Steven Feld's study of appropriations of Central African "pygmy music" in Western popular culture (cf. Feld 1996) — are, of course, evident in the promotion of Africa as a prod-uct on the cultural market. Signs are, after all, open to appropriation, and par-ticularly advertisements are grounded in a binary logic that works with ob-vious contrasts to attract people's attention. As Lefebvre (with an audible un-dertone of cultural pessimism) remarked:

[P]ublicity is the poetry of Modernity, the reason and pretext for all successful displays. It takes possession of art, literature, all available signifiers and vacant signifieds; it is art and literature, it gleans the leavings of the Festival to recondition them for its own ends; as with trade, which it takes to its logical limits, it confers on all things and on all beings the plentitude of duality and duplicity, the dual value of object (utility value) and of consumer goods (trade value), by carefully organized confusion of these "values" to the advantage of the latter. (Lefebvre [1971] 2004:107)

Acknowledging that images appropriated in publicity put binary oppositions into play, intended to serve selling particular products, the question whether we find the meaning of these images solely in their duality is nonetheless open. Regarded in the way above described, representations — irrespective whether they are appropriated in advertisements or by whomsoever — appear first of all as a textual strategy. But are images and representations really encountered this way in social space? On the level of social interaction the logic of binary oppositions seems to be an oversimplification. While style is quite obviously a part of economic strategies — we might refer to this aspect as the "macropolitics of style" —, it is at the same time an aspect of social interaction. On the level of a "micropolitics of style," that is, in its appropriated forms integrated into the practices of everyday life such as the performance of roles, style is an expression of social relations. And these, we said earlier, resist simple oppositions.

If we consider the image of an "authentic Africa," which, as Connell and Gibson argue, exemplifies a fetishization of marginality par excellence, we have seen that the same image has not only been appropriated by a dominant "white West" and the tourist industry, but likewise by African Americans as well as African nationalist and pan-African movements. Far from denying that the macropolitics of style produces potent images based on a binary logic, on a micropolitical level the seemingly simple workings of domination and suppression, of appropriation and counter-appropriation, are subverted and contradicted. This is to say that structural interpretations do often not go beyond the assumed binary oppositions that form the starting point of such analyses. Yet still, as a performative practice styles are of a relational nature. Performance is, as Ebron (2002:11) noted, "lived representation"; performance brings representation as a social practice to life. As a performative practice of everyday life, the micropolitics of style is part of the negotiation of social differences along the vectors of age, gender, ethnicity, class, and others. It is in this sense that styles are relational while they cannot be reduced to simple binaries.

Symbolic economies produce, then, signs and images that are open to appropriation and that are also integrated, reenacted, and transformed in everyday-life practices. Nonetheless, in the dissemination of signs media play a crucial role. Media are central nodes in the production of styles and also and important means to navigate musical scenes. For the cultural economy of a city like Berlin there are for example general event magazines such as *zitty*, one of the established bi-weekly papers listing parties, performances, addresses, and so on. Musical events appearing in these magazines are stylistically characterized to help people making their choices where and how to go out. They also include announcements for courses, classes and workshops in the most diverse fields of interest, among them African drumming and dancing. Local radio stations also play their part, though for the Afro scene they are of only minor importance. There are numerous websites providing information about upcoming events in the Afro scene.[1] But more important than such published media are the information networks within the scene itself. Once you are in the scene, images and representations advertising events come your way, for example, in the form of flyers. As a mobile network of images, flyers follow the logic of the networks of musical scenes in that they represent themselves a "moving interconnectedness."

In times when "standard cultural reproduction" has become "an endangered activity that succeeds only by conscious design and political will, where it succeeds at all" (Appadurai 1996:54), style, we could argue, often becomes a substitute for culture. Culture has itself become a political and economic activity today. Taking the importance of media networks for today's cultural processes into account, particularly in urban society symbolic economies produce a relative cultural stability in terms of vocabularies of style and the employment of images and representations of a highly stylized nature. No matter where you come from, whether you are "cosmopolitan," a "migrant," or a "scenester" — today cultural identities are often as much a matter of "lifestyle" and attitude as they are of cultural heritage, a matter of political standpoint, economic strategy, conscious design, and self-creation.

---

[1] Some examples are "Afrika Start" at http://www.afrika-start.de or "Africa live" at http://www.africa-live.de. Sites with a more regional focus are "Afropott" at http://www.afropott.de focusing on the Ruhr area and the event magazine "jali" at http://www.jali.de specifically for the Afro scene in Berlin (all sites accessed on April 13, 2007).

Strategic Positions

Coming to Europe as a young man, Asamoah remembered, was "like a first class trip."[2] He got to know some people from Sheffield who invited him to England. From there he came to Germany in 1981. Thinking about his journey from Africa to Europe now, it sometimes seemed unbelievable to him.

> I've been born in a village in Ghana. No cars, no electricity, no flowing water. As kids we used to drum, we started on cooking pots. Later we founded a theater group. You grow up with drumming. When I was ten, twelve years old — my grandmother has a church. In our church there was also drumming and dancing. [...] I can show you my village. And from this village to Europe — it's hard to imagine.

Many Africans I met in Berlin as well as in Accra told me about "their village." Similarly, most people I encountered who were involved in culture told me that drumming and dancing would basically be a "family thing," that nobody in particular taught them how to drum and dance and they just grew up with it. In an average European mind like mine such biographical accounts evoke powerful images: people drumming and dancing in remote villages somewhere in Africa, mostly in the glow of campfires or the full moon (or even better both). These were the images employed in the advertisements for the "jungle night" in Leipzig, images that paradigmatically represented "Pongoland." As for most of the people who gave me such biographical accounts, after inquiring into more detail, the "family thing" drumming and dancing turned out to be cultural activities they got involved with through groups at youth centers or in the school, groups which were led by someone who also functioned as teacher and where people taught each other drumming and dancing patterns according to their knowledge. Moreover, most people who said they are from some village happened to be either born or grew up in the city. And most of the "villages" where people claimed they came from and which I eventually did pay a visit turned out to be what I would refer to rather as a town or even a city.

This is not to say that the associative chain "Africa-village-drumming and dancing" is completely mistaken, but rather that such an image is highly rela-

---

[2] All quotations in the following are excerpts from an interview I conducted with Mark Kofi Asamoah in Berlin-Zehlendorf on April 14, 2004. The interview was conducted in German and the quotations represent my translations.

tive. To be sure, there are villages in Africa, and drumming and dancing are activities that go along with festivities in such villages. Knowing where you and your family come from is highly important for most Ghanaians, and people refer to their place of origin, even if they have not been there in their whole life. In addition, if you have been to funeral celebrations in, say, Anloga in the southern Volta Region (is Anloga a village or a small town?) — and there is every weekend one or more funerals in and around Anloga — and if you are not too ignorant, you will at least rudimentarily know how to dance *agbadza* afterwards. Anyone who grows up in Ghana encounters the same kind of cultural music also in performances throughout the cities, on the radio, in television programs, and at many other occasions. This is to say, people grow up with culture in Ghana just as people grow up with Beethoven in Germany. Though both are considered a part of the respective national heritage, knowing Beethoven does not mean that one is able to play the Pathétique or to read sheet music (which is nonetheless an integral part of the European classical tradition).

Coming back to Asamoah's journey, he founded his group Adikanfo at the beginning of 2000. Over the years he performed with a number of groups, among them the joint project Afrika Mma, which he initiated in 1990 together with musicians from Senegal, Nigeria, Ethiopia and Brazil. At the beginning of his time in Germany, in the 1980s, he played in a group called Bibiba, which he formed together with other Ghanaians and Germans. It was, as he remembered,

> the very first Afro-rock band in Berlin [...]. We brought African or Ghanaian highlife, and then the Germans were rock musicians. And we put up this project — it was really rock together with Ghanaian music, new in the music scene at that time. After that, I played with a number of groups.

In contrast to "fusion" projects such as Bibiba or Afrika Mma, the idea of Adikanfo was to put a group that presents "purely" traditional African music:

> If you put highlife on one side, then, on the other, there are pure, real traditional rhythms and dances — though you mostly hear this guitar music, and then hip hop and pop, which is to say, highlife. But you seldom hear something about traditional music. Normally, if people invite traditional groups, it is mostly the School of Performing Arts in Legon [at the University of Ghana], and they do every-

thing. But this is only for people or organizations with money, since
they will come with at least twenty to forty artists. But normal people
can't afford such groups, it is too expensive.

In contrast to stylistic mixes as one encounters them mostly within the scene,
for Asamoah the kind of music they perform with Adikanfo represents "pure
Africa." He has more generally built up a reputation as a "traditional man," as
he put it himself, within the music scene. He extensively draws on the image of
the traditionalist in his self-representations.[3] At the same time, he has much of
what David Rycroft once called a "continentalizer" (quoted in Agawu
2003:59). Understanding himself as a cultural broker and promoter of African
culture in a very general sense, he organizes workshops and seminars mostly in
schools to teach not only African drumming and music, but also to educate
young people about the African continent. As he explained:

> I am Ghanaian, but what happens in other countries in Africa —
> the cultures are similar. When I do programs with young people, I
> start with Ghana, mostly name giving and such things, and then I
> draw comparisons to other countries in Africa. So, you start with
> Ghana, but in the end, what happens in Ghana could as well hap-
> pen in other African countries, in Nigeria or Southern Africa. It is
> like that. One explains and presents pictures — and if you look at
> these pictures, you can see that the motives are almost the same, the
> same motives.

We can clearly see that stylistic decisions are led by strategic considerations
with regard to the market. Just as Afro rock in the 1980s was "new" in the
scene, engaging in "pure" traditional music and dance "in the colors of Africa"
(according to a self-advertisement of Adikanfo) was equally led by strategic
economic considerations for Asamoah. Meanwhile, people often occupy more
than just one strategic position. Presenting himself as a "traditional man" with
Adikanfo, Asamoah employs more of a "rocker" image when performing with
Afrika Mma (on the promotional photograph for the program outlined in the
previous chapter the members of Afrika Mma wear sunglasses and leather
caps). Thus, in addition to strategic positioning in particular locations, stylistic
broadness and the occupation of a number of positions is at the same time a
very common strategy. The different positions somebody occupies do not necessarily have to be compatible with each other.

---

[3] See his personal website at http://www.asamoah.de (accessed on January 17, 2007).

While expressive specialists from Africa commonly authenticate their performance and teaching practices with reference to their African origin (a strategy also employed by people who did not start drumming or dancing before they came to Europe), it should come with little surprise that another important element in positioning oneself on the market are references to professionalism and, as a part of this, to cosmopolitanism. The competition on the market is, after all, high, and when it comes to choosing a drumming or dancing teacher, people are well aware that no matter how "deep" someone might be rooted in whatever tradition, teaching students is a different business altogether. Consider for example the following promotional text for a workshop in African dance:

> Fanta Kaba descends from the tribe of the Malinke who have a rich treasure of traditional rhythms and dances. As a young girl she was discovered for the National Ballet of Guinea. She stayed there for 27 years, more than ten years as solo dancer of this famous "Ballet Africain," with which she then undertook seven world tours.[4]

The following excerpt from a flyer advertising weekly dance classes in Berlin-Kreuzberg is a similar text, where the reference to cultural heritage is combined with an account of the teacher's professional and cosmopolitan experience:

> Ofei Ankrah is a professional dancer from Ghana. For five years he traveled to many African countries with the National Dance Ensemble in order to perform traditional West African dances and music. He lives in Germany for three years and performs here with different groups. In the class Ofei wants to convey a part of his people's awareness of life to dance enthusiasts. The dancers are accompanied by live drumming. The dances are based on traditional as well as modern rhythms.[5]

---

[4] "Fanta Kaba stammt vom Volksstamm der Malinke ab, die über einen reichen Schatz an traditionellen Rhythmen und Tänzen verfügen. Sie wurde als junges Mädchen für das Nationalballett von Guinea entdeckt, blieb dort 27 Jahre, davon über 10 als Solotänzerin dieses berühmten 'Ballet Africain,' mit dem sie dann sieben Welttourneen unternommen hat" (Flyer promoting a workshop weekend in "African dance" in Berlin-Reinickendorf on June 12/13, 2004).

[5] "Ofei Ankrah ist ein professioneller Tänzer aus Ghana. Mit dem National Dance Ensemble hat er 5 Jahre lang viele Länder Afrikas bereist, um dort traditionelle westafrikanische Tänze und Musik aufzuführen. Seit drei Jahren lebt er in Deutschland und tritt mit verschiedenen Gruppen auf. In dem Kurs möchte Ofei Tanzbegeisterten ein [sic] Teil des

In the case of Ofei's dance classes we find an additional strategy that positions his product on the market. As his promotional text (which was written by Ofei's German wife Judith) continues:

> The classes start with a warm up. Afterwards the single dance steps are practiced which, one after the other, add up to a composition. At the end we do stretching and relaxation exercises. The course does not only inspire lovers of African music, but equally all those who enjoy exercising to spirited rhythms.[6]

The reference to exercise and sports opens a completely new market and must be seen in connection to the current fitness boom and people's growing "body awareness" (and Ofei's classes were exercise indeed). Apart from that, expressive specialists mostly put emphasis on their international experience and expertise in a variety of styles to attract students. At times, mobility itself seems to function as a form of expertise, which is true for Africans as well as Germans operating within the scene. Even more so for Germans engaged in the workshop business, references like "learned dance and percussion in Guinea," "many educational stays in Africa," "several stays in West Africa at the National Ballet of Mali, in Senegal and Ghana, as well as on Martinique," "intensive study of Malinke rhythms in Guinea (Conakry)" are commonly found in professional biographies. In this regard the creation of professional biographies in the Afro scene differs little from how other professionals, such as for example ethnomusicologists, construct their biographies. The production of professionalism, here, goes along with the evocation of what has been described as "ethnographic authority" (cf. Clifford 1988:21-54), an authority that has to be acquired by means of travel and through immersion into other "cultures."[7]

Apart from traditionalism, professionalism, and cosmopolitanism, another strategy to stylistically position oneself within the scene in relation to

---

Lebensgefühles seines Volkes vermitteln. Die Tänzer werden von Trommelmusik live begleitet. Die Tänze basieren auf traditionellen als auch modernen Rhythmen" (Flyer promoting weekly classes in "African dance" at the Percussion Art Center in Berlin-Kreuzberg in the year 2004).

[6] "Der Kurs beginnt mit einem Aufwärmungsteil. Danach werden die einzelnen Tanzschritte trainiert, die nach und nach eine Komposition ergeben. Zum Abschluss finden ein Stretching und Entspannungsübungen statt. Der Kurs begeistert nicht nur Liebhaber der afrikanischen Musik sondern auch alle, die sich gerne zu schwungvollen Rhythmen sportlich bewegen" (ibid.).

[7] For an account how ethnomusicologists rhetorically create cultural competence and establish their ethnographic authority through references to their "fieldwork experience," see Agawu (2003:43) or my own rhetoric strategies in the introduction of this book.

others is the highlighting of individualism. Being distinguishable is, after all, the aim of any promotional strategy. In the following excerpt from a promotional text of the drummer and teacher Gordon Odametey, for example, individualism is explicitly stressed:

> Gordon Odametey has his own individual style. On the basis of tradition and his longstanding experience in the most diverse styles, he creates his own music. He explores the tension between African rhythms and current music styles from all over the world. He is equipped with great skills and originality.[8]

In a personal communication Gordon told me that when he came to Germany in the 1980s, he used to teach rather "traditional" Ghanaian, "sometimes perhaps also some Senegalese drumming styles." But he changed his style of playing as well as teaching completely a few years ago. He had become, as he put it, "more international," promoting now a style of drumming he referred to as "European." Teaching African rhythms with their timelines and layering of different patterns played simultaneously, many of his German students had actually difficulties comprehending his music, "they just didn't get it." As we can see, then, strategic positions are subject to change and are basically determined in relation to other positions as well as to the demand on the market. Occupying more than just one stylistic position is a very common strategy, though diversity and broadness have to be balanced in order for expressive specialists to remain distinguishable. While single stylistic elements people employ can coincide and overlap, it is through the combination of a variety of elements that individual positions are created.

Identity Brokerage

Expressive specialists have often been described as cultural brokers, as mediators in processes of cultural transformation. Coplan (1985), for example, in his account of the development of urban popular culture in South Africa, describes the role of such cultural brokers in the emergence of distinctively urban

---

[8] "Gordon Odametey hat seinen ganz individuellen Stil. Auf der Basis der Tradition und aufgrund seiner langjährigen Erfahrung in den verschiedensten Stilen erschafft er seine eigene Musik. Diese bewegt sich im Spannungsfeld zwischen afrikanischen Rhythmen und aktuellen Musikrichtungen in aller Welt. Er verfügt über großes Können und Originalität" (quoted from a promotional brochure entitled "Spiritual Healing Drumming").

identities, who mediated between older ethnic and newer pan-ethnic identifications in the rapidly growing cities at the end of the nineteenth and beginning
of the twentieth century. Similarly, Waterman (1990) gives an account of the
social history of popular music in Nigeria and stresses the role of cultural brokers in processes of urbanization and the formation of urban society in West
Africa.[9] In the previous chapter we have emphasized the role of expressive
specialists as cultural brokers in the mediation between local and translocal
identities, in the negotiation of national and transnational, or, cosmopolitan
positions. In this section, now, I want to argue more generally for the role of
expressive specialists as what we might refer to as "identity brokers," that is,
mediators not only of collective cultural identities, but also of the self-identities
of individuals.

It is often through the exposed individualism of an expressive specialist
that his or her students and followers discover and experience their own individuality. Music and dance, or, more specifically, African music and dance are
the media in these individualizing processes. Thus, while expressive specialists
position themselves stylistically within the symbolic economy, what they offer,
or at least promise, is that by way of finding them, people eventually find
themselves. In a sense, then, they present themselves as a means of siting, as in
the following example:

> Gordon's experience can be felt in the way he teaches: Not the
> head, but the whole body appropriates a rhythm — drumming,
> keeping the rhythm, breathing, relaxation and a free mind go to-
> gether. The ear will be trained for the beat and the coordination of
> all participants. Drumming with Gordon means laughing a lot, fun,
> and discovering oneself on uncommon paths.[10]

There are many other examples for the marketing and promotion of the exploration of one's "inner self" and the discovery of one's body through African
rhythm, dance, and bodily movement more generally. This discourse is closely
related to the ideoscape of "New Age" and similar movements, which stress

---

[9] See also Coplan (1978) for an analysis of parallel processes in the coastal cities of present-
day Ghana.

[10] "Gordons Erfahrungen sind spürbar in der Art und Weise, wie er unterrichtet: Nicht der
Kopf, sondern der ganze Körper eignen [sic] sich einen Rhythmus an — Trommeln,
Rhythmus halten, Atmen, Entspannung und ein freier Kopf gehören zusammen. Das Ge-
hör wird geschult für den Beat und die Abstimmung aller Beteiligten. Mit Gordon zu
trommeln, bedeutet viel Lachen, Spaß und auf ungewöhnlichem Weg Neues über sich
selbst erfahren" (quoted from Gordon's promotional brochure "Spirit Healing Drumming").

naturalness, spirituality, and mysticism. This imagery has been well described for the discourse on world music. Fostered by what Taylor (1997:21-26) describes as the discourse of "authentic emotionality and experience," it plays a central role in the production of "Africanness." But beyond the reinforcement of dichotomies between Africa and Europe, between an exotic Other on the one hand and a superior Self on the other, such images are also a means for people to discover themselves. We have criticized the critique of representation as it is commonly put forth in the discourse on world music (cf. Feld 1994a; Frith 2000; Garofalo 1993; Guilbault 1997; Taylor 1997) for underrating world music as a practice of everyday life. What we mostly encounter in the Afro scene are quite idiosyncratic and eclectic mixtures of images and ideologies rather than purist versions of a romanticized and exoticized Africa. Images and symbols employed in representations are seldom consistent, which makes their reading as a consistent ideology also problematic. In the following example a kind of universal Rastafarianism is combined with references to music therapy and more unspecific forms of mysticism through which "you will find yourself":

> So here we go, in the name of I and I LORD. I got the power of healing out of my spiritual drumming. I was born into a drumming, dancing and spiritual family. Since more than 20 years drumming is a serious experiment for me, a communication with myself, with people, with the soul and the holy spirit of mankind. Heal your soul and you will find yourself! If you find yourself, you will find your way! Heal your soul to free yourself from darkness, from madness, and let the light shine in you. Healing Drumming brings you joy and spiritual power to the soul, confidence in the destiny and protection against bad evil force on your way and in times of confusion.[11]

Regarding the imagery of the Afro scene we are moving within a space where images of individualism, Africa and African music, esoteric ideologies such as New Age, but also insights from the realms of pedagogy, physiology, psychology, or music therapy meet and intermingle in manifold ways. We are therefore also confronted with questions like these: "What do dance and menstruation have to do with each other?" The answer follows prompt:

> Dance is movement with rhythm; movement is life; rhythm is a

---

[11] Quoted from the same promotional brochure by Gordon Odametey. English in the original.

Greek word and means "flow," "flowing." The womb creates life, it
is the source of making and creating; menstruation is flow. In this
workshop we will search for the connection between dance, movement, rhythm, and the cycle and flow of menstruation. We start with
easy steps from African dance, which will bring our whole body into
motion. African dance with its earth-bounding steps and movements
helps the body to open up, to "flow." The live music supports this
with sound and rhythm. In easy exercises and improvisations with
music we will try to feel the rhythm of our menstruation and the
movement of our womb, and to find an expression for the special
emotional states during menstruation, like restlessness, the need for
retreat, being comfortable, pain, etc. Finally, I would like to create
and dance together with you our own "menstruation dance."[12]

The above quoted workshop program is not untypical in that it stresses dance
as a bodily experience. As a matter of fact, the majority of the clientele for
dancing as well as drumming workshops happen to be women (cf. Fürst &
Grätschus 2002), though in advertisements women are mostly not approached
exclusively as it is the case here. What is sold or marketed is actually individuality through African music and dance, self-discovery through a musical exploration of the bodily self. We are dealing with a process of identity formation by
way of the (re)production of bodily space, since it is, as we have already noted,
"by means of the body that space is perceived, lived — and produced" (Lefebvre [1991] 2004). If the aesthetics of the Afro scene can be described as a
political economy of space, we have to consider it as a political economy of the
body in the first place.

---

[12] "Was haben Tanz und Menstruation miteinander zu tun? Tanz ist Bewegung mit
Rhythmus; Bewegung ist Leben; Rhythmus ist ein griechisches Wort und bedeutet 'Fluß,'
'fließen.' Die Gebärmutter schafft Leben, sie ist die Quelle des Schaffens und Erschaffens;
Menstruation ist Fluß. In diesem Workshop werden wir nach dem Zusammenhang von
Tanz, Bewegung, Rhythmus und dem Zyklus und Fluß der Menstruation suchen. Wir beginnen mit einfachen Schritten aus dem Afrikanischen [sic] Tanz, die unseren ganzen Körper in Bewegung bringen. Der Afrikanische Tanz mit seinen erdenden Schritten und Bewegungen hilft dem Körper, sich zu öffnen und 'fließen zu können.' Die Live-Musik unter-
stützt dies mit Klang und Rhythmus. In einfachen Übungen und Improvisationen mit Musik versuchen wir, den Rhythmus unserer Menstruation, die Bewegungen unserer Gebärmutter zu erspüren und Ausdruck zu finden für die besonderen Gefühlszustände während
der Menstruation, wie Bewegungsdrang, Bedürfnis nach Rückzug, wohlig-sein [sic],
Schmerzen usw. Zum Abschluss möchte ich mit Euch [sic] gemeinsam daraus unseren eigenen ,Menstruations-Tanz kreieren und tanzen" (quoted from a flyer promoting the dance
workshop "Tanz und Menstruation" led by Christa Flaig on September 18/19, 2004, at the
Tanzfabrik in Berlin-Kreuzberg).

References to rhythm as a very elemental human and, above all, bodily experience reappear over and over again in the promotional strategies of expressive specialists operating within the Afro scene. "Rhythm is a basic experience of every human being" we are for example informed. "Our heartbeat, our breath, tension, release, day and night."[13] Gordon's theory on rhythm, as he disclosed it in his weekly drumming classes and promotes it in his flyers, is that every human being is born with a natural rhythmic faculty. It is only that many people, particularly Westerners, "forget" or unlearn this natural faculty over the course of time. Part of his mission is then helping Germans to rediscover "their rhythm." Likewise, Mark Kofi Asamoah asks on his webpage: "Who has rhythm in his blood? […] Everyone on this earth has rhythm; it is just that many don't feel it. In my projects and workshops I show ways to feel rhythm, to sense and to live it — also for those who never experienced it!"[14]

Such a self-discovery of Europeans in expressive forms originating on the African continent is, of course, by no means a new phenomenon. The idea behind such processes of self-creation is closely tied to notions of the individual, individuality, and the importance of personal experience of the world as they were already developed in the romanticist movement in the eighteenth and nineteenth centuries (Hall 1992). We encounter similar conceptions of individualism and individual experience, of an essential Self which is identical only with itself, for example in the writings of Johann Gottfried Herder, such as in his *Ideas on the Philosophy of the History of Mankind* (cf. Carl 2004:89f.). The ideals of Historical Particularism as developed by Franz Boas and related notions of the uniqueness of "cultures" stand clearly in this tradition and we could argue that the discourse on world music has borrowed extensively from these, in the first place, academic ideologies. Hannerz reminds us that, from an anthropological point of view, individualism is by no means an individual, but rather a social affair, which is to say that individuality makes only sense in relation to others. Ideas about individuality and the individual must, in other words, be regarded "not as something residual, something outside the domain of culture, but at least in part as a product of cultural organization" (1996:39).

The forms of self-exploration and the production of individuality as we described them for the Afro scene are also reminiscent of earlier primitivist movements as they took place in Germany and Europe at the beginning of the

---

[13] Quoted from a flyer promoting a weekly course in African drumming organized by Babette Schwahlen in Berlin in 2004.

[14] "Wer hat Rhythmus im Blut? […] Jeder auf dieser Erde hat Rhythmus, nur fühlen viele ihn nicht. In meinen Projekten und Workshops zeige ich Wege auf, Rhythmus zu fühlen, zu spüren und zu leben — auch für diejenigen, die ihn noch nie erlebt haben!" (http://www.asamoah.de, accessed on July 08, 2007).

twentieth century — at the same time when Hornbostel (1928) was inventing African music as the ultimate Other. Meanwhile, other authors found Africa not all that different. In the world of art, African expressive forms and symbolism inspired cubism. A statement by Leo Frobenius is revealing with regard to how Africa impressed the youth and "back to nature" movements in the 1920s:

> For me the strangest thing about this Africa always appears to be the fact that its inside is so familiar to us. The most honorable Schweinfurth [a German traveler] used to call the Africans "summer Europeans." And who really apprehended this essence of Africa will understand the infinitely deep sense of the word. [...] Our youth demands nature; rediscovery of the oldest and simplest connections to nature, a return to naturalness. Art is calling for simplification. And out of this longing, the for us only now awakening style touches us in an opposed impulse: in the yearning for our own originality, which, out of this being Africa, out of this coarse stumpiness, this childlike naturalism, seems to be kindred to our own childhood.[15]

All in all, examining representational patterns employed within the Afro scene, it is true that we encounter common clichés about Africa and African music, images that clearly have their roots in earlier colonial discourses. Romantic visions of Africa are not only reinforced in advertising texts, they also appear as vivid images in the form of sunsets, beaches, palm trees, and so on.[16] If we think of the YAAM, which we portrayed in the previous chapter, we could argue that the representational space of this location is partly a reconstruction of a romanticized Africa (or, for that matter, the Caribbean). We find romanticized images of rural Africa as early as in the nineteenth century such as in travel literature (Carl 2004:62ff). African American utopias of the "motherland" are clearly inspired by such images, and they are also excessively used by

---

[15] "Als das Merkwürdigste an diesem Afrika erscheint mir immer wieder, daß sein Inneres uns so verwandt ist. Der ehrwürdigste Schweinfurth pflegte die Afrikaner ‚Sommereuropäer' zu nennen. Und wer dieses Wesen Afrikas innerlich erfaßt hat, ersieht den unendlich tiefen Sinn dieses Wortes. [...] Unsere Jugend fordert Natur. Wiederentdeckung ältester schlichter Naturverbindungen, Rückkehr zur Natürlichkeit. Die Kunst ruft nach Vereinfachung. Und aus diesem Sehnen heraus berührt uns der jetzt erst erwachende Stil in dem entgegengesetzten Triebe: im Drang nach eigener Ursprünglichkeit, die aus diesem Wesen Afrika, aus dieser ungeschlachten Plumpheit, diesem kindlichen Naturalismus heraus uns selbst, unserer eigenen Kindheit verwandt erscheint" (Frobenius 1923:4).
[16] The dance club Tam-Tam, for example, uses the "sunset and palm trees" image extensively on its flyers.

the tourist industry. Closely related are images of spirituality as we outlined them here. The African body as a somehow natural body and also as an object of erotic desire is similarly highlighted in many representations. Africa appears mostly as a "natural" and "authentic" entity in contrast to the "artificial" and "inauthentic" metropolis in these visions — just as the "African being" in Frobenius' text (which, by the way, clearly had an impact on African philosophies such as Négritude).

But at the same time it is important to note that it is not merely "Africa" and "African rhythm," but rather the Africa and African rhythm "in all of us" we keep reencountering within the symbolic economy of the Afro scene. As for African rhythm, it has well been noted that it is one of the most pervasive images associated with African music (Agawu 2003:55-70). Already Hornbostel in his account of *African Negro Music* (1928) remarked that "we [the Whites] proceed from hearing, they [the Blacks] from motion" (ibid.:26). In the third chapter we outlined the colonial discourse on African music and how the "primitive" was constructed against a superior European self by way of the ascription of an extraordinary rhythmic and mimetic faculty. While we agree with Agawu that "'African rhythm' […] is an invention, a construction, a fiction, a myth, ultimately a lie" (2003:61), the idea of the natural rhythmic ability of Africans is nevertheless common. Many participants in drumming and dancing workshops whom I spoke to reproduced the assumption that rhythm is somehow "in their blood" (*Det ham die doch im Blut!*). Through their self-accounts African expressive specialists reinforce such a view often enough. The macropolitics of style clearly highlights the basic binary opposition between "us" and "them." It is, however, important to bring to mind that drumming and dancing, as practiced in workshops as well as less structured jam sessions, are group activities; "African rhythm" is here a collective musical experience and not a representation.

Performing Performativity

In contrast to the common argument that a "primitive" Africa is invented as an exotic Other in order to reinforce a superior sense of a European Self, as a "lived representation" or performative practice African music takes place in a "space between" Self and Other. As outlined earlier, Taussig describes this process of identification as mimesis, that is, "the nature that culture uses to create second nature, the faculty to copy, imitate, make models, explore difference, yield into and become Other" (1993:xiii). What he calls the "wonder of mimesis" is more than just the evocation of dualisms in which Self and Other are opposed. This view reduces mimesis to a mere rhetorical strategy. Yet mimesis creates an affective link, a complex mutual relation and dependency between two elements. We described such a mimetic moment in the third chapter, when Portuguese explorers encountered local people at the Cape of Good Hope. The performance of music in that situation does not so much reinforce the opposition between Europeans and Africans, but rather represents the mutually dependent process of becoming human. For Taussig mimesis has a magical moment:

> To ponder mimesis is to become sooner or later caught […] in sticky webs of copy and contact, image and bodily involvement of the perceiver in the image, a complexity we too easily elide as nonmysterious, with our facile use of terms such as identification, representation, expression, and so forth — terms which simultaneously depend upon and erase all that is powerful and obscure in the network of associations conjured by the notion of the mimetic. (Taussig 1993:21)

Heading for the same end, though talking about it in slightly different terms, Deleuze and Guattari describe the formation of so-called "rhizomes" as such processes of becoming. For them, however,

> [m]imicry is a very bad concept, since it relies on a binary logic to describe phenomena of an entirely different nature. The crocodile does not reproduce a tree trunk, any more than the chameleon reproduces the colors of its surroundings. The Pink Panther imitates nothing, it reproduces nothing, it paints the world its color, pink on pink; this is its becoming-world, carried out in such a way that it becomes imperceptible itself, asignifying, makes its rupture, its own line of flight, follows its "apparallel evolution" through to the end. (Deleuze & Guattari 1987:11)

Whatever terms we employ for what Taussig calls "space between" and Deleuze and Guattari conceptualize as "rhizome," we are restricted to the realm of language and therefore caught up in the binary logic we are, at the same time, trying to overcome. Lived space, the space where "becoming-world," as Deleuze and Guattari in their somewhat esoteric rhetoric put it, takes place, is heterogeneous and cannot be reduced to matters of black and white or good and bad. To quote Foucault's account of heterotopic space once again:

> [W]e do not live in a kind of void, inside of which we could place
> individuals and things. We do not live inside a void that could be
> colored with diverse shades of light, we live inside a set of relations
> that delineates sites which are irreducible to one another and ab-
> solutely not superimposable on one another. (1986:23)

Tellingly Taussig as well as Deleuze and Guattari stress the role of music and
sensual phenomena in processes of transformation. "Music has always sent out
lines of flight, like so many 'transformational multiplicities,' even overturning
the very codes that structure or arborify it; that is why musical form, right
down to its ruptures and proliferations, is comparable to a weed, a rhizome"
(Deleuze & Guattari 1987:11f). Highlighting sensual experience, Taussig
writes, "contact and copy merge to become virtually identical, different mo-
ments of the one process of sensing; seeing something or hearing something is
to be in contact with that something" (1993:21). Though arguing from a quite
different philosophical angle, Gadamer (1998) has developed a similar view on
the process of hearing, and particularly with regard to the African-German
encounter Carl (2006) has stressed the catalytic nature of music in processes of
bodily transformation.

The neatly ordered space of the representational realm becomes much
more complex and messy when we encounter it as a lived experience. This
was the paradox of colonial space, and it is that of the contemporary culture
industry. For "scenesters" and participants in workshops, African music is not
something they solely, and not even primarily encounter in the form of textual
or symbolical representations, but as a practice that is commonly mediated by
an expressive specialist. Afro events as we described them in the previous
chapter are consciously staged as "holistic" sensual experiences and include
music, dance, food and other sensually pleasurable forms. We have noted that
a major characteristic feature of Afro events is the active involvement of the
audience in performances. Participation and collectivity are qualities that are
more generally ascribed to African music. In many of the "classical" publications on African music it is stressed that we are dealing with an essentially
communal affair.[17] Just like "rhythm," "participation" is a perpetual metaphor
of African music. We mentioned audience performances taking place at Afro
events, where dancers and also instrumentalists spontaneously join the performers on or in front of the stage, particularly towards the end of concerts.

---

[17] See for example Nketia (1974) or Chernoff (1979).

Ebron made similar observations with regard to performances of Madinka music in North American settings. She describes for example one performance, which was categorized as world music or New Age event. When the concert started and the music went on for a while, "a few young white people got up and started to dance in the aisles, throwing their bodies around with an abandonment that suggested they were listening to a different melody or set of tunes than those of us who remained in our seats" (2002:57). As she continues to explain,

> the dancers re-imagined [the music] within their hearing of "African music." Such dancers had been affectionately referred to by a colleague of mine as "the organic dancers" when we watched a similar event. The audience performers were not an unfamiliar sight; they often appear at world music events, dressed with a fashion sense most immediately derived from the 1960s. [...] The dancers appeared to seek a release from the restraints of everyday life. Moreover, their display seemed part of an already prepared script. Their response to the music reminded me of [...] popular ideas about African music [...]: it is rhythm; it transcends reason to touch the spirit. Their response, although awkward in relation to the music, resonated with broader configurations of "The Africa." (ibid:57f)

We have probably all an idea about what kind of people Ebron is talking here. I would nevertheless argue that what is performed here is not the mimicry of an image of African music, re-imagined by the "organic dancers" as a rhythmic and spiritual affair. If that would be the case, world music would indeed be not much more than "an 'empty' semantic field" (Erlmann 1999:181). As Erlmann, in a general critique of "globalized" forms of music, further writes: "[T]he globalized and rampant musics of late modernity are arbitrary indeed and no longer mediate [...] culture specific processes of appropriation of the external world" (ibid.:187). And he continues to argue:

> What makes such musics a-semantic is the transformation that has occurred in the meaning, as it were, of meaning. Meaning itself recedes into the spaces between different spheres of meaning. Difference itself is the meaning; it is the fact that different cultural repertoires are being put into the global circulation. Global musical sounds, then, do not speak. World beat is no messenger. Rather, it is action — action that mediates nothing but action. (ibid.:189)

Regarded this way, a performance like the above described would be more or less meaningless, a mere embodiment of difference for difference's sake. At best, we could see it as an expression of the alienation of "Western" audiences from themselves, leading a meaningless life in the meaningless world of "late modernity." This is, of course, an exaggeration, but the way "globalized musics" are discussed in the quoted passages reveals the major shortcoming of the discourse on world music. The assumed consumers of so-called world music appear as a taken-for-granted mass of "Western listeners," generally surmising homogeneity in background, taste, and aesthetic preferences. Such a view is ultimately related to simplified notions of a fundamental difference between Europe and Africa, "the West" and "the rest," white and black, in that it constructs a binary opposition between "us" and "them" — here in the form of good (critical) listeners and bad (uncritical) listeners, adherents of the aesthetically valuable and adherents of "trash."

In contrast to Erlmann, Ebron acknowledges the performative nature of reception and refers to the releasing quality of the audience performance she describes. But I disagree with her reading of the performance as a mere reenactment of representational modes. It is not so much the common images of Africa and African music that are represented or reenacted through performance. The musical forms circulating in the Afro scene are appropriated and transformed in the process of performance beyond their representation. What is performed, I would argue, is performativity itself — not as a reenactment of the most obvious and pervasive themes associated with African music, but as the act of becoming a performer oneself.

As a matter of fact, it is through African music and more particularly through an expressive specialist that many people discover their own capabilities as a musical performer. For the majority of participants in drumming workshops I spoke to drumming was actually their first experience in active music-making and they considered themselves rather "not musical" in the first place. Notions of a "natural" musical ability and African performativity are relativized by the experience that the quality of performance rests largely on practice. There are, after all, many Germans who have become decent drummers, some of them offering workshops themselves. For students of African music the choice of a teacher who meets their individual needs and abilities is more important than vague notions of African musicality, and differences in style are well noted. Somebody told me for example that she preferred "Ga rhythms from Ghana" to the "Malinke style" mostly taught by Senegalese and Gambians, which she considered "old-fashioned." The Ghanaian rhythms would match better with her predilection for electro festivals, where she would also drum. This brings to mind a statement by Feld quoted earlier, namely that "appropriation means that the question 'Whose music?' is submerged, supplanted, and subverted by the assertion 'Our/my music'" (Feld 1994a:238). What is at the heart of performances as the one outlined by Ebron or like the concert at the Werkstatt der Kulturen we described in the previous chapter is not so much the enactment of an "us" versus a "them," or, as Erlmann has it, of "difference itself," but rather the performance of performativity, the performed assertion that "this is my music, this is me."

8 Traveling With Culture

In Search of Africa

The first time I traveled to the Volta Region was in late 2004. A friend of mine, Charles, took me to his "village" or "hometown," to Tegbi in the Keta District. While in Accra I had been the *oburoni* or, depending in which part of the city I was, people called me *brofonyo*, in the Volta Region I became a *yevu*. People welcomed me, "Yevu, woezor," as we walked through the sandy alleys of Tegbi, and the children who followed us sang "Yevu, yevu, ge yibor, ta, ta, ge yibor" ("White man, white man with the black beard..."). For the children our presence was a welcome change in the otherwise rather eventless town of Tegbi. Keta, which is the district capital, literally means "on top of the sand" in Ewe, which describes the geographical location of the towns in this part of the country, strung along the narrow tongue of land between the Gulf of Guinea and the Keta Lagoon, quite well.

Between the 1900 and the 1990s, before the "sea defense project" was put into place, large parts of the settlements around the Lagoon slowly disappeared in the water due to erosion caused by the sea. Many people lost their houses and had to be relocated. And many just left the area to try their luck in the city. Though it appears quite tidy, this part of the country is considered "deprived" and jobs are rare. Apart from a few guesthouses, the potentials for tourism have not been developed yet, though the road to Accra is now in a very good condition and it takes only roughly two hours to Ghana's capital. Most people who got somewhere, that is, who were capable of accumulating at least a little wealth, live either in Accra or abroad nowadays. Not a few houses in this area are empty most of the time. The properties are left to aged relatives and house keepers, and it is only for the funerals at weekends, when somebody has died, that people come back — often even as far as from North America or Europe. The out-migration of labor force in the southern Volta Region is high.[1]

---

[1] See statistical data on the Keta district on the website http://www.ghanadistricts.com (accessed on June 5, 2007). For an excellent eco-social history of the southern Volta Region see Akyeampong (2001).

Two weeks later, also in December 2004, Charles and I traveled to the area again, this time to attend a funeral in Anloga. The grandfather of a friend of Charles whose family comes from Anloga passed away, and she therefore invited us to her hometown. She and Charles and a couple of other friends who also attended the funeral were all members of the Dance Factory, the junior ensemble of the National Theatre. We arrived in Anloga on a Friday afternoon. At the funeral celebration, in the yard of the family house in which the corpse was laid out, a local drumming group performed and people danced *agbadza* — a dance that I also learned (more or less by force) that afternoon. In the evening, then, a sound system took over to entertain the guests, and we enjoyed ourselves oscillating between the family house, where people danced to the latest highlife and hiplife hits, and the drinking spot around the corner.

The next day, on Saturday, the celebration continued in a similar manner. In the afternoon the local drumming group played again. Since people knew that some "culture people" from Accra were present at the funeral, the members of the Dance Factory were asked to give a small performance as well. They started presenting some "modern" dances of almost acrobatic nature, which they danced to a recorded tape they had brought, and which combined the most diverse elements, from breakdance to more traditional African patterns. Then they switched to a more traditional repertoire, and after a while the local drumming group simultaneously began to play again. From that point onward the whole performance took more the shape of a competition. Everybody wanted to show his or her skills. People particularly enjoyed the dancing and showed their appreciation by "dashing" money to the dancers. Two of the dancers who were originally from Accra and couldn't understand the Ewe language told me afterwards that they felt quite uncomfortable during the performance. They were actually worried that the local people could spiritually cause them harm. The Ewe, they told me, are good in "those things." In Ghana they have indeed the reputation of being rather "traditional" people, people who stick to their customs (which is probably why ethnologists like studying them so much).

Be that as it may, when we came to the Volta Region this time — it was already late January 2005 — we were on a different mission. For the last two months since Ofei and I had arrived in Ghana, Ofei had been busy reorganizing his group. Mostly I followed him on his endless tours through Accra, visiting group members to convince them to rejoin Nortseme. Following Ofei was the best way for me to get to know the city, the geography of which confused me for several weeks due to the complete lack of landmarks — except for a few higher buildings in the city center. My presence during what was largely Ofei's mission seemed natural enough to most people. Everybody knew that the

Whites had a special interest in African culture, and for Ofei to bring a white student from Europe was also a way of doing his people a favor. Charles, the master drummer of Nortseme who was supposed to become my drumming teacher, but who in the end mostly took me around and linked me up with people, surely profited the most from me. And I undoubtedly profited the most from him. Teaching and taking white students around, he told me, was his job. He had done this before, mostly for Americans. For me in turn, as ethnomusicologist "in the field," being taken around was somehow my job, so the two of us complemented one another excellently.

Still in Berlin Ofei had repeatedly told me how much he missed his group in Ghana and that he wanted to bring them to Germany. When he told me that he would travel to Ghana to produce a promotional video with them and asked me whether I would like to accompany him, I didn't have to think twice. Now, after the sometimes stressful efforts of the proceeding weeks to bring the people back together, I actually wondered whether Ofei didn't wish himself back to Germany sometimes. Ofei had assumed that Nortseme continued to rehearse in his absence, which was not the case. Thus, the first two weeks or so after our arrival in Accra, before Nortseme even started to practice again, there were endless discussions and meetings. Ofei had to explain to the group members why it was necessary to produce another promotional video, and why the first one they had done two years before had not led to the desired success. There was tension and mistrust between Ofei and the group members. Some suspected Ofei of doing his own business with the video CDs, selling them in Europe without sharing the profit with the rest of the group. Ofei tried to explain that the material they had was just "too local," that they needed better recordings in order to promote Nortseme successfully. In any case, the plans to get the group a chance to travel abroad remained an unfulfilled promise.

We had explored the area around Anyako, located on the northern banks of the Keta Lagoon, on New Year's Day. "I want something antique for the video coverage," Ofei told me, something like a "real" African village as he imagined it to be in the "olden days," before there was electric light, television, and the like. This had been the image we had also used as backdrop for the scenes we recorded at the training ground in Teshie in Accra, where Ofei managed to organize a huge cloth from the requisites of the National Theatre on which the "classical" African village scene — a round hut and a baobab tree — was painted. It turned out to be much more difficult than we thought to find this imagined African idyll in reality (not to mention the fact that huts in southern Ghana had always been square-cut and not round, even in the "olden days"). A friend of Charles, who lived in Anyako, served as "location scout" in the area that neither Ofei nor Charles knew very well. After they had explained what we were looking for, we sifted through the surrounding area, inspecting different dwellings and homesteads, until we found an old barn built of mud with a thatched roof. The building seemed to meet what Ofei had meant by "antique" or "traditional," though the people who depended on the structure economically considered it probably just antiquated. Maybe they used the (comparatively little) money Ofei gave them for using their premises as a setting for his video to buy a new aluminum roof for the barn after we left the place.

The shooting of all scenes for the promotional video took roughly a week, including the scenes we recorded in Accra as well as those in the Volta Region. My job was that of the second cameraman. And even though Ofei sometimes doubted whether he would ever accomplish this goal, on January 18, 2005, Nortseme finally traveled from Accra to Anyako in the group's old Mercedes Benz bus (by then the journey still took about three and a half hours, since the new road was not completed yet). Right after we arrived at the old barn Ofei had chosen as background for the recordings, we began unpacking the drums from the roof of the bus and putting up the equipment. Ofei's parents-in-law, who specially came from Germany to Ghana to help Ofei with his video (his wife's father was a passionate amateur film-maker and therefore had the proper equipment), were at first a little worried that filming in "the village" could include images which would be "too brutal" for a German audience, since one might see too much poverty on them. But just as the recordings we did in Teshie conveyed, after all, "a quite nice illusion of Africa, just as one would imagine it," as his father-in-law put it, our only problem with the old barn was actually to keep the overhead power lines that showed up behind the thatch and which didn't fit into the "antique Africa" we tried to cover out of the picture.

We continued to record different songs and dances the next day, but in a different location. It was a mere coincidence that Ofei discovered these three or four "antique" houses or huts, at least as old as the barn, in the middle of the landscape when we passed by — a meager dwelling place without flowing water or electricity. Perfect! So he spontaneously decided to do some more recordings. After bargaining with the old residents who sat in front of one of the houses we began to unpack the instruments and equipment again. We should only make sure, the old people told Ofei, not to step into their shrine (which was one of the structures) and also not into the small forest which adjoined the yard in between the houses on one side. These spaces were reserved for their ancestral spirits. That wouldn't be a problem. Only for some of the group members the idea of being surrounded by spiritual forces they didn't really know left an uncanny feeling. But Ofei was the boss. It took about three or four hours, until early afternoon, to complete all recordings, and the sun got hotter and hotter. The batteries for the camera would not have taken us much further anyway. While at first the old residents amusedly watched our activities in their yard, they soon went back to normal and most of them dozed off in the midday heat.

After we finished with the recordings everyone was exhausted. We must have exhibited a bizarre picture as we sat in the shadow of the Mercedes bus, a horde of townspeople drinking lukewarm "pure water" from these small plastic sachets one gets everywhere in Ghana, around us the clucking of hens, and in the background the shrine and the dozing residents. Somebody had tuned in to a Togolese station in the car radio, which played a strange mixture of French chansons, German Schlager, and American country music and which, after all the Ga "folk music" and other "traditional" Ghanaian music and dance, made the whole scene even more absurd. I received a text message on my mobile phone from a friend in Germany. While my phone had reception and I could call Germany from this place, the people who lived there didn't even have electric light. This is probably what they call globalization. I think I replied to my friend in Germany, telling him about the absurdity of the moment, before we packed our things and drove back to Accra.

Tradition and Culture. Or: Learning How To Fly

Performing and teaching African music or dance in the periphery of Europe's world music economy is not what the "average" Ghanaian would necessarily strive for. As we already discussed in connection with the social types of the *burger* and the *beento*, which epitomize the successful migrant, "making it big" abroad is a potent image in Ghanaian social discourse. "Doing culture," in contrast, is at best regarded an agreeable hobby for schoolchildren in Ghana, but in terms of achieving a prosperous living many consider it useless or even counterproductive. Drummers and dancers I talked to in Accra as well as Berlin repeatedly told me how much their parents disliked the fact that they put more efforts into learning "culture" than studying science and math. On campus, at the University of Ghana in Legon, classes in dancing and drumming or other African instruments, as they are taught in the School of Performing Arts, are derogatorily referred to as "dondology" — the *dondo* being an hourglass, or, "talking" drum — and music and dance students are looked down on by fellow students in other departments and schools.

As much as the cultural heritage of the country is highlighted when it comes to celebrating Independence Day and the nation, in everyday life drumming and dancing in Ghana is often considered something for people who did not learn anything better — and for the Whites, of course, who travel as far as from Europe, Australia, or North America to learn about "African culture." This is the paradox of what is referred to "culture" in Ghana: While musicologist J. H. Kwabena Nketia, professor emeritus at Legon who introduced African studies as an academic discipline at the University of Ghana and, thereby, contributed to not an insignificant degree to the formation of a national identity, received an award at the "Ghana@50 Music Awards" festival for his lifetime achievements (Agyei-Twum 2007), some fathers would beat their children if they hear that they dream of becoming a drummer or a dancer rather than a lawyer, an engineer, a finance accountant, or a medical practitioner.

Nonetheless, "culture" is a means to get in contact with Europeans (which means it is a potential source of income), and it is also a means to travel abroad. A dancer in Accra told me that it was only when he had the chance to travel to Italy, France, and Spain as a member of a cultural group that his father accepted what he is doing. In a conversation I had with Kay and Ofei in Berlin, Kay compared the culture scene in Accra to football. Culture, he explained, is like football. There would be hundreds of young men who claim to be drummers and whose ultimate goal is to travel abroad. Since the job opportunities are few, particularly for those with little education, the competition among drummers and dancers would be very high. Just like in football, everybody would dream of becoming a star abroad. But unlike football — at least as far as the national team, the "Black Stars", is concerned —, politicians in Ghana have mostly lost their interest in cultural politics. As Nketia said, "Nkrumah begun to think of culture in institutional terms. The strategy of cultural action in the post-colonial era was inclusive." In contrast to that, nowadays "culture has ceased to be a political priority" (quoted in Atafori 2006). In an interview I conducted in Accra, a dancer put it this way:

> Normally, here in Africa, our presidents don't sponsor us. They only put their mind on football. […] We culture [people], we struggle before we travel. It's hard for us to get a visa to travel. But, if a president is coming from Europe […] they come and invite a cultural troupe to come and dance for him. But our president […] puts his mind on football. So I wish, in my mind, one day, if a president is coming, they should invite the footballers to […] the airport to go

and play football there.[2]

There is, as people explained to me, a basic difference between what is considered "tradition" and what is referred to as "culture" in Ghana. This difference is embodied in the performance at Anloga as I recounted it in the first section of this chapter. Both groups that performed at the funeral, the local drumming group and the Dance Factory, relied on similar resources. But "tradition," as a drummer in Accra put it, is "raw" while "culture" is "polished" or "choreographed." The group in Anloga performed "traditional" Ewe music; the Dance Factory's repertoire includes dances from all regions in Ghana and beyond, as well as "contemporary" dances and "dance dramas" combining a number of dances in a single choreography. Culture, then, is choreographed tradition. For cultural groups in Accra — and there are, today, virtually hundreds of such groups — broadness and diversity in repertoire as well as inventiveness and creatively developing one's own ideas on the basis of "traditional" material are widely shared aesthetic ideals. Traditional groups usually stick to the repertoire of a particular region.[3]

Travel as a means of learning and expand one's repertoire by visiting different places is therefore an integral part of the concept of culture in Ghana. "You have to move around, the groups that are surrounding you. You have to move", the leader of a cultural group in Accra told me, "you have to make friends among the people in the culture. Maybe [someone] knows something I don't know."[4] It is not only the idea that performing "culture" might help to travel to Europe or North America; travel in the sense of educative study trips was a concept most drummers, dancers, and other people involved in the cultural business whom I spoke to in Accra highlighted. Many had traveled to other African countries mostly in West Africa, such as Togo, Benin, or Ivory Coast in order to learn different styles of drumming and dancing. A dancer in Accra explained to me:

ANSWER: [There are] the traditional dances. And we have the creative dance, and we have the contemporary dance, mixed with cas-

---

[2] The interview was conducted on January 16, 2005.
[3] This, I should stress, is basically the perspective of people active in cultural groups in Accra. As we discussed in chapter five, there is, and has probably always been, an exchange and reciprocity between performing groups and their repertoires in the cities and in rural areas. Unlike the "typical" cultural group, which will perform dances from all regions in Ghana and maybe from other African countries, there are also ethnic associations in Accra that concentrate on a single tradition, for example Ewe groups performing only *borborbor* music from the northern Volta Region.
[4] Quoted from an interview conducted on January 25, 2005.

sette and music.

QUESTION: So you do all those things?

ANSWER: I do all those things. I do traditional dances and contemporary. Yeah, I do those things, both. Because, nowadays, if you want to learn only one side, you fall in some trouble. Because, you go to some place, you go and meet different group. They'll be doing different things. Maybe you haven't done those things before — it will be very hard for you. So these days, it's not like… You will be doing most of the things, like contemporary dances and… in Africa… Because most of the Whites came down to come and learn our drumming and that kind of thing. Why doesn't we also learn about their dancing and that kind of thing? Especially people in Senegal, they dance a Senegalese dance, they flick, they jump, and that kind of thing. So, you also have to learn how to fly. They dance on their knees, so you also have to study that kind of thing. […] If you are a dancer, you have to study many dances. If you go to Togo, they have different traditional dancing in Togo. If you go to Benin, they have different dancing in Benin. And at the same time in Côte d'Ivoire. The same with Senegal. If you come to South Africa — different thing. So, you have to go to some places and study the dancing.[5]

In a way, individuals and groups in the cultural scene have an academic approach to performance and the acquisition of knowledge about performance practices, which parallels the approach to "music culture" promoted by disciplines like ethnomusicology. "Culture" in the sense of choreographed traditional drumming and dancing can, after all, be regarded as a popularized academic tradition, just as the usage of the culture concept in everyday discourse. It is no coincidence that the cultural troupes as we find them in Ghana today are modeled after the first state-sponsored group initiated by Nketia, the Ghana Dance Ensemble, which was initially attached to the then School of Music and Drama at the University of Ghana in Legon. This was also one of the first groups to travel abroad to promote Ghanaian drumming and dancing. As Mustapha Tettey Addy, today a widely recognized performer of Ghanaian music, who studied at Legon in the early 1960s, remembered:

ANSWER: I learned from my brothers. My older brothers were drummers, dancers. […] Then I went to university.

---

[5] The interview was conducted on December 16, 2004.

QUESTION: Here in Legon?

ANSWER: Yeah, the School of Music and Drama by then. For four years. I met so many cultures, from Ghana and from Nigeria, from Togo, you know. So I became very interested in… 1963 — that was the time of the School of Music and Drama. […] Professor Nketia was the master, the president of all the… business. He was the father, the teacher, the founder… of all this business about African studies. […] Sixty-four I went with the School of Music and Drama to East Germany, West Germany, Russia, Poland, and Hungary, you know. That was 1964, when the School of Music and Drama […] assembled so many music and dance from Ghana. So we went out to show the rest of the world. When we came back they […] turned it into the Ghana Dance Ensemble. And then later they moved to National Theatre.

QUESTION: How was that experience to travel, particularly in those days when not many people had this opportunity?

ANSWER: During those days a lot of Ghanaians went outside, especially Germany. Doctors, they studied medicine… you know, a lot of Ghanaians were traveling long, long time before sixty-three, sixty-four… because… I remember most of my friends, they got scholarship to study medicine in Germany, in Hungary, Russia. They traveled a lot. But this kind of business, drumming and dancing, I would say the School of Music and Drama were the first to do this traveling with culture.[6]

Addy was not only among the first to "travel with culture" after independence, he was also one of the first to organize workshops for African drumming in Germany in the 1970s and to bring students from Europe to Ghana to study drumming and dancing.

My first major concert [in Germany] was at the Olympic Games in Munich in 1972. I first settled in Essen, later I moved to Düsseldorf. I started to form my own band called Ehimomo. This was the band that included my nephew Aja Addy. At that time I met a German percussion enthusiast who had this idea to establish the Werkstatt, a center for African arts, dance, theater and music [today the Tanzhaus NRW]. In this center we organized a lot of workshops

---

[6] The interview was conducted at Kokrobitey, where Mustapha Tettey Addy founded the Academy of African Music and Arts, on January 23, 2005.

and concerts. In 1980 I started to bring percussion students to
Ghana: I think that people who are interested in African drumming
should study it in its natural surrounding, where they can practice
better and more often. After that everyone started to do workshops
in Ghana, but I was the first.[7]

There are a number of schools and "cultural centers" in Accra and along the
Ghanaian coast today, which were modeled after the School of Performing
Arts as well as Addy's Academy of African music and Arts, such as the Kasapa
Centre, Akuma Village, or the Odehe Centre. Most of these projects combine
workshops in drumming and dancing with other offers in cultural tourism.[8]
Just as in Addy's case, these centers and the attached cultural groups are managed in a similar fashion, that is, they are organized around a per-
former/teacher who is commonly based abroad. A German-Ghanaian couple
that initially worked together with Mustapha Tettey Addy initiated the Kasapa
project, for example, and Odehe is lead by Emmanuel Gomado who lives in
Bremen, Germany. His Odehe Dance Company tours in Germany and other
parts of the world every year to perform at festivals and other occasions. In
most cities they perform they also give workshops in African drumming and
dance.

It is interesting to note that former students of Mustapha Tettey Addy
founded many of the drumming schools we find in the area around Düsseldorf
today. It is not only Africans or Ghanaians who copied what Addy claims was
his initial idea, but there are also many schools run by Germans.[9] This was,
after all, a general complaint I heard from African drummers and dancers,
that "first you teach them what you know, and then they start their own workshops." It might sound paradox at first, but in a way Germans have even an
advantage on the cultural market. As Whites, being ethnically or racially unmarked, they cannot promote themselves with reference to their African heritage. This "racial neutrality" allows white Germans, at the same time, to offer
a greater stylistic diversity, including not only all sorts of African styles, but in
addition also Latin American percussion (by far the most popular drumming

[7] Quoted from an interview published at http://www.weltwunder.com/mta.html (accessed on June 10, 2007). See also the biography of Mustapha Tettey Addy on the same webpage.
[8] See the websites http://www.kasapa.de, http://www.akumavillage.com and http://www.odehe.com (all accessed on June 10, 2007). Akuma village, in addition to a cultural program and offering workshops in drumming and dancing, lately also introduced yoga, meditation and massage.
[9] To give but a few examples see the webpages http://www.trommeln-in-duesseldorf.de, http://www.trommelschule.de, or http://www.ubuntu-krefeld.de (all accessed on June 11, 2007).

style in Germany at the moment is Brazilian samba percussion). On the other hand, performers like Mustapha Addy feel that also some Africans spoil the market by offering poor quality and taking advantage of the fact that as Africans they are perceived as "natural" musicians by many Germans. As he said:

ANSWER: Some of the Germans are fools, because any African they see, they think it's a drummer. So they believe all this what they play […]. So any motherfucker African will go there and say: "Oh, I'm a drummer!" And they believe it, you know. […] Nowadays, it's too many fake drummers around. […] I have a German guy who is professor in percussion. He was here [at Kokrobitey] for three months, four months… a friend of mine. They are very good. The German drummers, they are very, very good. I have women, women who — I teach them here, they have a women group in Germany. When they play kpanlogo, you hear that it's proper, original.

QUESTION: In how far would you say this culture thing changed over the years? Nowadays, I saw there are many, many groups in Accra.

ANSWER: It has changed a lot. The original things… Like I said, it is going to come from Germany. The original drummers are coming to teach, next time, in the next years, they are coming from America and Germany to teach Ghana people here. It is going to happen like that. Because… You see, we are not serious any more. We want everything from Europe, from America. So we are going to loose all those things. […] It's going to be different. Only few people are going to be playing drums in Africa one day, few. Because, when they go to university, they qualify, they become engineer, they stop drumming. […] They become pastor, pastor… the preachers, you know. It's going to be like that. Especially we have some people in America who are very serious. They study the original, the old Ghanaian drumming, or, African drumming, or… They are all over Africa! These people — most of them are white people, but they are serious. Because they know what is going to happen in future… of course. Nobody can stop it.[10]

Many other people told me about "fake drummers." Talking about other drummers who are not "serious," who would not know how to drum properly, is for many people in the scene certainly a strategy to legitimize their own

---

[10] Interview on January 23, 2005.

skills. On a different level, what we see in such statements is also a fear of cultural loss that goes beyond mere competition on the global cultural market. We are basically dealing with a dilemma, a development that "nobody can stop," as Addy put it. On the one hand the competition among people in the cultural scene in Ghana is much higher today than it might have been in the 1960s. People confirmed to me that in terms of mere quantity, there are much more people involved in the business than thirty or forty years ago, and there are much more cultural groups to be found in Accra. This has to do with an increase in tourism, and it forces individuals to be more inventive and original — not in the sense of practicing the "real" or "authentic" tradition, but in the sense to have "one's own style" in order to be distinguishable, as we discussed it in the previous chapter. On the other hand these circumstances bring about the feeling of cultural loss generally associated with processes of globalization, the feeling that things are not done "properly" any more. But, and this might be worse, due to the fact that some tourists come particularly to learn African drumming and dancing, there is also a feeling that Whites now take over the last refuge of what was once considered quintessentially African, namely, drumming and dancing.

Imagining the White Man's Land

Anxieties about cultural loss are associated with the (felt as well as real) act of "selling one's culture." In an interview one drummer even referred to what he is doing as "selling himself." Focusing on the West African cultural institution of the *jali*, or griot, Ebron (2002:167ff) describes these ambivalences for The Gambia and shows how postcolonial discourses intersect with the dilemmas that become apparent in the wake of different forms of contemporary tourism. On a theoretical level the ambiguities that are involved here have been described as the dialectics of the global and the local (Appadurai 1996:178ff) or by some authors as the dialectics of "flow and closure" (Geschiere & Meyer 1999).[11] This concerns issues about the uneven distribution of power in the globalized world, the fact that cultural production and the distribution of knowledge are inseparable from questions of political, economic, and technological power.

---

[11] Connell and Gibson have developed a similar approach in their attempt to develop a musical geography and suggest thinking about music in terms of fluidity and fixity (2003:9-11).

It is important to note that the very concept on which constructions of collective identity are based, namely "culture," is an imported one in West Africa, which causes a contradiction that goes to the heart of any cultural identity. And if we look into the history of the concept, culture turns out to be something which is always already lost, something that has to be (re)discovered or restored (Fabian 1983; Stocking 1982). We mostly remember "our culture," when we feel that we do not "have" it any more, or, at least to a lesser degree. The concept of culture evolved with modern travel practices as they were professionalized in academic disciplines such as anthropology or ethnology (Clifford 1992), and eventually also in ethnomusicology. For Europeans in the nineteenth century the search for their own "lost cultural past" led them, among other places, to Africa where they found the assumed "contemporary ancestors." For Europeans and Africans in search of culture and tradition today, the same search likewise leads them out of the cities into remote areas, into villages that are supposedly less "contaminated" by Western lifestyle.

When asked about culture, people in Ghana initially gave me some sort of Taylorian definition of the term, understood as a "whole way of life." For example: "Culture is how we live, how we dress, how we eat, how we talk, how we walk, et cetera, et cetera. That mean[s] culture. Culture is not only one thing, it's a lot of things."[12] Yet, in conversations it became apparent that culture as a "way of doing things" really meant a "way how things were done" originally, in an imagined and somehow sterile cultural past. "We've turned ourselves to Babylon, to the European way of life," somebody commented for example. The cultural self is imagined as a primordial self. In addition, culture, which Europeans ever since the nineteenth century invented as the Other, is imagined as a quality Africans posses while Europeans do not, or at least to a lesser degree. As somebody (referring to "culture" in the sense of "cultural repertoire") commented: "Africans, we have the talent in culture [more] than the Whites. It's true. You know, the culture that is going on in this world, the majority [is] from Africa. The majority from Africa."[13]

Some aspects that are involved in this discourse already came up in our discussions in previous chapters, for example in our outline of the debate about president Kufuor's dress code on Independence Day. What is concerned here is basically the question: What is African culture, and how is Africa positioned against the dominance of the West? This quest for identity, the search for the "African personality," as Nkrumah coined it (in the wake of the fiftieth anniversary celebrations, the term "Ghanaian personality" also popped

---

[12] Quoted from an interview with a dancer in Accra on January 16, 2005.
[13] Quoted from an interview conducted on January 25, 2005.

up frequently in the Ghanaian media), which was answered in nationalistic and culturalist terms in the early post-independence Ghana, is increasingly discussed with regard to the conditions of a globalized world. And these questions are discussed in highly racialized terms as well. It is not only in view of European (post)colonial domination that questions of an African — and that means an essentially black — identity are negotiated; a globalized mediascape, debates on "cultural imperialism," and the presence of Lebanese, Chinese, or Indian immigrants in a country like Ghana likewise contribute to this discourse.[14]

While in the previous chapters we discussed questions of racialized identities primarily with regard to the construction of blackness — the debates around "African" performances in the zoo were most obviously concerned with questions how blackness is constructed vis-à-vis an unracialized, European Self —, there is also a growing body of literature on the question how whiteness is constructed.[15] In an instructive essay Nyamnjoh and Page (2002), for example, have outlined the discourse on Whites and constructions of whiteness in Cameroon. Their general observations with regard to Cameroonian identity constructions hold also true for Ghanaian social discourse. They write:

> In the 'West' to be 'white' is not to have a race. In Cameroon to be white is to be sufficiently different to be constantly remarked upon. Just as white gazes on black, so black, also, gazes on white. Yet, all too often, discussions of alterity have portrayed only the 'Occident' as the bearer of the gaze and the maker of meaning, whilst the 'Orient', the 'African' or the 'Other' is left as the passive object of Western curiosity. The interlocking of gazes is ignored. (Nyamnjoh & Page 2002:608f)

We thus have to consider that "both white and non-white are the makers of the meaning of whiteness" and, just as for black identity constructions in Cameroon, the (black) Ghanaian self is "maintained through the production of the white as other" (ibid.:609). Both studies of blackness and whiteness are based on the assumption that "race is given meaning through the agency of

---

[14] For a revealing article how these questions are negotiated in the context of charismatic Christianity in Ghana see Meyer (1999). On questions of identity in a globalized context more generally see Geschiere & Meyer (1999). Particularly on the Lebanese diaspora in West Africa and especially in Ghana, see Akyeampong (2000:200-203 and 2006).

[15] For an overview on "critical whiteness studies" and the introduction of this approach in German academia see Arndt et al. (2005).

human beings in concrete historical and social contexts, and is not a biological or natural category" (Roediger 1994:2). In Ghanaian discourse, whiteness is discussed in a number of terms and, parallel to the Cameroonian case, also with regard to the "imaginative geography of the 'whiteman kontri,'" as Nyamnjoh and Page (2002:609) put it. I became acquainted with this imagined geography on my first trip to Ghana. When I was about to return to Germany, somebody asked me whether I could deliver a letter for him. He had a friend in the U.S. and since he didn't trust the Ghana Postal Service, he wanted to ask me this favor, assuming I would travel to the same place where his friend lived. I tried to explain that Germany and the U.S. are on two different continents. Yet, on many Ghanaian imaginary maps terms like U.S., U.K., New York, London, Germany, Hamburg, Netherlands, Italy, and so on, all denote the same territory: the white man's land. This imagined territory evokes powerful and contradictory images — a land of inconceivable riches and an easy living, yet at the same time a land of selfishness, immorality, and materialistic excess.

If in the West to be white means not to have a race, in West Africa you are constantly reminded that you are white and, therefore, different. The white body causes fear and curiosity; some people try to touch your hair or your skin. There are a number of myths circulating about the white body, and while on one level Whites and light skinned persons (labeled "half-castes" in Ghana) are admired (as a white man in Ghana, it might happen that women on the street will ask you not only to marry them and take them to Europe, which is often the case, but sometimes just to impregnate them, to give them a white baby), Whites are at the same time detested. As Nyamnjoh and Page, summarizing some of the common prejudices against Whites, write:

> Whites are seen as cruel, exploitative, selfish, arrogant, jealous, ignorant, racist, hypocritical, violent, unemotional, physically weak, cunning, deaf to rhythm, unable to eat African food, not very attractive, cold, shabby, unnatural, unreliable in friendship, far behind in terms of body hygiene, and incapable of putting in full tackles in football. (2002:615)

At the same time Whites are seen a means to have a good life and travel to the West. "If only I could find a white girl to marry, I could solve at least some of my problems," was a comment I heard in this and other forms many times from men in Ghana. As Nyamnjoh and Page argue for Cameroon:

> Whites continue to be perceived both as vehicles for, and obstacles

to, the realization of dreams of the West and Western "way of life."
[...] The *whiteman*, seen essentially as 'a wallet on legs' or a ticket to
the good life, is the centre of competing struggles by young ladies
dreaming of future abundance, first in a high-class residential area
somewhere in Douala or Yaoundé (the local epicentres of modern
metropolitan sophistication), and subsequently in Europe or North
America. Every visit to the nightclubs, bars, cafés, or beaches frequented by whites, seems like playing the American citizenship lottery. (Nyamnjoh & Page 2002:612)

There are a number of terms that are used for Europeans in Ghana, such as
Akwasi Broni, oburoni, White man, White, brofonyo, among others. *Oburoni* or *brofonyo*, the first being from the Akan language, the latter derived from Ga, are
mostly translated as "white man" or just "White" (the terms are used for men
and women alike). Yet, these terms are not the linguistic equivalents to racial
constructions as we find them in European languages, if we compare it to the
(still often heard) German term *Neger* ("Negro"), for example, which clearly
denotes a "black" person, not to speak of the offensive connotations and associated inferiority it implies. Though often translated this way, *oburoni* does literally not mean "a white person." The term is, for example, also employed for
African Americans or Afro-Germans and likewise for Asians. As Roediger observed in Ghana:

> It is not possible to travel far without encountering vivid evidence
> that race is a socially constructed ideology rather than a biologically
> determined category. In Ghana's Ashanti Region, where this is be-
> ing written, we are greeted on the streets by children who chant
> '*Oburoni koko maakye*'. English-speaking Ashantis often translate this as
> 'Red white man, good morning'. Similarly, *oburoni wawu*, the term
> for used Western clothing, is charmingly translated as 'the white
> men, they have died'. However, *oburoni* derives from *Aburokyere*, the
> Akan word for 'from across the waters', and is thus not the equiva-
> lent of Euro-American usages of *white*. The many Chinese, Koreans
> and Japanese now in Ghana are generally also termed *oburoni*. But in
> discussing translations Ashantis will point out that this is not just be-
> cause they are 'from across the sea' but because they 'are white' —
> that is, they are perceived as looking and acting like Europeans and
> Americans. African American visitors present an intriguing case be-
> cause they literally have crossed the waters to reach Ashanti. In most
> cases today only the fairest of such visitors would be called *oburoni*.

But in the recent past there apparently was some tendency to apply the term to them according to its original derivation. Thus it is intriguing in a number of ways that British listeners to Malcolm X's talks in Ghana on his celebrated pilgrimage to Mecca tell me that Ghanaians expressed surprise to them that an *oburoni* could say such things. Indeed one listener recalls hearing Malcolm described as a *white man* with astonishing ideas. Whatever strong elements of playfulness run through such characterizations, they ought to alert us to the complexity and the reality of the social construction of race. (Roediger 1994:4)

Ebron has made the same observation for The Gambia where she traveled with a group of African American tourists who, just like white Americans, are categorized as *toubob*, and notes that "the mark of difference is wealth and mobility" (2002:184) rather than the color of the skin. As such, African Americans or Afro-Europeans are equally seen as a means to access wealth and mobility or the white man's land, though in the case of Whites their socio-economic difference might be more obvious at first glance.

Professional Friends

The ambivalence attached to whiteness and the West in Ghanaian society is the subject of a number of popular stories. In Accra, when I sat and chatted with people, I came across stories about relationships between Blacks and Whites and about people who had traveled to Europe or the United States. While I took them just as anecdotes about particular persons at first, after a while I realized that there are certain themes that run through these stories. These anecdotes are part of a larger body of tales that deal with the ambivalences associated with the contact to Westerners and the West, and the process that is generally perceived as "Westernization." My insights about the wider significance of such stories, understood as social commentary, owes a lot to Ebron's exploration of sociological studies of tourism and their intersection

with tales […] about men, women, and tourism. […] Their repetition, frequency, and accompanying commentary suggested that these stories could be appreciated outside the bounds of the tourist industry as parables that expressed national anxieties over power differences between Africa and Europe, and between men and women.

(2002:168)

Most of the stories I collected in Ghana are of a similar character like those recounted by Ebron (2002:180ff). They are located on and around the beaches, in nightclubs, and in similar settings, that is, in the potential "contact zones" where tourists and Ghanaians meet.[16] These contact zones are, at the same time, also a central focus of the cultural economy. The territories of "culture" in Ghana often coincide with tourist locations such as hotels, beach resorts, and tourist markets along the coast. And these settings are also strongly associated with the more negative outgrowths of contemporary tourism such as prostitution and drug consumption. Understood as social commentary, the stories people tell about the encounters in these settings often stand as warnings about the temptations, dangers, and ultimately destructive nature of what is seen as a Western lifestyle, hence they commonly end with the downfall of the protagonist.

One of the stories I was told, for example, is about a young Ghanaian man and a young white lady from the United States (I encountered a number of variations of this story, but the baseline of the different versions was always the same). They got to know each other on the beach and fell in love. The American woman truly loved the young man, and since she was quite rich, she did everything she could to support her boyfriend. She rented a luxurious apartment (including personnel) and also bought him a car. "The way he dressed by that time, you would have thought he came straight from the U.S.," I was told, "but in fact he had never been abroad." When the woman had to return to her country, she continued sending money, and they frequently spoke on phone. They were already making plans to get married. But after a while, the young man started to spend the money his girlfriend sent to him mindlessly: he went out to nightclubs, started taking drugs, gave excessive parties in his house and met "expensive girls." So, anytime his American girlfriend sent money, which was supposed to suffice for a whole month, it got finished within a week or two, and the young man asked for more. This went on for a while, until the woman got suspicious. She knew that life in Ghana couldn't be that expensive. So, one day she called him and told him that she had got a new job, and therefore had to move. As soon as she would reach her new place, she would call him to give him her new contact. And that was the

---

[16] On my first three-months stay in Ghana in 2004/05 I lived in Labadi, not far from two of the most prestigious beach hotels in Accra, Labadi Beach Hotel and La Palm Beach Hotel. Thus, many of the stories occurred in connection with this setting. The public beach La Pleasure Beach is one of the main beaches in the city where foreigners as well as locals go at weekends, and where beach parties are organized on public holidays.

last time the Ghanaian man heard from his American girlfriend. He had to move out of the apartment, sell his car, and in the end he lost everything. As someone commented, "he is walking around in only slippers now — he can't even afford proper shoes."

Another story, yet in many respects very similar, is about a Ghanaian Rastaman who used to hang around at the beach with his drum. Sometimes he had some white students whom he taught drumming. He also performed in a cultural group. He was, so the story goes, a "real" Rasta, that is, he didn't drink alcohol and he also didn't eat meat. One day a white man came to the beach and heard the Rasta with his group playing. He liked them and coincidently turned out to be a promoter, so he helped them to travel to Europe. They went for a whole year and performed in different countries. Things were going well for the group, and through the newly established contacts, they managed to travel and perform abroad again the next year. After they came back, the people in the group started to set up businesses with the money they had saved. They bought cars to work as taxis for them, set up restaurants and shops. They brought television sets and stereo systems, DVD players and the like. Except for the Rastaman. He was still living as he used to live before he had traveled. "He was still living in his single room; you didn't see a TV or a stereo, nothing." He also still used to go to the beach looking for Whites who might take a drum lesson. After a while the group got the chance to travel again, including the Rastaman. But again, unlike the other group members, the Rastaman brought nothing home from this trip either. What actually happened was that the Rasta "lived big" abroad. He drove expensive cars and frequented prostitutes. He eventually became addicted to drugs and spent all the money he had got. "If you see him now you think it's a mad person. You would never think that he ever traveled."

A common picture around tourist locations in Ghana such as hotels and beach resorts are young men with long dread locks. Young men search the beaches for tourists who might be interested in buying souvenirs, taking drumming lessons, being taken around, or who are just looking for company. These people belong to a group Ebron, following the anthropologist Ulla Wagner, refers to as "professional friends," whom she describes as an "outgrowth of the service industry" and "who move alongside tourism yet outside many of the formal aspects of the system" (Ebron 2002:176). Such "professional friends," sometimes also referred to as "bumpsters," can be found not only in The Gambia and Ghana, but in many countries in sub-Saharan Africa where a tourist sector has been established. For the unemployed youths of these countries, establishing informal contacts to Western tourists is often the only way to participate in the tourist economies. A common scene, which

Ebron describes for The Gambia, could also take place in Ghana. As she writes:

> These young men comb the beaches and hang around hotels in search of potential "friends". They are often prohibited from entering hotels. Thus they stand outside hotel entrances waiting for tourists who, upon exiting, encounter a number of boys and men approaching with such welcoming phrases as "Hello, I want to be your friend; I want to show you around The Gambia. I can make your stay very nice." Relationships formed between tourists and bumpsters can include a number of activities. They act as tour guides to both men and women, as interpreters and negotiators between local people and tourists, as facilitators of sexual liaisons for male travelers who seek female companions, and as escorts for tourist women to the night life in The Gambia. Some bumpsters also seek involvement in romantic affairs with women tourists who potentially have the resources to help them travel. [...] From the perspective of these professional friends, all tourist women are potential sexual partners. (Ebron 2002:176)

"Culture" is often a means of establishing relationships to tourists and therefore an integral part of the informal economy around tourist locations. Whites, so the common picture, are highly interested in culture, be it in the form of drumming and dancing performances, sight seeing, or just souvenirs. In an interview I conducted in Labadi with somebody who sold drums on the beaches in and around Accra, he described the activities of "professional friends" from his perspective, a conversation which is worth quoting at some length.

> QUESTION: You told me that you sold drums on the beach. When did you start selling like this? You just walk around...?
> ANSWER: The problem is, getting a store at the beach. A stand at the beach, it costs. [...] Not all white men who go to shop, the craft shop, to buy. [...] So, if you are holding it [the drum] and he passing by, he might be interested [...].
> QUESTION: So then you just take your drums and walk around and see whether somebody is interested?
> ANSWER: Yeah.
> QUESTION: How would you do it?
> ANSWER: [laughs]

QUESTION: Just for me to imagine.

ANSWER: Hmm [pauses]. We call it... It's a business! It's a business to us. It's difficult to do it, but... if you know what you are doing, what you are towards to do... and then also... because of my school problem, I have to force. There is no money in my pocket. My father traveled, and then, left with my mom... then, my grandmom is, too, now old. So, from sitting at one place, nobody comes to me. If he [the white man] comes, he say: I buy this, I buy this — Oh, I don't manage [...]. So I say: Okay, let me try this, going around. Maybe somebody is interested in it... so... at times I walk, nobody calls me... I will sit with them [the tourists], I will chat with them... they will play. [...]

QUESTION: Are there many people on the beach doing this business?

ANSWER: Yeah. Much people. Much Blacks.

QUESTION: What kind of people is it?

ANSWER: Not all of them do the drum business. Some doing the necklace. Some also on... hmm... the painting. Some also on cigarettes... others just walk, maybe a white man needs something, and then... [...] maybe... befriend with them. Maybe they need something. Maybe want to know: Where is Kumasi? Where is... I mean... to know much about the place, to know much about Ghana. Some people are there, they know much history about Ghana. [...]

QUESTION: What kind of people is it? Is it... young people? Old people?

ANSWER: Both.

QUESTION: Women? Men?

ANSWER: No. Women not do. The women who do is the Rastamen — Rastawomen.

QUESTION: Rastawomen?

ANSWER: Yeah, it's the Rastawomen who do such a business... necklace business... much Rastamen they do necklaces. But the maximum people is the young and then... children... [...] age of nine. You can see nine-years boy doing the business. Yeah. [...] You know, Rastas, they deal with tourists, they do culture. They know much about culture.

QUESTION: What kind of culture?

ANSWER: Their hairs. How they got to do the dread locks. And then the necklace, yes. So, there are Rastamen at the beach who can do the dread locks for you. And then, also people… some are there to, I mean, to get a white lady. […] Some move from hotels to hotels, nightclubs.[17]

In The Gambia, as Ebron reports, such "bumpsters" became the target of campaigns initiated by government officials who were concerned about the nation's reputation. Efforts to by the ministry of tourism to officially register these young men and give them identity badges and uniforms failed, because the bumpsters refused to register. "In a more recent sweep that was part of one of the government's clean-up campaigns," she adds, "prostitutes and cannabis smokers — that is, men with long dread locks — were targeted and their heads were shaved" (Ebron 2002:177). Though I haven't heard about any such campaign in Ghana, the ambivalence that is attached to these forms of "professional friendship" is the same.

Ebron reminds us that there are also complex gender constructions at play in the relationships between mostly black African men and white European or American women. Assumed male-female power relations are at times reversed in the encounter between Africans and Europeans, though we shouldn't make the mistake to victimize African men who go for white female tourists. Just as constructions of race, as we discussed them in the previous section, are more complex and far beyond a simple distinction between black and white, questions of gender construction in the European-African encounter are more complicated. In the same way as for Europeans seeking romantic affairs with Africans, the attraction of the "exotic" body is also a motive for Africans to look for sexual adventure with Whites, along with considerations of enhancing one's social status. As Nyamnjoh and Page observe for Cameroonian nightlife:

> Bars and nightclubs become a location for unrelenting bids by young men to entice the *whiteman woman* with an exuberant display of highly suggestive local dancing styles such as *zengue*, *zaiko*, and *bikutsi*, fuelled not only by universal desires but also by the particular attraction of the exotic body and the liberating material opportunities it provokes in the mind. (2002:612)

It is interesting to note that in Ghana such behavior is tolerated for men sooner than for women, which has to do with the role models ascribed to men and women. Men are considered sexually adventurous anyway, while "decent

---

[17] The interview was conducted on January 24, 2005.

women" are not supposed to look after men, whether white or black. Though the dream of many, not least due to the material advantages associated with it, Ghanaian women who go for white men are mostly seen as prostitutes. As somebody explained, "before a lady can get a white man [...], they have to pass through [...] prostitution business." The same observation holds true for Cameroon: "Cameroonian family members might look down on a Cameroonian woman who marries a white man. Such relationships are seen as akin to prostitution because of their implicit economic basis" (Nyamnjoh & Page 2002:624).

These implicit ambivalences that are attached to interracial relationships are, after all, also an inherent quality of culture and its connotations, as it is intimately linked to the tourist industry. It is the people who are dealing with tourists who are, at the same time, "doing culture" — often young men with dread locks. And the beach, where these Rastamen operate, as one of the contact zones between Blacks and Whites, is also a territory of immoral and criminal activities. "Through culture we communicate with white people, we get tourists, they understand about culture," somebody explained. And he continued:

> And then, the disadvantage is: through communicating we are befriending with them... There are some people [...] who don't understand the business. [...] They came for money. As we call it: they are the 419 people. [...] They deal with the women, the prostitute women. Maybe they say: Okay, there is a white man there. I think he is loaded [with money]. So the girls will go and then befriend with the white man. Or maybe the white man need some woman to accompany him. And then, later, they come; they have address and this thing; she will give it to the 419 people. They will go straight, they rob you, and then they share the money.[18]

Such activities are mostly associated with foreigners, particularly Nigerians who come to Ghana to engage in dubious economic activities. Likewise, the market in illegal drugs is said to be controlled by foreigners, since

> not all the tourists who came here are good. Some are gangsters. Some people come and then do that kind of cocaine business here. Ganja business. [...] [Some] people they don't come to see how the beach is, but — maybe they need some ganja to smoke. Or they

---

[18] Interview conducted on January 24, 2005.

need some place where they can buy some kind of cocaine. [...]
Mostly they do it, Rastaman people. 'Cause the Rastas, they know
much about this business. [...] They do the ganja and then the
necklace [...] to get the tourists, to get the white man.[19]

It is within this ambivalence that also professional travelers such as anthropologists and ethnomusicologists move — whether we like it or not. We said
earlier that "culture" in Ghana as well as elsewhere in the postcolonial world
could be regarded as a popularized academic tradition. Ever since the nineteenth century, it has been anthropologists and ethnologists in search of "exotic cultures" who also fostered the commoditization of objects and practices
of "ethnographic" interest, and eventually of "culture" itself. We have to be
very self-critical, therefore, when it comes to reflecting our own role as researchers in a postcolonial setting, with all the implications that are involved in
the relationships we set up. Whether we are in a German zoo, an African village, or conurbations like Accra or Berlin, we cannot escape the discourses
and power relations prescribed in space. We are never passive in the
(re)production of space, and should therefore consciously take advantage of
our strategic positions in setting up relations in space.

    The figure of the "professional friend" has his precursor and methodo-
logical counterpart in the "informant," a highly problematic figure in ethnographic literature, as Clifford (1992:100f) reminds us. As "researchers" looking
for information in "the field" we, in turn, also take the role of a "professional
friend" vis-à-vis many of the people we are dealing with. Though it might not
be completely impossible, it is probably only in the minority of cases that
"real" friendship (whatever that might be) results from the professional relations we set up. Culture is, after all, a business, and we are, and have always
been, an integral part of the business with travel and culture.

---

[19] Quoted from the same interview.

9 Conclusion: Music, Power, Space

Throughout the preceding chapters we have argued for the constitutive role of musical practices in the production of space. To make our point clear, we should perhaps stress once again that when we talk about musical practice, we refer to the social practice Christopher Small (1998) coined "musicking." Small urges us to think about music not so much as a noun, but rather as a verb, "to music," since the "fundamental nature and meaning of music lie not in objects, not in musical works at all, but in action, in what people do" (ibid.:8). Through musical performance, people set up relations, they reenact, reinforce, as well as transform (at least potentially) the social order within which musical performances take place, an order which musical performance, in the soundscapes that come into being through it, at the same time transcends. To music, in this sense, is to live space. Space, we have said, is at once the precondition and the outcome of social action. It is, therefore, also the precondition and outcome of musical action. Musicking encompasses not only all activities directly aiming at the production of sound, but everything that is involved in singing, playing, listening, creating, talking, writing, representing, and even thinking music.

Ethnomusicologists often stress that their focus is on "music-culture," on the study of music in or as culture, following Merriam's (1964) seminal definition of "the anthropology of music," a definition which for our field has served to cut us off from other branches in musicology for several decades now. Disregarding Merriam's rather functionalist view that specific musics always serve a specific purpose within a specific culture, in the wake of this shift of ethnomusicology towards cultural anthropology, it was particularly the notion of "context," which became prominent. Thus, generations of ethnomusicologists worked on "contextualizing" musical practices as embedded within specific cultures. The notion of culture on which such contextual approaches are based is what I deliberately tried to argue against in the preceding chapters. The concept of culture understood as a distinct meaning system absorbs notions of space, place, and time, and it conceals the fact that cultural constellations are interrelated and mutually dependent, rather than isolated entities in space. In order to unveil the power relations that are at the heart of any cultural representation, we are, as far as the cultural study of music is concerned, in need of theorizations of space.

If culture refers to the culture of a particular group of people, I have indeed been "writing against culture" (Abu-Lughod 1991) throughout the preceding chapters. Notions pursued by liberals such as the "cultural mosaic" or "multiculture," but also nationalistic conceptions of a *Kulturnation* or that of a *Leitkultur*, as they are employed in German political debates, are equally grounded in a principal isomorphism space, place, and culture, and little help, I would argue, to understand the cultural complexity of an interconnected world. Such notions of culture are ideological and political devices, but they are not analytical. Instead, when I speak of culture, it is in the general sense of the "social organization of meaning" (Hannerz 1992), that is, the way how space is symbolically structured. I therefore agree with Hannerz that "the idea of culture in the singular, encompassing the entire more or less organized diversity of ideas and expressions, may become more important than it has been, as we explore the way humanity inhabits the global ecumene" (1996:23). Focusing on transnational social spaces, a metaphor which might be more helpful than the "cultural mosaic," which implies a multitude of disconnected cultural entities in their coexistence, is that of "habitats of meaning." As Hannerz writes:

> In the global ecumene, some people may indeed share much the same habitats of meaning, but these can also become quite idiosyncratic. The places we have been to and the people we have met in them, the books and newspapers we read, the television channels we zap to, all these make a difference. My own daily habitat of meaning changed the day our apartment building installed cable TV, and I suddenly had access to British, French, German, Turkish, American, and Russian programming apart from the Swedish channels. Yet our habitats of meaning will of course depend not only on what in some physical sense we are exposed to, but also on the capabilities we have built up for coping with it knowledgeably: the languages we understand, write, or speak, our levels of literacy with respect to other symbolic forms, and so on. (Ibid.)

Regarded this way, culture is a matter of physical and intellectual mobility, of relationships, and a matter of competence. It is the cultural realm that renders musical forms and practices meaningful, and the meaning of the same musical forms and practices can indeed be highly diverse if we consider them in different habitats of meaning. In order to get these different habitats into focus we have to approach culture spatially. To demonstrate this diversity and show what happens to and with a, in the first place, discursively constructed entity such as "African music" in various habitats of meaning was one of the aims of this ethnography. How African music is produced as a meaningful space, how it produces culture itself as an ideological and political space, was therefore one of my prime concerns throughout this thesis. What we were not concerned with here is the question what African music or African culture "really" is. Just as notions of what black and white genuinely is can differ considerably, as we have outlined in the last chapter, the answer to what African music is depends on circumstances, perspective, and at least to some extent political program. The question about the essence of African music, black music, or similar categories, actually gives us a hint as to how racialized spaces are produced. The invention of African music is part of musical discourse, of musicking, and therefore of the production of space. The following excerpt from an interview I conducted in Accra with the leader of a cultural troupe might be revealing in this regard:

> ANSWER: It's not that there is a difference between black and white, and that is why… No. But, if something is in your country, you are doing it. The Whites have something that, if they are doing it now and you tell the Blacks to go and do it, it will be difficult — something like… this dance, what is it called? It's not rock and roll… […] I forgot the dance's name. I have one of my sisters, she is learning it. And when … if I go to the training ground and the Whites are dancing, I'm happy. But when my sister gets in … I'm annoyed.
> QUESTION: But you're not talking about salsa?
> ANSWER: Very good! Salsa!
> QUESTION: You mean salsa?
> ANSWER: Yeah! For the Blacks, to learn, it's very, very difficult. But the Whites, they do it easily. They just move and go. But the Black — you know. Even the step to turn… it's always difficult for the Blacks. So, everybody has… you know… the thing that he can do easily… and the thing he finds very, very difficult to do. Everybody.[1]

How much culture and musical forms are "made," and the way we are always involved in producing and reproducing cultural space, became clear to me in an encounter I had in 2004 in New Town, Accra. Having been trained within a tradition of cultural relativism that sometimes goes as far as relativizing and ridiculing itself, I had been asked about what I was working on, about what

---

[1] The interview was conducted on January 25, 2005.

exactly I was doing. I circuitously started to explain my project on music and migration, explicating my views on the coherencies of music, travel, and the production of social spaces, when the man, a Ghanaian who had lived in Sweden for the past twenty years and who passed his vacation in Ghana mainly in drinking huge amounts of local liquor, complaining about his Swedish wife, and annoying his relatives by bossing them around, languidly interrupted my vain attempts, saying, "So, you're doing culture?" Well, I think his comment hit the nail right on the head. And this is mainly what I have been doing above, I "did" culture as I scrutinized how other people do culture, drawing on a largely constructivist discourse that aims at exploring different habitats of meaning. Parallel to Small's approach to music as social practice we can maybe best think of culture as a verb, as something we always do by way making sense of the world.

Ethnographic constructivism, as it has been promoted in cultural anthropology since the 1980s (cf. Clifford 1988; Clifford & Marcus 1986; Marcus & Fischer 1986), definitely has its shortcomings and limits. But while it might not provide the answers to the basic dilemma in the human sciences that results from the discrepancies between the aspiration to objectively describe the cultural and social realities of the world on the one hand, and the epistemological insight that we can never arrive at this reality by way of description, analysis, and interpretation on the other, for me a conscious and well-balanced constructivism seems still a good way of being self-critically connected to one's own doings. If we manage to make clear the assumptions and paradigms on which our accounts are based, I think that ethnography, particularly in times of "globalization," when scholars start developing the "grand" models again to explain the world (the tale of the "clash" of different meaning systems, for example, is a manifestly popular one), can offer valuable insights, a "microscopic" counterpoint to the generalizing narratives of modernization, globalization, and cultural homogenization. Ethnography is a way, in other words, to render the abstractions we are operating with concrete, and to provide the data and material that is needed for a theory of practice (cf. Bourdieu 1977; de Certeau 1984).

*   *   *

We started our journey in the second chapter as we outlined the setting of the zoo as one of the sites where African music and culture emblematically appears — in the form of ethnographic shows in the nineteenth and early twentieth century, and in the form of folklore and world music in the twentieth and twenty-first century. As we have seen, the "village" seems to be a vivid image, in which the African continent is caught. Some of the most heated debates concerning the politics of representing Africa arose around the metaphor of the village and particularly its placement in the zoo. We asked about the continuities and the discontinuities with regard to the performance and representation of African music within the setting of the zoo, and said that in contrast to former ethnographic shows, where Africans were exhibited themselves as "living objects," at events like the "African Village" in the Augsburg zoo or the "jungle night" in Leipzig, human beings were not themselves put on display.

Nonetheless, considering the appearance and reappearance of Africa in the zoo also illustrated its highly ambivalent position within the global cultural economy. Representations and performances of Africa continue to occupy a paradoxical space between myth and reality, past and present, here and there. Such paradoxical representations of space have clearly an impact on and are connected to the realities of sociocultural space and they foster processes of racialization. While Africans and people of African descent were not put on display in Augsburg or in Leipzig in any strict sense, the bodily space that is reserved for Blacks within such settings is a racialized one, while the spaces of the white body appear racially neutral. We can see that in this context being black indeed means to have a race, while being white means to be "raceless." A further contradiction produced by the cultural economy is the fact that racialized products apparently sell better than racially unmarked ones, at least in the examples we considered. We might put it as simply as: "Ethno," the ethnic, and racial difference sells. The commercialization of race under the pretence of cultural difference is, after all, a phenomenon that connects performances by Africans in Europe over the course of at least the last one and a half centuries or so.

In the third chapter, then, we considered the history of the paradox attached to African music in more detail and scrutinized the role of academic disciplines in the production of African music as the racially Other. At the same time we grounded our line of argument more explicitly in a theory of space as it has been formulated by Lefebvre ([1991] 2004). We have seen that in the nineteenth century African music represented the place of the "primitive"; "primitive music" was the epitome of the primordial origins of music and musical practice. In the nineteenth century the primitive marked the mythical beginnings of time-space, a position which was conceptualized as the identical yet non-identical mirror image of the "civilized." In the space of history, as it dominated nineteenth-century thinking (cf. Foucault 1973), Africa and Europe were conceptually connected at the same time as they were denied coevalness (cf. Fabian 1983).

This Hegelian line of reasoning, in which the cultural advancement of humankind appeared as an organic development of a *Weltgeist*, was eventually superimposed by a more technologized rationale (Kittler 1995). With the media revolution at the end of the nineteenth century African music enters, we have argued, the space of the Real. In real time temporal distance in the sense of history does not exist, and representations of the Other as remote in time-space are therefore obsolete. This media revolution, for the study of music most importantly associated with Thomas Edison's invention of the cylinder phonograph, marks the beginning of what Foucault (1986) calls the "epoch of space." Therefore, in newly emerging descriptions and analyses based on phonographic recordings such as those by Hornbostel, African music appears as fundamentally different to European music, a difference that represents an essential "racial" gap rather than a temporal distance in time-space. And this difference is continually reproduced by Europeans as well as Africans. In his highly critical essay on the "invention of African rhythm," Agawu (2003:55-70) therefore asks:

> When was the last time an ethnomusicologist went out to hunt for sameness rather than difference? When did we last encourage our students to go and do fieldwork not in order to come back and paint the picture of a different Africa, but of an Africa that, after all the necessary adjustments have been made for material divergence, is remarkably like the West? So strong and powerful is the founding premise of difference that the ongoing invention and reinvention of African rhythm, far from buttressing epistemological claims, presents the writer with a mirror image of the dictates of this very ideology of difference. (Ibid.:64)

The history of the discovery, exploration, and appropriation of African music, which is to say, the history of its invention, is at the same time the history of its commercialization. We have seen that African culture in the form of a consumable commodity already sold well in the nineteenth century. As recorded sound, African music is today probably one of the most widely appreciated cultural products worldwide. As Collins remarked, "the black musics of the Americas and Africa are the nearest thing this planet has to a global twentieth-century sound," and "black diasporic and African dance music has become the mainstream style for both the Old and the New World, East and West, North and South" (1992b:330). While recording technology was a crucial factor in the process of its deterritorialization, the reterritorialization of African music within the global cultural economy stretches across a vast space today.

As an image as well as a practice African music connects sites on almost all continents in multiple ways. In this reverse process of reterritorialization, technology plays an equally crucial role.

In our more theoretical exploration of space at the end of the third chapter, we discussed "siting" as one of the prime concerns that Foucault (1986) identified in what he calls the "epoch of space." Siting, that is, the mapping of sites in space, constitutes more generally the framework of our exploration of the place(s) of African music in contemporary popular culture. On a practical as well as political level, siting fundamentally concerns the categorization of people and things into manageable groups and classes. It concerns, in this sense, processes of identity formation as well as demography, particularly under conditions of an increased mobility of people and things. Siting occurs mostly as a form of restricting and disciplining movement. Siting is, we said, in a very general sense about the distribution of elements in time-space. With regard to the global cultural economy we are dealing with the distribution of meaning and meaningful forms, that is, processes of deterritorialization as well as reterritorialization of culture. The problem of siting concerns both the theoretical conceptualization of space as well as our practical approach to it. Siting or mapping therefore forms the intersection between theory and practice for musical geography.

In the fourth chapter, then, we approached urban space. Taking imaginary walks in the streets of Berlin as a way of "reading" the city, we considered at first different lifeworlds in an immigrant society such as Germany, and reviewed some of the debates that surround the country's multiethnic reality. The polemics we outlined illustrate well, in a way, the opposition between "the pious descendants of time and the determined inhabitants of space," which Foucault (1986:22) draws attention to. As a heterotopic space, the encounter with the Other, we argued, is an inherent quality of urban society. Urban space is appropriated by the most diverse groups, and its terrains as well as the representations of it are contested. As a concrete example for the production of heterotopic space we considered a Ghanaian outdooring in Berlin-Kreuzberg. As a manifestation of the heterochronic aspects of urban space and the contradictions and conflicts that the inscription of history in space brings about, we read colonial space in the streets of Mitte and Wedding.

The production of the abstract transnational space that reaches from Berlin to Accra concretizes not only in the transnational social networks that interlink Ghana with diasporic communities in Germany and a city like Berlin, but this production of space is likewise manifest in the physical remnants of history within urban space, be it architecture or the naming of city quarters and streets. For example, the "colony Togo," of which present-day Ghana's Volta Region was once a part, is still to be found in Berlin's district Wedding in the form of what in Germany is known as *Schrebergartenkolonie*, that is, a colony of allotment gardens. It was founded in the 1920s and named "Togo" after the former German protectorate in the wake of the colonial revisionist movement. For Ghanaians living in Berlin today, the city's ill-reputed neighborhoods represent "Nima," which epitomizes another heterotopia in urban space.

We ended our discussion in the fourth chapter with methodological considerations concerning multi-sited ethnography as a way of approaching urban space and urban society. Tellingly, the "African Village" we encountered in the Augsburg and Leipzig zoos (and then again in the eighth chapter in Ghana's Volta Region) in its popularized and commercialized form, was for a long time also the central methodological focus of ethnographical efforts. As a form of mapping at the same time as focusing attention on other people's attempts to map space, we discussed a multiply situated ethnography (Marcus 1995) and the implied strategic methodology, encompassing various forms of "tracking," as one possible alternative to more anachronistic equations of the field of ethnography with hermetic cultures.

Chapter five dealt with the spaces of what Gilroy (1993) coined the Black Atlantic. Gilroy conceptualizes the Black Atlantic as a transcultural formation that evolved with the dispersion of Africans, which took its beginnings in the transatlantic slave trade from the fifteenth century onward. We outlined the history of the African diaspora in Germany, and the country's place within the networks of the Black Atlantic. For Gilroy the expressive forms that evolved within the Black Atlantic represent a "counterculture" to the totalizing tendencies of modernity. As such, he argues, African or black musical forms can serve as a model for the theorization of hybridity that stands against the nationalization and racialization of culture. But the spaces of the Black Atlantic are equally contested, and in black nationalist movements there have repeatedly been attempts to essentialize black expressive forms and indeed the identity of a racialized "black subject." Thus, while for African Americans in search of their roots the African continent is at times envisioned as a romanticized cultural past, a utopia not unlike nineteenth-century accounts of the space of the primitive, we also find a creative exchange between American and African modernism that resists simple binaries of the pure versus the impure, hybridity versus a sterile cultural past. In its resistance to dichotomizations, the exchange and mutual inspirations, as they are manifest in popular cultural forms around the Atlantic, exemplify the complexities and interdependencies of the production of space. Yet also within the spaces of the Black Atlantic we cannot escape the permeating ambivalence that results from the commercialization of expressive forms and cultural identities, or from the promotion of what Ebron calls "sponsored identities" (2002:208).

Looking at the production of space through musical practice and movement from a quite different angle, the sixth chapter scrutinized the networks of people, places, and musical practices that constitute Berlin's Afro scene. Musical scenes are decidedly urban phenomena, we argued, in that they depend on a critical mass of people with similar preferences for particular styles. Musical scenes depend on diversity, that is, the coexistence of different things and people within a limited space, as it is the case in larger cities. As one of its characteristic features, the Afro scene centers around expressive forms that are held to have some innate African quality, however vague the notion of such an "Africanness" might be. In contrast to other accounts of "subcultures," which have mostly been portrayed as exclusively "youth cultures," the age structure of the Afro scene is quite diverse. Its networks distinguish themselves from other social constellations rather through specific gender relations, which correlate at same time with the racial makeup of the scene. In its interethnic or interracial structure, the Afro scene reflects and expresses the demographic realities of urban society, though in the case of Berlin's Afro scene we are dealing, at the same time, with an overrepresentation of Blacks and highly stylized images of an interracial society.

We scrutinized the role of expressive specialists within the networks of musical scenes and discussed their wider significance in the production of metropolitanism as one of the most vivid representations of urban space. In a way expressive specialists can be seen as an embodiment of the metropolis, and their role is to mediate transnational and cosmopolitan identities. In the last section of chapter six we looked more concretely at how urban space comes into existence through what Schwanhäußer (2005) calls a "culture of drifting." We have argued that the musical practices within the scene constitute the city itself as a place out of the ordinary. The form of musicking practiced by scensters not only in the Afro scene, but in musical scenes more generally, celebrates and "festivalizes" urban space. In this connection we also discussed how particular places establish themselves as extraordinary spaces, indeed as materialization of a heterotopia.

The image of the city, which is celebrated in the Afro scene, stands in sharp contrast to representations of Africa as a rustic and rural space, an image which most concisely crystallizes in the cloistered village. We dealt with this ambivalence in our discussion of the politics of style in chapter seven, where we identified style as a strategic moment in the production of space. By distinguishing between the macro- and the micropolitics of style, we tried to

make sense of the evident inconsistencies in stylistic representations. While
many accounts of the symbolic economy of so-called world music analyze its
representational modes and patterns in terms of the basic dualism between
Self and Other, we argued that by looking at stylistic representations as social
practice on the micro level, the politics of style express much more complex
relations in space than the "grand narrative" of domination and subordination, appropriation and counter-appropriation, suggests. We reencounter here
again the fundamental ambivalence that results from the dialectic of the
authentic and the inauthentic, or, the commercialized and alienated.

Following Straw's ([1991] 1997) basic line of argument, we suggested that
with regard to style we might not, or, at least not solely, deal with simple processes of appropriation and counter-appropriation, but rather with a complex
entanglement of spatial relations that are expressed and established through
style. Style, in this sense, is a way of positioning oneself strategically within social networks. And as such it is also a means of self-identification. An often un-
derrated aspect in accounts of the symbolic economies of popular culture is the
fact that styles not merely represent, but that they are actually performed and
lived. Style is often looked at as a mere textual strategy and not as social practice. Musical styles are, after all, a form of musicking. Thus, in the last section
of chapter four we concerned ourselves with one of the perpetual metaphors of
African music, which is performance itself. While Ebron (2002), for example,
argues that through performance the image of performativity is reenacted or
"re-imagined," I would rather say it is not an abstract image or a representation that is crucial in the performative practices within the Afro scene, but the
act of being a performer itself, as a way to live space. We mentioned that musical practice in a narrower sense is highly important in the Afro scene. I
would indeed argue that through drumming and dancing, as it is practiced
and celebrated in the scene, people discover themselves as performers. This is
in line with Small's critique of the pervasive image of musical practice as a
specialist tradition. In the Afro scene everybody is a (potential) musician, a
drummer or a dancer. As Small writes,

> I am certain, first, that to take part in a music act is of central impor-
> tance to our very humanness, as important as taking part in the act
> of speech [...] and second, that everyone, every normally endowed
> human being, is born with the gift of music no less than with the gift
> of speech. If that is so, then our present-day concert life, whether
> "classical" or "popular," in which the "talented" few are empowered
> to produce music for the "untalented" majority, is based on a false-
> hood. It means that our powers of making music for ourselves have

been hijacked and the majority of people robbed of the musicality that is theirs by right of birth, while a few stars, and their handlers, grow rich and famous through selling us what we have been led to believe we lack. (1998:8)

While there might be "stars" in the Afro scene, we are not dealing with "untouchable" pop stars, on the contrary. Mediating musicality and the faculty to rhythmically move as a general human feature is one of the important roles African expressive specialists play in Germany's musical landscape.

In the last chapter, then, we turned our attention more specifically to the Ghanaian cultural market and looked at the meanings and contradictions of culture and the cultural business. Culture in the form of choreographed tradition has been invented in Ghana in the wake of independence and was an integral part of nation-building processes (cf. Agawu 2003:17ff; Schramm 2000). As staged performance, culture stands today for a multi-ethnic canon of traditional music and dance, which is also an integral part of the tourist industry. Though on the African continent the implications of multi-ethnicity are not necessarily congruent with the multiethnic realities of urban society in European metropolises, there are nonetheless parallels in the production of space through African culture in the musical scenes in Berlin and Accra. In both cases we are dealing with urban phenomena. There are, moreover, very concrete connections as the constitutive networks of these musical scenes coincide in individual expressive specialists who operate transnationally.

As a symbolic space, culture is produced as the antithesis to Western modernity, and also in the African context the image of the "village" appears as a compelling metaphor. In our discussion of constructions of whiteness and the "white man's land," which are of course mutually dependent on constructions of blackness as we discussed them in the previous chapters, the ambivalences that are attached to images of Western modernity, and that are also implicit in the culture business, became apparent. As a sociocultural space, culture establishes itself as a contact zone where Ghanaians and foreigners, Blacks and Whites, meet. This represents another parallel to the German Afro scene, and shows that culture and cultural processes constitute themselves as a "space between," as Taussig (1993) describes it in *Mimesis and Alterity*. We thus returned once again to culture's essentially relational nature in favor of which we argued throughout this thesis. And it is in this sense, namely in setting up and defining relationships to oneself and others, that musicking also can be regarded an integral part of the production of social space.

What the preceding discussion shows — among other things — is that the ambivalences that are associated with a category such as African music, and African culture more generally, are (at least) as old as the colonial project. Whichever way and in whatever habitat of meaning we look at it, the impact of colonialism and colonial discourses on a category like African music cannot be overlooked (cf. Agawu 2003). The inherent ambivalences of the very idea of Africa always point to processes of racialization (cf. Mudimbe 1994). Regarded from the viewpoint of representational politics, African music necessarily produces racialized spaces, that is, a fundamental difference between white and black. This dualistic logic is in fact the principle of any representation. Yet, the implied power relations structural analyses of this sort postulate hardly go beyond the identification of a binary opposition between a dominant subject (the one that represents) and a repressed one (the represented). As a critique of representation such insights might be helpful, yet they are neither particularly new nor very exciting. But as soon as we look beyond the neatly ordered spaces of the symbolic realm, the relations constituted by music as a spatial practice and its role in the production of space becomes much more complex and at times maybe even irrational. Describing and representing this realm is not a simple task; this is, in the end, where any written account must fail.

The critique of representations of space is nonetheless necessary, since it reveals the mutual dependence of the production of knowledge and the production of space. The question about the interplay between the academic production of knowledge and the performance of music and culture was, therefore, a persistent theme throughout our discussion. Representation always means reduction, and as long as we feel called upon to write, we cannot escape reductionism to at least a certain extent. And we have to be aware that, as Lefebvre has noted, "reduction can reach very far indeed in its implications." As he continues to explain: "Many people, members of a variety of groups and classes, suffer (albeit unevenly) the effects of a multiplicity of reductions bearing on their capacities, ideas, 'values' and, ultimately on their possibilities, their space and their bodies" ([1991] 2004). Representation is, in this sense, a practice of siting and important means in the production of space. Siting is often a means to discipline, to control, and to restrict movement. It is therefore also an instrument to exercise power. I do not think that it is possible to locate power in simple binaries, as all too simplistic structural analysis might suggest. Power is, we have argued, hard to localize in a deterritorialized world; we will hardly be able to identify the "dominant class" or the center of the system, from where power is exercised.

Nevertheless, power is one of the central aspects in the production of space. Any constructivism is therefore necessarily a political endeavor. What we have been dealing with throughout this thesis is the role of musical practice in a political economy of space. Considering that it is, as Lefebvre writes, "by means of the body that space is perceived, lived — and produced" ([1991] 2004), the political economy of space is at the same time a political economy of the body, producing bodily spaces that you can only enter if you belong to a certain group or class. We discussed examples where musical practice is quite obviously an exercise of power, as it was the case in the colonial encounter. It seems that we can localize power only on a micropolitical level; power occurs always in concrete relations. This is what Foucault (1979) called the "micro-physics of power," of which music is always a part. In this respect power and music as power take place at the margins, the front lines, in between, in the border zones — and the power of music divides as much as it unites. After all, some people's authenticities will always be other people's inauthenticities. These are not so much matters of "emic" and "etic" viewpoints, of cultural understanding, or immersion into different cultural realms, but as a political endeavor it is rather a question of who's side you are on, a question of political opportunism, sympathy, and social distinction.

As we have seen, representations of space as they are contained in terms like Africa, Europe, the West, or the global, always comprise temporal and spatial paradoxes. The production of space is a contradictory and an essen-tially relational process. Representations always entail relations and denote social distinctions. This is true for older representations of Africa as the primi-tive as well as modernist visions of metropolitanism through African expressive forms, as they are also embodied in the social type of the *burger*. It could be ar-gued that both of these distinctions, the one embodied by the primitive as well as that embodied by the *burger*, have their root in a fundamental opposition between nature and culture, between the rural and the urban, the uncivilized and the civilized (based on the Latin word *civitas*, that is, the city). Like the "beento" in Nigeria, who "stands, as it were, at the intersection where Waller-stein meets Bourdieu," as Hannerz puts it, the *burger* also points to "a charis-matic geography, arranged around the bright lights of the metropolis" (Han-nerz 1992:229). *Burger* and *beento* are the antithesis of the bush (cf. ibid.:228ff). Similarly, as Mudimbe explicates, the antipode of the civilized, namely the "primitive" or the

> "savage" (Silvaticus) is the one living in the bush, in the forest, in-deed away from the *polis*, the *urbs*; and, by extension, "savage" can designate any marginal being, foreigner, the unknown, whoever is different and who as such becomes the unthinkable, whose symbolic

or real presence in the *polis* or the *urbs* appears in itself as a cultural
event. (Mudimbe 1994:15)

In times when, as we said at the outset of this book with reference to Clifford's
characterization of ethnographic modernity, the "'exotic' is uncannily close,"
when "[d]ifference is encountered in the adjoining neighborhood" and "the
familiar turns up at the ends of the earth" (Clifford 1988:13f), it might indeed
be time to get away with particular images that are linked to particular percep-
tions and expectations concerning the order of space. If you want to insult
someone in Ghana, you can call him *akuraseni*, that is, "villager" or "bush boy"
— bush being more generally "an epithet for ignorance and rustic, unso-
phisticated, uncouth conduct" (Hannerz 1992:229) in English-speaking West
Africa. You can insult an Afro-German by commenting on his or her accent-
free mastery of the German language, as it often happens as black Germans
again and again report. Afro-German, just as other hyphenated and therefore
hybrid, seemingly "impure" identities, are still being "the unthinkable" for
some people, who trust in the isomorphism of space, place, and culture.
Maybe they would expect Blacks rather in some village in the jungle of Africa
— or was it Pongoland?

References

Abraham, Otto & Erich M. von Hornbostel [1904] 1975. "On the Significance of the Phonograph for Comparative Musicology." English translation by Ray Giles. In: Erich M. von Hornbostel. *Opera Omnia*, vol. 1. Edited by Klaus P. Wachsmann, Dieter Christensen & Hans-Peter Reinecke. Den Haag: Nijhoff, pp. 184-202.

— 1909/10. "Vorschläge für die Transkription exotischer Melodien." *Sammelbände der Internationalen Musikgesellschaft* 11:1-25.

Abu-Lughod, Lila 1991. "Writing Against Culture." In: R. Fox (ed.). *Recapturing Anthropology. Working in the Present*. Santa Fe, NM: School of American Research Press.

Achiaw, Nehemia Owusu 2007. "President Dismisses Criticisms On His Attire." Article in the newspaper *Daily Graphic*, March 08, 2007.

Adesiyan, Frauke 2006. "Diesseits von Afrika." Article in the daily newspaper *die tageszeitung*, April 4, 2006.

Adogame, A. 1997. "A Home Away From Home. The Proliferation of the Celestial Church of Christ (CCC) in Diaspora-Europe." *Africana Marburgensia* 30:3-22.

Adorno, Theodor W. 1941. "On Popular Music." *Zeitschrift für Sozialforschung* 9(1):17-49.

Adorno, Theodor W. & Max Horkheimer 1972. *Dialectic of Enlightenment*. Translated by John Cumming. New York: Continuum.

Agawu, Kofi 2003. *Representing African music. Postcolonial Notes, Queries, Positions*. New York: Routledge.

Agyei-Twum, Frank 2007. "Ghana Music Awards festival takes off." Article in the daily newspaper *The Statesman*, May 05, 2007.

Aikins, Joshua Kwesi 2005. "Wer mit Feuer spielt... Aneignung und Widerstand — Schwarze Musik/Kulturen in Deutschlands *weißem* Mainstream." In: Maureen Maisha Eggers, Grado Kilomba, Peggy Piesche & Susan Arndt (eds.). *Mythen, Masken und Subjekte. Kritische Weißseinsforschung in Deutschland*. Münster: Unrast, pp. 283-300.

Akyeampong, Emmanuel K. 2006. "Race, Identity and Citizenship in Black Africa: The Case of the Lebanese in Ghana." *The Journal of the International*

African Institute 76(3):297-323.

— 2001. *Between the Sea and the Lagoon: An Eco-Social History of the Anlo of Southeastern Ghana, c. 1850 to Recent Times*. Athens: Ohio University Press.

— 2000. "Africans in the Diaspora: The Diaspora and Africa." *African Affairs* 99:183-215.

Alvarez-Pereyre, Frank & Simha Arom 1993. "Ethnomusicology and the Emic/Etic Issue." *The World of Music* 35(1):7-33.

am Orde, Sabine 2004. "Keine Angstdebatten, bitte!" Article in the daily newspaper *taz Berlin lokal* November 16, 2004.

Ankermann, Bernhard [1901] 1976. *Die afrikanischen Musikinstrumente*. Photomechanical reprint of the original publication. Leipzig: Zentralantiquariat der Deutschen Demokratischen Republik.

Appadurai, Arjun 1996. *Modernity at Large: Cultural Dimensions of Globalization*. Minneapolis & London: University of Minnesota Press.

— (ed.) [1986] 2003. *The Social Life of Things. Commodities in Cultural Perspective*. Cambridge: Cambridge University Press.

Arndt, Susan, Maureen Maisha Eggers, Grada Kilomba & Peggy Piesche (eds.) 2005. *Mythen, Masken und Subjekte. Kritische Weißseinsforschung in Deutschland*. Münster: Unrast.

Arnold, Stefan 1995. "Propaganda mit Menschen aus Übersee: Kolonialausstellungen in Deutschland, 1896-1940." In: Robert Debusmann & János Riesz (eds.). *Kolonialausstellungen — Begegnungen mit Afrika?* Frankfurt/M.: IKO (Verlag für Interkulturelle Kommunikation), pp. 1-24.

Asad, Talal (ed.) 1973. *Anthropology and the Colonial Encounter*. New York: Humanities Press.

Atafori, Ayuure Kapini 2006. "Prof Nketia: Policy cannot promote culture." Article in the daily newspaper *The Statesman*, September 21, 2006.

Augé, Marc 1995. *Non-Places. Introduction to an Anthropology of Supermodernity*. Translated by John Howe. London & New York: Verso.

Ausländerbeauftragte 2005. *Bericht der Beauftragten der Bundesregierung für Migration, Flüchtlinge und Integration über die Lage der Ausländerinnen und Ausländer in Deutschland*. Berlin, Juni 2005. http://www.bundesregierung.de/nn_56708/Content/DE/Publikation/IB/migrationsbericht-2005.html (accessed November 22, 2008)

Avorgbedor, Daniel K. 1983. "The Place of the 'Folk' in Ghanaian Popular Music." *Popular Music and Society* 9(2):35-44.

Bade, Klaus J. (ed.) 1992. *Deutsche im Ausland — Fremde in Deutschland: Migration in Geschichte und Gegenwart*. Munich: Beck.

Ballantine, Christopher 1992. *Marabi Nights. Early South African Jazz and Vaudeville*. Braamfontein: Ravan.

Barber, Karin 1997. *Readings in African Popular Culture*. Bloomington: Indiana University Press.

Barley, Nigel 1983. *The Innocent Anthropologist. Notes From a Mud Hut*. London: British Museum Publications.

Barz, Gregory F. & Timothy J. Cooley (eds.) 1997. *Shadows in the Field: New Perspectives for Fieldwork in Ethnomusicology*. New York & Oxford: Oxford University Press.

Bauman, Zygmunt 2000. *Liquid Modernity*. Cambridge: Polity Press.

Baumann, Max Peter (ed.) 1985. *Musik der Türken in Deutschland*. Kassel: Landeck.

— 1979. *Musikalische Streiflichter einer Großstadt*. Berlin: Vergleichende Musikwissenschaft des FB 14 der Freien Universität Berlin.

Bechhaus-Gerst, Marianne 2004. "'Wir hatten nicht gedacht, dass die Deutschen so eine Art haben'. AfrikanerInnen in Deutschland zwischen 1880 und 1945." In: AntiDiskriminierungsBüro (ADB) Köln von Öffentlichkeit gegen Gewalt e.V. & cyberNomads (cbN) (eds.). *TheBlackBook. Deutschlands Häutungen*. Frankfurt/M. & London: IKO, pp. 21-33.

Béhague, Gerard H. 1994. *Music and Black Ethnicity. The Caribbean and South America*. New Brunswick & London: Transaction.

Benjamin, Walter 1969. "The Work of Art in the Age of Mechanical Reproduction." In: *Illuminations*. Edited by Hannah Arendt. Translated by Harry Zohn. New York: Schocken, pp. 217-51.

Blum, Stephen 1991. "European Musical Terminology and the Music of Africa." In: Philip V. Bohlman & Bruno Nettl (eds.). *Comparative Musicology and Anthropology of Music. Essays on the History of Ethnomusicology*. Chicago & London: The University of Chicago Press, pp. 3-36.

Bohlman, Philip V. & Ronald Radano (eds.) 2000. *Music and the Racial Imagination*. With a Foreword by Houston A. Baker, Jr. Chicago & London: The University of Chicago Press.

Born, Georgina & David Hesmondhalgh (eds.) 2000. *Western Music and Its Others. Difference, Representation, and Appropriation in Music*. Berkeley, Los Angeles & London: University of California Press.

Bourdieu, Pierre 1977. *Outline of a Theory of Practice*. Translated by Richard Nice. Cambridge & New York: Cambridge University Press.

Brady, Erika 1999. *A Spiral Way: How the Phonograph Changed Ethnography*. Jackson: University Press of Mississippi.

Brändle, Rea 1995. *Wildfremd, hautnah: Völkerschauen und Schauplätze, Zürich 1880-1960. Bilder und Geschichten*. Zürich: Rotpunktverlag.

Brettell, Caroline B. 2000. "Theorizing Migration in Anthropology: The Social Construction of Networks, Identities, Communities, and Globalscapes."

In: Caroline B. Brettell & James F. Hollifield (eds.). *Migration Theory. Talking Across Disciplines*. New York: Routledge, pp. 97-135.

Bücher, Karl [1896] 1924. *Arbeit und Rhythmus*. Leipzig: Reinicke.

Bullion, Constanze von 2005. "In den Fängen einer türkischen Familie — Muslimische Dorfmoral in der Berliner Moderne: Die Geschichte eines brutalen Zusammenpralls der Kulturen." Article in the daily newspaper *Süddeutsche Zeitung*, February 26, 2005.

Carl, Florian 2006. "Reisen im kolonialen Raum. Musik, Macht und die Transformation des weißen Körpers." In: Marianne Bechhaus-Gerst & Sunna Gieseke (eds.). *Koloniale und postkoloniale Konstruktionen von Afrika und Menschen afrikanischer Herkunft in der deutschen Alltagskultur*. Berlin: Peter Lang, pp. 215-230.

— 2004. *Was bedeutet uns Afrika? Zur Darstellung afrikanischer Musik im deutschsprachigen Diskurs des 19. und frühen 20. Jahrhunderts*. Münster: LIT.

Carl, Florian, Raimund Vogels & Martin Ziegler forthcoming. "Die Musik ghanaischer Migranten in Deutschland." Article based on a paper presented at the international conference *Music and Cultural Identity* in Weimar, September 21, 2004.

Castles, Stephen & Mark J. Miller 1993. *The Age of Migration: International Population Movements in the Modern World*. London: Macmillan.

Chernoff, John Miller 1979. *African Rhythm and African Sensibility: Aesthetics and Social Action in African musical Idioms*. Chicago & London: The University of Chicago Press.

Clifford, James 1994. "Diasporas." *Cultural Anthropology* 9(3):302-338.

— 1992. "Traveling Cultures." In: Lawrence Grossberg, Cary Nelson & Paula Treichler (eds.). *Cultural Studies*. New York & London: Routledge, pp. 96-112.

— 1988. *The Predicament of Culture: Twentieth-Century Ethnography, Literature, and Art*. Cambridge & London: Harvard University Press.

Clifford, James & George E. Marcus (eds.) 1986. *Writing Culture: The Poetics and Politics of Ethnography*. Berkeley, Los Angeles & London: University of California Press.

Coleman, S. 2000. *The Globalisation of Charismatic Christianity*. Cambridge: Cambridge University Press.

Collins, John 1997. "Gospel Highlife: Ghana's New Response to Urban Anxiety." Paper presented at the International Conference on *Music and Healing in Africa and the Diaspora* held at the University of Ghana, Legon, September 3-5, 1997.

— 1994. *Highlife Time*. Accra: Anansesem Publications.

— 1992a. "Some Anti-Hegemonic Aspects of African Popular Music." In:

Reebee Garofalo (ed.). *Rockin' the Boat. Mass Music and Mass Movements*. Boston: South End Press, pp. 185-194.

— 1992b. *West African Pop Roots*. Philadelphia: Temple University Press.

— 1986. *E. T. Mensah, King of Highlife*. London: Off the Record Press.

Connell, John & Chris Gibson 2003. *Sound Tracks: Popular Music, Identity and Place*. London & New York: Routledge.

Cooley, Timothy J. 1997. "Casting Shadows in the Field. An Introduction." In: Gregory F. Barz & Timothy J. Cooley (eds.). *Shadows in the Field: New Perspectives for Fieldwork in Ethnomusicology*. New York & Oxford: Oxford University Press, pp. 3-19.

Coplan, David 1994. *In the Time of Cannibals. The Word Music of South Africa's Basotho Migrants*. Chicago & London: The University of Chicago Press.

— 1985. *In Township Tonight! South Africa's Black City Music and Theater*. Johannesburg: Ravan Press.

— 1978. "Go to My Town, Cape Coast! The Social History of Ghanaian Highlife." In: Bruno Nettl (ed.). *Eight Urban Musical Cultures*. Urbana, Chicago & London: University of Illinois Press, pp. 96-113.

Darko, Amma 1995. *Beyond the Horizon*. Oxford: Heinemann.

Darwin, Charles [1871] 1998. *The Descent of Man; and Selection in Relation to Sex*. With an introduction by H. James Birx. New York: Prometheus.

Dea, Data, Markus Höhne & Nina Glick Schiller 2005. "Afrikanische Kultur und der Zoo im 21. Jahrhundert. Eine ethnologische Perspektive auf das 'African Village' im Augsburger Zoo." Bericht an das Max-Planck-Institut für ethnologische Forschung, Halle. Published online at http://www.eth.mpg.de (accessed on March 05, 2007).

Debusmann, Robert & János Riesz (eds.) 1995. *Kolonialausstellungen — Begegnungen mit Afrika?* Frankfurt/M.: IKO (Verlag für interkulturelle Kommunikation).

de Certeau, Michel 1984. *Practice of Everyday Life*. Translated by Steven Randall. Berkeley: University of California Press.

Degbéon, André 2005. "Wenn wir uns nicht selbst vertreten, vertritt uns niemand." Interview with André Degbéon, chief editor of Afro-Berlin-TV. *Lo'Nam* 2:18-20.

Deleuze, Gilles & Felix Guattari 1987. *A Thousand Plateaus*. Translated by Brian Massumi. Minneapolis: University of Minnesota Press.

Diehl, Sarah Verena, Jörg Sundermeier & Werner Labisch (eds.) 2003. *Neuköllnbuch*. Berlin: Verbrecher Verlag.

— 2002. *Kreuzbergbuch*. Berlin: Verbrecher Verlag.

Ebron, Paulla A. 2002. *Performing Africa*. Princeton & Oxford: Princeton University Press.

Eger, Matthias 2005. "Hardly Heard. African music in East Germany Before and After the Wall." Paper presented at the international conference of the Society of Ethnomusicology held in Atlanta/Georgia, November 18, 2005.

El-Tayeb, Fatima 2004. "Medien, Machos und Mädchenrap: *Tic Tac Toe* und deutsche Debatten um *race* und *gender*." In: AntiDiskriminierungsBüro (ADB) Köln von Öffentlichkeit gegen Gewalt e.V. & cyberNomads (cbN) (eds.). *TheBlackBook. Deutschlands Häutungen*. Frankfurt/M. & London: IKO, pp. 308-312.

Essner, Cornelia 1985. *Deutsche Afrikareisende im neunzehnten Jahrhundert. Zur Sozialgeschichte des Reisens*. Stuttgart: Steiner.

Erlmann, Veit 1999. *Music, Modernity, and the Global Imagination*. London & Oxford: Oxford University Press.

— 1993. "The Politics and Aesthetics of Transnational Musics." *The World of Music* 35(2):3-15.

— 1991. *African Stars. Studies in Black South African Performance*. Chicago & London: The University of Chicago Press.

Eze, Emmanuel Chukwudi (ed.) 2000. *Race and the Enlightenment: A Reader*. Malden & Oxford: Blackwell.

Fabian, Johannes 2000. *Out of Our Minds. Reason and Madness in the Exploration of Central Africa*. Berkeley: University of California Press.

— 1983. *Time and the Other: How Anthropology Makes Its Object*. New York: Columbia University Press.

Feld, Steven 1996. "Pygmy POP. A Genealogy of Schizophonic Mimesis." *Yearbook for Traditional Music* 28:1-35.

— 1994a. "Notes on 'World Beat.'" In: Steven Feld & Charles Keil. *Music Grooves. Essays and Dialogues*. Chicago & London: The University of Chicago Press, pp. 238-246.

— 1994b. "From Schizophonia to Schismogenesis: On the Discourses and Commodification Practices of 'World Music' and 'World Beat.'" In: Steven Feld & Charles Keil. *Music Grooves. Essays and Dialogues*. Chicago & London: The University of Chicago Press, pp. 257-289.

Fikentscher, Kai 2000. *"You Better Work!"* — *Underground Dance Music in New York City*. Hanover & London: Wesleyan University Press.

Firla, Monika & Hermann Forkl 1995. "Afrikaner und Africana am württembergischen Herzogshof im 17. Jahrhundert." *Tribus* 44:149-193.

Flores, Juan 2000. *From Bomba to Hip-Hop: Puerto Rican Culture and Latino Identity*. New York: Columbia University Press.

Foucault, Michel 1986. "Of Other Spaces." Translated by Jay Miskowiec. *Diacritics* 16(1):22-27.

— 1980. *Power/Knowledge*. New York: Pantheon.

— 1979. *Discipline and Punish*. Translated by Alan Sheridan. New York: Vintage Press.

— 1973. *The Order of Things*. New York: Vintage Press.

Frei, Kerstin 2003. *Wer sich maskiert, wird integriert. Der Karneval der Kulturen in Berlin*. Berlin: Hans Schiler.

Fremgen, Gisela 1984. *... und wenn du dazu noch schwarz bist. Berichte schwarzer Frauen in der Bundesrepublik*. Bremen: edition CON.

Frith, Simon 2000. "The Discourse of World Music." In: Georgina Born & David Hesmondhalgh (eds.). *Western Music and Its Others*. Berkeley, Los Angeles & London: University of California Press, pp. 305-322.

— 1996. "Music and Identity." In: Stuart Hall & Paul du Gay (eds.). *Questions of Cultural Identity*. London, Thousand Oaks & New Delhi: Sage, pp. 108-127.

Frobenius, Leo 1923. *Das Unbekannte Afrika. Aufhellung der Schicksale eines Erdteils*. Munich: Beck.

Fürst, Anneke & Esther Grätschus 2002. "Afrikanisches Trommeln — Untersuchung der geschlechtsspezifischen Herangehensweise Lernender und der Didaktik/Methodik afrikanischer und europäischer Lehrender." Research report at the University of Oldenburg, published online at http://www.uni-oldenburg.de/musik-for (accessed on March 18, 2007).

Gadamer, Hans-Georg 1998. "Über das Hören." In: Thomas Vogel (ed.). *Über das Hören: Einem Phänomen auf der Spur*. Tübingen: Attempto, pp. 197-205.

Garofalo, Reebee 1993. "Whose World, What Beat: The Transnational Music Industry, Identity, and Cultural Imperialism." *The World of Music* 35(2):16-31.

Geertz, Clifford 1973. *The Interpretation of Cultures. Selected Essays*. New York: Basic Books.

Gelder, Ken & Sarah Thornton (eds.) 1997. *The Subcultures Reader*. London & New York: Routledge.

Geschiere, Peter & Birgit Meyer (eds.) 1999. *Globalization and Identity. Dialectics of Flow and Closure*. Malden & Oxford: Blackwell.

Giddens, Anthony 1990. *The Consequences of Modernity*. Oxford: Polity Press.

Gilroy, Paul 2004. "Der Schwarze Atlantik: ein negativer Kontinent." In: Haus der Kulturen der Welt (ed.). Brochure of the program *Black Atlantic*, September 17 to November 15, 2004, at the *Haus der Kulturen der Welt* in Berlin. Berlin, p. 4.

— 1993. *The Black Atlantic: Modernity and Double Consciousness*. Cambridge: Harvard University Press.

Greve, Martin 2003. *Die Musik der imaginären Türkei: Musik und Musikleben im Kontext der Migration aus der Türkei in Deutschland*. Stuttgart & Weimar: Metzler.

Grosse, Pascal 2002. "Koloniale Lebenswelten in Berlin 1885-1945." In: Ulrich van der Heyden & Joachim Zeller (eds.). *Kolonialmetropole Berlin. Eine Spurensuche*. Berlin: Berlin Edition, pp. 195-201.

Gründer, Horst 2002. "Der 'Wettlauf' um Afrika und die Berliner Westafrika-Konferenz 1884/85." In: Ulrich van der Heyden & Joachim Zeller (eds.). *Kolonialmetropole Berlin. Eine Spurensuche*. Berlin: Berlin Edition, pp. 19-23.

— 1995. *Geschichte der deutschen Kolonien*. 3., verbesserte und ergänzte Auflage mit neuer Bibliographie. Paderborn & München: Schöningh.

Grupe, Gerd 1998. "E. M. von Hornbostel und die Erforschung afrikanischer Musik aus der *armchair*-Perspektive." In: Sebastian Klotz (ed.). *Vom tönenden Wirbel menschlichen Tuns: Erich M. von Hornbostel als Gestaltpsychologe, Archivar und Musikwissenschafter*. Berlin & Milow: Schibri.

Guilbault, Jocelyne 1997. "Interpreting World Music: A Challenge in Theory and Practice." *Popular Music* 16(1):31-47.

— 1993. "On Redefining the 'Local' Through World Music." *The World of Music* 35(2):33-47.

Gupta, Akhil & James Ferguson 1997. "Beyond 'Culture': Space, Identity, and the Politics of Difference." In: Akhil Gupta & James Ferguson (eds.). *Culture, Power, Place: Explorations in Critical Anthropology*. Durham & London: Duke University Press, pp. 33-51.

Ha, Kien Nghi 2003. "Die kolonialen Muster deutscher Arbeitsmigrationspolitik." In: Encarnación Gutiérrez Rodriguez & Hito Steyerl (eds.). *Spricht die Subalterne deutsch? Migration und postkoloniale Kritik*. Münster: Unrast, pp. 56-107.

Haberland, Wolfgang 1988. "'Diese Indianer sind falsch' — Neun Bella Coola im Deutschen Reich 1885/86." *Archiv für Völkerkunde* 42:3-67.

Hagenbeck, Carl [1909] 1928. *Von Tieren und Menschen. Erlebnisse und Erfahrungen*. Leipzig: List.

Hale, Thomas A. 1999. *Griots and Griottes. Masters of Words and Music*. Bloomington: University of Indiana Press.

Hall, Stuart 1992. "The Question of Cultural Identity." In: Stuart Hall, David Held & Tony McGrew (eds.). *Modernity and its Futures*. Cambridge: Polity Press, pp. 273-316.

Hamm, Charles 1995. *Putting Popular Music in Its Place*. Cambridge: Cambridge University Press.

Hanslick, Eduard [1854] 1902. *Vom Musikalisch-Schönen. Ein Beitrag zur Revision der Ästhetik der Tonkunst*. Leipzig: Breitkopf & Härtel.

Hannerz, Ulf 1996. *Transnational Connections. Culture, People, Places*. London & New York: Routledge.

— 1992. *Cultural Complexity. Studies in the Social Organisation of Meaning*. New

York: Columbia University Press.

— 1980. *Exploring the City. Inquiries Toward an Urban Anthropology*. New York: Columbia University Press.

Harvey, David 1989. *The Condition of Postmodernity*. Oxford: Blackwell.

Hawley, Charles 2005. "'African Village' Accused of Putting Humans on Display." Article in the newsmagazine *Spiegel Online*, published online on June 09, 2005, at http://www.spiegel.de (accessed on March 06, 2007).

Hebdige, Dick 1987. *Cut 'n' Mix. Culture, Identity and Caribbean Music*. London & New York: Comedia.

— 1979. *Subculture. The Meaning of Style*. London: Methuen.

Hegel, Georg Wilhelm Friedrich [1822-28] 1986. *Vorlesungen über die Philosophie der Geschichte*. Werke, vol. 12. Frankfurt/M.: Suhrkamp.

Hermetek, Ursula 2001. *Mosaik der Klänge*. Wien: Böhlau.

Herkenhoff, Michael 1990. *Der dunkle Kontinent. Das Afrikabild im Mittelalter bis zum 12. Jahrhundert*. Pfaffenweiler: Centaurus.

Hessel, Franz [1929] 1984. *Ein Flaneur in Berlin* (mit Fotografien von Friedrich Seidenstücker). Berlin: Das Arsenal.

Hochschild, Adam 1998. *King Leopold's Ghost. A Story of Greed, Terror, and Heroism in Colonial Africa*. New York: Houghton Mifflin.

Hopkins, Leroy T. Jr. 1999. "Race, Nationality and Culture: The African Diaspora in Germany." In: Leroy T. Hopkins (ed.). *Who Is a German? Historical and Modern Perspectives on Africans in Germany*. Harry & Helen Gray Humanities Program Series, Volume 5. Washington, D.C.: American Institute for Contemporary German Studies, pp. 1-31.

Hornbostel, Erich M. 1928. "African Negro Music." *Africa* 1(1):3-35.

— 1921. "Musikalischer Exotismus." *Melos* 2:175-182.

— 1917. "Gesänge aus Ruanda." In: Jan Czekanowski. *Forschungen im Nil-Kongo-Zwischengebiet*, vol. 1. Leipzig: Klinkhardt & Biermann, pp. 375-412.

— 1913. "Musik." In: Günter Tessmann. *Die Pangwe. Monographie eines westafrikanischen Negerstammes*, vol. 2. Berlin: Hansa, pp. 320-357.

— 1911. "U.S.A. National Music." *Zeitschrift der Internationalen Musikgesellschaft* 12(3):64-68.

— 1910. "Wasukuma-Melodie nach der Aufnahme von Dr. J. Czekanowski". *Bulletin de l'Académie des Sciences de Cracovie, Classe des Sciences Mathématique et Naturelles* 7:711-713.

— 1909. "Wanyamwezi-Gesänge." *Anthropos* 4:781-800 & 1033-1052.

Hülskötter, C. & R. Klostermann 2003. "Diese Wüsten-Sonne! Werden wir alle Afrikaner?" Article in the daily newspaper *Bild*, August 12, 2003.

Inda, Jonathan Xavier & Renato Rosaldo (eds.) 2002. *The Anthropology of Globalization. A Reader*. Malden & Oxford: Blackwell.

Keil, Charles 1994. "'Ethnic' Music Traditions in the USA (Black Music; Country Music; Others; All). *Popular Music* 13(2):175-178.

Keller, Ulrike (ed.) 2000. *Reisende in Südafrika, 1497-1990. Ein kulturhistorisches Lesebuch*. Vienna: Promedia.

Kessen, Peter 2001. "Schwarze Heimat Nord-Neukölln." Article in the daily newspaper *die tageszeitung*, July 24, 2001.

Kirshenblatt-Gimblett, Barbara 1991. "Objects of Ethnography." In: Ivan Karp & Steven D. Lavine (eds.). *Exhibiting Cultures. The Poetics and Politics of Museum Display*. Washington & London: Smithsonian Institution Press, pp. 386-443.

Kisliuk, Michelle 1997. "(Un)Doing Fieldwork." In: Gregory Barz & Timothy J. Cooley (eds.). *Shadows in the Field: New Perspectives for Fieldwork in Ethnomusicology*. New York & Oxford: Oxford University Press, pp. 23-44.

Kittler, Friedrich 1995. *Aufschreibesysteme 1800 · 1900*. Munich: Fink.

— 1986. *Grammophon, Film, Typewriter*. Berlin: Brinkmann & Bose.

Klein, Tobias Robert 2004. "'Drawing on musical ideas with a dazzling eclecticism' — Preliminary sketches on postcolonialism in African and Ghanaian music." Paper presented at the VAD conference held in Hanover, Germany, from June 02-05, 2004.

Kleßmann, Eckart 1987. "Der Mohr in der Literatur der Aufklärung." In: Institut für Auslandsbeziehungen & Württembergischer Kunstverein (eds.). *Exotische Welten — Europäische Phantasien*. Stuttgart: Edition Cantz, pp. 236-241.

Knauer, Wolfram (ed.) 1996. *Jazz in Deutschland*. Darmstädter Beiträge zur Jazzforschung Band 3. Hofheim: Wolke.

Knecht, Michi & Levent Soysal (eds.) 2005. *Plausible Vielfalt. Wie der Karneval der Kulturen denkt, lernt und Kultur schafft*. Berlin: Panama.

Koischwitz, Christine 2005. "Hier reimt die Unterschicht." Article in the weekly newsmagazine *Der Spiegel* 14/2005.

Kubik, Gerhard 2001. "Africa." In: Stanley Sadie (ed.). *The New Grove Dictionary of Music and Musicians*. Second Edition, vol. 1. London & New York: Macmillan, pp. 190-210.

— 1998. *Kalimba, Nsansi, Mbira — Lamellophone in Afrika*. Berlin: Museum für Völkerkunde.

Kunzemann, Thilo 2002. "Die Polizei will nicht rassistisch sein." Article in the daily newspaper *taz Berlin lokal*, March 02, 2002.

Kwarteng, E. Kojo 2006. "Remittances from abroad to hit $8bn." Article in the daily newspaper *Daily Graphic* August 5:16.

Lefebvre, Henri 2003. *The Urban Revolution*. Translated by Robert Bononno. Foreword by Neil Smith. Minneapolis & London: University of Minnesota

Press.

— [1991] 2004. *The Production of Space*. Translated by Donald Nicholson-Smith. Malden, Oxford & Carlton: Blackwell.

— [1971] 2004. *Everyday Life in the Modern World*. Translated by Sacha Rabino-vitch. With a New Introduction by Philip Wander. New Brunswick & London: Transaction.

Lindfors, Bernth 1999. "Charles Dickens and the Zulus." In: Bernth Lindfors (ed.). *Africans on Stage: Studies in Ethnological Show Business*. Bloomington & Indianapolis: Indiana University Press, pp. 62-80.

Lindfors, Bernth (ed.) 1999. *Africans on Stage: Studies in Ethnological Show Business*. Bloomington & Indianapolis: Indiana University Press.

Lomax, Alan 1976. *Cantometrics: A Method in Musical Anthropology*. Berkeley: University of California, Extension Media Center.

Low, Setha M. 1996. "The Anthropology of Cities: Imagining and Theorizing the City." *Annual Review of Anthropology* 25:383-409.

Marcus, George E. 1995. "Ethnography in/of the World System: The Emergence of Multi-Sited Ethnography." *Annual Review of Anthropology* 24:95-117.

Marcus, George E. & Michael M. J. Fischer 1986. *Anthropology as Cultural Critique. An Experimental Moment in the Human Sciences*. Second Edition. Chicago & London: The University of Chicago Press.

Meier, Arnim 1984. "Die Kolonialprofiteure oder 'Der Platz an der Sonne.'" In: Manfred O. Hinz, Helgard Patemann & Arnim Meier (ed.). *Weiss auf schwarz:100 Jahre Einmischung in Afrika — Deutscher Kolonialismus und afrikanischer Widerstand*. Berlin: Elefanten Press, pp. 56-60.

Meier-Braun, Karl-Heinz 2002. *Deutschland, Einwanderungsland*. Frankfurt/M.: Suhrkamp.

Meinecke, Gustav (ed.) 1897. *Deutschland und seine Kolonien im Jahre 1896. Amtlicher Bericht über die Erste Deutsche Kolonial-Ausstellung*. Herausgeben vom Arbeitsausschuss der Deutschen Kolonial-Ausstellung. Berlin: Reimer.

Mendívil, Julio 2006. "'Wenn die Trommel ruft': Zur Repräsentation von Afrika und Schwarzen im deutschen Schlager." In: Marianne Bechhaus-Gerst & Sunna Gieseke (eds.). *Koloniale und postkoloniale Konstruktionen von Afrika und Menschen afrikanischer Herkunft in der deutschen Alltagskultur*. Frankfurt/M.: Lang, pp. 307-313.

Merriam, Alan P. 1964. *The Anthropology of Music*. Evanston: Northwestern University Press.

Meyer, Birgit 1999. "Commodities and the Power of Prayer: Pentecostalist Attitudes Towards Consumption in Contemporary Ghana." In: Peter Geschiere & Birgit Meyer (eds.). *Globalization and Identity. Dialectics of Flow and Closure*. Malden & Oxford: Blackwell, pp. 151-176.

Mielke, Andreas 1999. "'Black Cherries Are Sweeter': A Note On African-German Erotic Relations." In: Leroy T. Hopkins (ed.). *Who Is a German? Historical and Modern Perspectives on Africans in Germany*. Harry & Helen Gray Humanities Program Series, Volume 5. Washington, D.C.: American Institute for Contemporary German Studies, pp. 55-75.

Miller, Tobias 1998. "Großeinsatz gegen Drogenszene in der Hasenheide." Article in the daily newspaper *Berliner Zeitung*, March 14, 1998.

Mitchell, J. Clyde 1956. *The Kalela Dance. Aspects of Social Relationships among Urban Africans in Northern Rhodesia*. Rhodes Livingstone Papers 27. Manchester: Manchester University Press.

Möhle, Heiko 2002. "Betreuung, Erfassung, Kontrolle — Die 'Deutsche Gesellschaft für Eingeborenenkunde.'" In: Ulrich van der Heyden & Joachim Zeller (eds.). *Kolonialmetropole Berlin. Eine Spurensuche*. Berlin: Berlin Edition, pp. 243-251.

Monson, Ingrid (ed.) 2000. *The African Diaspora. A Musical Perspective*. Critical and Cultural Musicology, Vol. 3. New York & London: Garland.

Mudimbe, V. Y. 1994. *The Idea of Africa*. Bloomington & Indianapolis: Indiana University Press.

— 1988. *The Invention of Africa. Gnosis, Philosophy, and the Order of Knowledge*. Bloomington & Indianapolis: Indiana University Press.

Mugglestone, Erica 1982. "The Gora and the 'Grand' Gom-Gom: A Reappraisal of Kolb's Account of Khoikhoi Musical Bows." *African music* 6(2):94-115.

Nederveen Pieterse, Jan 1998. *White on Black. Images of Africa and Blacks in Western Popular Culture*. New Haven & London: Yale University Press.

Nketia, J. H. Kwabena 1974. *The Music of Africa*. New York: Norton.

Nnaemeka, Obioma 2005. "Bodies That Don't Matter: Black Bodies and the European Gaze." In: Maureen Maisha Eggers, Grado Kilomba, Peggy Piesche & Susan Arndt (eds.). *Mythen, Masken und Subjekte. Kritische Weißseinsforschung in Deutschland*. Münster: Unrast, pp. 90-104.

Nyamnjoh, Francis B. & Ben Page 2002. "*Whiteman Kontri* and the Enduring Allure of Modernity Among Cameroonian Youth." *African Affairs* 101:607-634.

Oguntoye, Katharina 2004. "Afrikanische Zuwanderung nach Deutschland zwischen 1884 und 1945." In: AntiDiskriminierungsBüro (ADB) Köln von Öffentlichkeit gegen Gewalt e.V. & cyberNomads (cbN) (eds.). *TheBlackBook. Deutschlands Häutungen*. Frankfurt/M. & London: IKO, pp. 15-19.

Oguntoye, Katharina, May Opitz & Dagmar Schultz (eds.) 1986. *Farbe Bekennen. Afro-deutsche Frauen auf den Spuren ihrer Geschichte*. Berlin: Orlanda Frauenverlag.

Oltmer, Thorsten 2007. "Die Hottentotten-Venus. Das Schicksal der Saartje Baartman als koloniale Zirkusattraktion." Article in the newsmagazine *Spiegel online*, May 22, 2007. Published at http://www.spiegel.de (accessed on June 25, 2007).

Park, Mungo [1799] 2000. *Travels in the Interior Districts of Africa*. Edited with an Introduction by Kate Ferguson Masters. Durham & London: Duke University Press.

Peil, Margaret 1995. "Ghanaians Abroad." *African Affairs* 94:345-367.

Peters, Carl [1891] 1907. *Die deutsche Emin Pascha-Expedition* (Volksausgabe). Hamburg & Braunschweig: Deutscher Kolonialverlag (Mumm).

Plarre, Plutonia 2004. "'Ich stehe zu meinen Äußerungen.' Mit ein paar deutlichen Worten schaffte es Neuköllns Bürgermeister auf alle TV-Kanäle." Article in the daily newspaper *die tageszeitung*, November 11, 2004.

Pogge von Strandmann, Hartmut 2002. "'Deutsches Land in fremder Hand' — Der Kolonialrevisionismus." In: Ulrich van der Heyden & Joachim Zeller (eds.). *Kolonialmetropole Berlin. Eine Spurensuche*. Berlin: Berlin Edition, pp. 232-239.

Radano, Ronald 2000. "Hot Fantasies: American Modernism and the Idea of Black Rhythm." In: Philip V. Bohlman & Ronald Radano (eds.). *Music and the Racial Imagination*. Chicago & London: The University of Chicago Press, pp. 459-480.

Reed-Anderson, Paulette 2000. *Berlin and the African Diaspora. Rewriting the Footnotes*. Berlin: Die Ausländerbeauftragte des Senats.

Reyes, Adelaida 1999. *Songs of the Caged, Songs of the Free. Music and the Vietnamese Refugee Experience*. Philadelphia: Temple University Press.

Roediger, David R. 1994. *Towards the Abolition of Whiteness. Essays on Race, Politics and Working-Class History*. London & New York: Verso.

Roller, Kathrin 2002a. "'Wir sind Deutsche, wir sind Weiße und wollen Weiße bleiben' — Reichtagsdebatten über koloniale 'Rassenmischung.'" In: Ulrich van der Heyden & Joachim Zeller (eds.). *Kolonialmetropole Berlin. Eine Spurensuche*. Berlin: Berlin Edition, pp. 73-79.

— 2002b. "Der Rassenbiologe Eugen Fischer." In: Ulrich van der Heyden & Joachim Zeller (eds.). *Kolonialmetropole Berlin. Eine Spurensuche*. Berlin: Berlin Edition, pp. 130-133.

Rotberg, Robert I. (ed.) 1970. *Africa and Its Explorers: Motives, Methods, and Impact*. Cambridge: Harvard University Press.

Sachs, Curt 1929. *Geist und Werden der Musikinstrumente*. Berlin: Reimer.

Said, Edward W. [1979] 1995. *Orientalism. Western Conceptions of the Orient*. With a New Afterword. London: Penguin.

Savishinsky, Neil J. 1993. *Rastafari in the promised land. The spread of a Jamaican socio-religious movement and its music and culture among the youth of Ghana and Senegambia.* PhD thesis, Columbia University.

Schallenberg, Jörg 2005. "Heiße Luft aus Afrika im Augsburger Zoo." Article in the daily newspaper *die tageszeitung,* June 11, 2005.

Schedtler, Susanne 1999. *Das Eigene in der Fremde. Einwanderer-Musikkulturen in Hamburg.* Münster: LIT.

Schirmeyer, Guido 2002. "Neuköllner Nächte sind schwarz." Article in the daily newspaper *Frankfurter Rundschau*, March 02, 2002.

Schramm, Katharina 2000. *Dancing the Nation. Ghanaische Kulturpolitik im Spannungsfeld zwischen Nation und globaler Herausforderung.* Münster: LIT.

Schröter, Almut 2003. "Reisebegleiter in die Weltstadt. Die Werkstatt der Kulturen wird 10 und bekommt einen Preis." Article in the daily newspaper *Neues Deutschland*, October 22, 2003.

Schwanhäußer, Anja 2005. "Die Stadt als Abenteuerspielplatz." In: Ingo Bader & Albert Scharenberg (eds.). *Der Sound der Stadt. Musikindustrie und Subkultur in Berlin.* Münster: Westfälisches Dampfboot, pp. 160-173.

Schwarzer, Anke 2005. "Proteste gegen das 'African Village' im Zoo." Article in the daily newspaper *Frankfurter Rundschau*, May 28, 2005.

Simon, Artur (ed.) 2000. *Das Berliner Phonogramm-Archiv 1900-2000: Sammlungen der traditionellen Musik der Welt.* Berlin: VWB (Verlag für Wissenschaft und Bildung).

Slobin, Mark [1993] 2000. *Subcultural Sounds. Micromusics of the West.* With a new preface. Hanover & London: Wesleyan University Press.

Small, Christopher 1998. *Musicking. The Meanings of Performing and Listening.* Hanover & London: Wesleyan University press.

Smith, Woodruff D. 1978. *The German Colonial Empire.* Chapel Hill: University of North Carolina Press.

Staehelin, Balthasar 1994. *Völkerschauen im Zoologischen Garten Basel 1879-1935.* Basel: Basler Afrika Bibliographien.

Stewart, Gary 2000. *Rumba on the River. A History of the Popular Music of the Two Congos.* London & New York: Verso.

Stocking, George W. 1982. *Race, Culture, and Evolution. Essays in the History of Anthropology.* Chicago & London: The University of Chicago Press.

Stokes, Martin (ed.) 1994. *Ethnicity, Identity and Music: The Musical Construction of Place.* Oxford & Providence: Berg.

Straw, Will [1991] 1997. "Communities and Scenes in Popular Music." In: Ken Gelder & Sarah Thornton (eds.). *The Subcultures Reader.* London & New York: Routledge, pp. 494-505.

Stumpf, Carl 1886. "Lieder der Bellakula-Indianer." *Vierteljahrsschrift für Musikwissenschaft* 2:349-405.

Taussig, Michael 1993. *Mimesis and Alterity. A Particular History of the Senses.* New York & London: Routledge.

Taylor, Charles 1992. *Multiculturalism and 'The Politics of Recognition.'* Princeton: Princeton University Press.

Taylor, Timothy D. 1997. *Global Pop: World Music, World Markets.* New York & London: Routledge.

Ter Haar, G. 1998. *Halfway to Paradise.* Cardiff: Cardiff Academic Press.

Thode-Arora, Hilke 2002. "Völkerschauen in Berlin." In: Ulrich van der Heyden & Joachim Zeller (eds.). *Kolonialmetropole Berlin. Eine Spurensuche.* Berlin: Berlin Edition, pp. 149-154.

— 1989. *Für fünfzig Pfennig um die Welt. Die Hagenbeckschen Völkerschauen.* Frankfurt/M. & New York: Campus.

Trüper, Ursula 2000. "Afrikaner in Berlin." Article in the newsmagazine *tazmag*, May 6-7, 2000.

Turino, Thomas 2000. *Nationalists, Cosmopolitans and Popular Music in Zimbabwe.* Chicago & London: The University of Chicago Press.

— 1993. *Moving Away From Silence: Music of the Peruvian Altiplano and the Experience of Urban Migration.* Chicago & London: The University of Chicago Press.

Van Dijk, R. 1997. "From Camp to Encompassment: Discourses of Transsubjectivity." *Journal of Religion in Africa* 27:135-159.

van der Heyden, Ulrich 2002a. "Das brandenburgische Kolonialabenteuer unter dem Großen Kurfürsten." In: Ulrich van der Heyden & Joachim Zeller (eds.). *Kolonialmetropole Berlin. Eine Spurensuche.* Berlin: Berlin Edition, pp. 15-18.

— 2002b. "Die Kolonial- und die Transvaal-Ausstellung 1896/97." In: Ulrich van der Heyden & Joachim Zeller (eds.). *Kolonialmetropole Berlin. Eine Spurensuche.* Berlin: Berlin Edition, pp. 135-142.

— 2002c. "Die Mohrenstraße." In: Ulrich van der Heyden & Joachim Zeller (eds.). *Kolonialmetropole Berlin. Eine Spurensuche.* Berlin: Berlin Edition, pp. 188-189.

— 2002d. "Das Afrikanische Viertel." In: Ulrich van der Heyden & Joachim Zeller (eds.). *Kolonialmetropole Berlin. Eine Spurensuche.* Berlin: Berlin Edition, pp. 261-263.

van der Heyden, Ulrich & Joachim Zeller (eds.) 2002. *Kolonialmetropole Berlin. Eine Spurensuche.* Berlin: Berlin Edition.

Vogels, Raimund 2005. "Between *Leitkultur* and *Überfremdung.* Musical Ethnography in Contemporary Germany." Paper presented at the international conference of the *Society of Ethnomusicology* held in Atlanta/Georgia, November 18, 2005.

— 2001. "Instrumentalsprache." In: Jacob E. Mabe (ed.). *Das Afrika-Lexikon:*

Ein Kontinent in 1000 Stichwörtern. Weimar & Wuppertal: Metzler & Hammer,
    pp. 259-260.

Wallaschek, Richard 1893. *Primitive Music. An Inquiry into the Origin and Develop-*
    ment of Music, Songs, Instruments, Dances, and Pantomimes of Savage Races. London
    & New York: Longman.

— 1892. "Das musikalische Gedächtnis und seine Leistung bei Katalepsie, im
    Traum und in der Hypnose." *Vierteljahrsschrift für Musikwissenschaft* 8:204-251.

Waterman, Christopher A. 2000. "Race Music: Bo Chatmon, 'Corrine
    Corrina', and the Excluded Middle." In: Philip V. Bohlman & Ronald
    Radano (eds.). *Music and the Racial Imagination.* Chicago & London: The Uni-
    versity of Chicago Press, pp. 167-205.

— 1991. "The Uneven Development of Africanist Ethnomusicology. Three
    Issues and a Critique." In: Philip V. Bohlman & Bruno Nettl (eds.). *Compara-*
    tive Musicology and Anthropology of Music. Essays on the History of Ethnomusicology.
    Chicago & London: The University of Chicago Press, pp. 169-186.

— 1990. *Jùjú. A Social History and Ethnography of an African Popular Music.* Chicago
    & London: The University of Chicago Press.

Wellershaus, Elisabeth 2004. "Hello Africa. Das Haus der Kulturen feiert den
    Black Atlantic. Wie steht es hierzulande um die Schwarze Identität?" Article
    in the biweekly magazine *zitty* 20/2004:28-29.

Weule, Karl 1908. *Negerleben in Ostafrika. Ergebnisse einer ethnologischen For-*
    schungsreise. Leipzig: Brockhaus.

Wieben, Uwe 2000. *Carl Peters. Das Leben eines deutschen Kolonialisten.* Rostock:
    Neuer Hochschulschriftenverlag.

Wiedenroth-Coulibaly, Eleonore & Sascha Zinflou 2004. "20 Jahre Schwarze
    Organisierung in Deutschland — Ein Abriss." In: AntiDiskriminierungsBü-
    ro (ADB) Köln von Öffentlichkeit gegen Gewalt e.V. & cyberNomads (cbN)
    (eds.). *TheBlackBook. Deutschlands Häutungen.* Frankfurt/M. & London: IKO,
    pp. 133-144.

Wissmann, Hermann von, Ludwig Wolf, Curt von François & Hans Mueller
    1891. *Im Innern Afrikas. Die Erforschung des Kassai während der Jahre 1883, 1884*
    und 1885. Leipzig: Brockhaus.

Yakpo, Kofi a.k.a. Linguist (Advanced Chemistry) 2004. "'Denn ich bin kein
    Einzelfall, sondern einer von vielen.' Afrodeutsche Rapkünstler in der Hip
    Hop Gründerzeit." In: AntiDiskriminierungsBüro (ADB) Köln von Öffent-
    lichkeit gegen Gewalt e.V. & cyberNomads (cbN) (eds.). *TheBlackBook.*
    Deutschlands Häutungen. Frankfurt/M. & London: IKO, pp. 332-339.

Zekri, Sonja 2005. "Das ist kein 'afrikanisches Dorf,' sondern ein 'African Vil-
    lage'!" Article in the daily newspaper *Süddeutsche Zeitung*, June 10, 2005.

Zeller, Joachim 2002. "Das Berliner Kolonialpanorama." In: In: Ulrich van der Heyden & Joachim Zeller (eds.). *Kolonialmetropole Berlin. Eine Spurensuche.* Berlin: Berlin Edition, pp. 154-158.

Ziegler, Susanne 1998. "Erich M. von Hornbostel und das Berliner Phono-gramm-Archiv." In: Sebastian Klotz (ed.). *Vom tönenden Wirbel menschlichen Tuns: Erich M. von Hornbostel als Gestaltpsychologe, Archivar und Musikwissenschaft-ler; Studien und Dokumente.* Berlin & Milow: Schibri, pp. 148-168.

Martin Blindow

Orgelgeschichte der Stadt Dortmund

Eine Dokumentation von den Anfängen bis ins 20. Jahrhundert

Musik: Forschung und Wissenschaft

LIT

Martin Blindow
Orgelgeschichte der Stadt Dortmund
Eine Dokumentation von den Anfängen bis ins 20. Jahrhundert
Bis zum 19. Jhdt besaß Dortmund nur eine Großorgel. In den meisten alten Kirchen standen kleine Instrumente ohne Pedal. Mit der rapiden Entwicklung zur Industriestadt und dem Bau neuer Kirchen verband sich eine große Orgelbegeisterung. Diese Veröffentlichung hält die Geschichte aller Orgeln fest, um die Bedeutung der Orgelstadt Dortmund für den deutschen Raum zu unterstreichen. Leider haben die Zerstörungen und Umbauten wegen des allzuraschen Fortschritts ihre Instrumente vernichtet. Umso wichtiger ist eine Dokumentation dieser Orgelgeschichte anhand bisher unbekannter Archivalien.
Bd. 2, 2008, 264 S., 24,90 €, br., ISBN 978-3-8258-0895-2

LIT Verlag Berlin – Münster – Wien – Zürich – London
Auslieferung Deutschland / Österreich / Schweiz: siehe Impressumsseite